THE 100 BEST Stocks to Own FOR UNDER $25

SECOND EDITION

Gene Walden

DEARBORN™
TRADE

A **Kaplan Professional** Company

This publication is designed to provide accurate and authoritative information in regard to the subject matter covered. It is sold with the understanding that the publisher is not engaged in rendering legal, accounting, or other professional service. If legal advice or other expert assistance is required, the services of a competent professional person should be sought.

Publisher: Cynthia A. Zigmund
Senior Managing Editor: Jack Kiburz
Interior Design: Lucy Jenkins
Cover Design: Jody Billert, Billert Communications
Typesetting: the dotted i

Library of Congress Cataloging-in-Publication Data

Walden, Gene.
    The 100 best stocks to own for under $25 / Gene Walden.— 2nd ed.
        p.   cm.
    Includes index.
    ISBN 0-7931-3826-4 (6x9 pbk.)
    1. Small capitalization stocks.   I. Title: One hundred best stocks to own
for under $25.   II.   Title.
HG4971 .W35   2000
332.63′22—dc21
                                                    00-011060

Dearborn Trade books are available at special quantity discounts to use as premiums and sales promotions, or for use in corporate training programs. For more information, please call the Special Sales Manager at 800-621-9621, ext. 4514, or write to Dearborn Financial Publishing, Inc., 155 North Wacker Drive, Chicago, IL 60606-1719.

Dedication

To Bob and Charles, Ruth and Joanne

Contents

Alphabetical Listing of the 100 Best Stocks Under $25   ix

Preface   xi

Acknowledgments   xiii

Introduction   xv

1   North American Scientific, Inc.   1

2   Advanced Digital Information Corp.   4

3   Optibase, Ltd.   7

4   Richton International Corp.   10

5   Concord Camera Corp.   13

6   AstroPower, Inc.   16

7   Akorn, Inc.   19

8   Exactech, Inc.   22

9   Actrade International, Ltd.   25

10   Tidel Technologies, Inc.   28

11   Integral Systems, Inc.   31

12   Embrex, Inc.   34

13   InnerDyne, Inc.   37

14   Candela Corp.   40

15   CompuDyne Corp.   43

16   Daktronics, Inc.   46

17   ePresence, Inc.   49

18   V3 Semiconductor, Inc.   52

19   Comtech Telecommunications Corp.   55

20   Gentner Communications   58

21   PW Eagle, Inc.   61

22   SpectraLink Corp.   64

23   Abaxis, Inc.   67

24   Abercrombie & Fitch Co.   70

25   Novadigm, Inc.   73

26   Summa Industries   76

27	Opinion Research Corp.	**79**
28	Hauppauge Digital, Inc.	**82**
29	Kensey Nash Corp.	**85**
30	Radyne ComStream, Inc.	**88**
31	Galileo Technology Ltd.	**91**
32	Trend Micro, Inc.	**94**
33	The InterCept Group, Inc.	**97**
34	TD Waterhouse Group, Inc.	**100**
35	International FiberCom	**103**
36	Ameritrade Holding Corp.	**106**
37	Take-Two Interactive Software, Inc.	**109**
38	Global Imaging Systems, Inc.	**112**
39	LaserVision Centers, Inc.	**115**
40	Sonic Automotive, Inc.	**118**
41	Citizens Financial Corp.	**121**
42	AmeriCredit Corp.	**124**
43	AmeriPath, Inc.	**127**
44	Standard Pacific Corp.	**130**
45	NETsilicon, Inc.	**133**
46	Avant! Corp.	**136**
47	Somera Communications	**139**
48	NetScout Systems, Inc.	**142**
49	Manatron, Inc.	**145**
50	Extended Stay America	**148**
51	AmSurg Corp.	**151**
52	Dataram Corp.	**154**
53	Taro Pharmaceuticals Industries Ltd.	**157**
54	BackWeb Technologies Ltd.	**160**
55	Monterey Pasta Company	**163**
56	STV Group, Inc.	**166**
57	Southwest Water Company	**169**
58	Genesis Microchip, Inc.	**172**
59	Moldflow Corp.	**175**
60	Spectrum Control, Inc.	**178**
61	Drexler Technology Corp.	**181**

62	Atrion Corp.	**184**
63	Cheap Tickets, Inc.	**187**
64	EarthLink, Inc.	**190**
65	Rubio's Restaurants, Inc.	**193**
66	Del Global Technologies Corp.	**196**
67	Catellus Development Corp.	**199**
68	Bell Microproducts, Inc.	**202**
69	Hello Direct, Inc.	**205**
70	California Micro Devices Corp.	**208**
71	Camtek, Ltd.	**211**
72	ANSYS Inc.	**214**
73	Digital Video Systems, Inc.	**217**
74	Sound Advice, Inc.	**220**
75	Mail-Well, Inc.	**223**
76	International Home Foods, Inc.	**226**
77	Chinadotcom Corp.	**229**
78	PFF Bancorp, Inc.	**232**
79	White Electronic Designs Corp.	**235**
80	Alpha Technologies Group, Inc.	**238**
81	Interliant, Inc.	**241**
82	InSilicon Corp.	**244**
83	Computer Network Technology	**247**
84	Kewaunee Scientific Corp.	**250**
85	Mitek Systems, Inc.	**253**
86	Gehl Company	**256**
87	Amtech Systems, Inc.	**259**
88	Channell Commercial Corp.	**262**
89	BTU International Inc.	**265**
90	AltiGen Communications	**268**
91	All American Semiconductor, Inc.	**271**
92	Network Access Solutions	**274**
93	Sage, Inc.	**277**
94	Semitool, Inc.	**280**
95	ESS Technology, Inc.	**283**
96	Ace*Comm Corp.	**286**

97   CollaGenex Pharmaceuticals, Inc.   **289**
 98   Xicor, Inc.   **292**
 99   Wabash National Corp.   **295**
100   Sevenson Environmental Services, Inc.   **298**
       The 100 Best Stocks Under $25 by State/Country   **301**
       The 100 Best Stocks Under $25 by Industry Group   **307**
       Index   **311**

Alphabetical Listing of the 100 Best Stocks Under $25

Abaxis, Inc. (23)
Abercrombie & Fitch Co. (24)
Ace*Comm Corp. (96)
Actrade International, Ltd. (9)
Advanced Digital Information
    Corp. (2)
Akorn, Inc. (7)
All American Semiconductor, Inc.
    (91)
Alpha Technologies Group, Inc.
    (80)
AltiGen Communications (90)
AmeriCredit Corp. (42)
AmeriPath, Inc. (43)
Ameritrade Holding Corp. (36)
AmSurg Corp. (51)
Amtech Systems, Inc. (87)
ANSYS Inc. (72)
AstroPower, Inc. (6)
Atrion Corp. (62)
Avant! Corp. (46)
BackWeb Technologies Ltd. (54)
Bell Microproducts, Inc. (68)
BTU International Inc. (89)
California Micro Devices Corp.
    (70)
Camtek, Ltd. (71)
Candela Corp. (14)
Catellus Development Corp. (67)
Channell Commercial Corp. (88)
Cheap Tickets, Inc. (63)
Chinadotcom Corp. (77)
Citizens Financial Corp. (41)
CollaGenex Pharmaceuticals, Inc.
    (97)

CompuDyne Corp. (15)
Computer Network Technology
    (83)
Comtech Telecommunications
    Corp. (19)
Concord Camera Corp. (5)
Daktronics, Inc. (16)
Dataram Corp. (52)
Del Global Technologies Corp.
    (66)
Digital Video Systems, Inc. (73)
Drexler Technology Corp. (61)
EarthLink, Inc. (64)
Embrex, Inc. (12)
ePresence, Inc. (17)
ESS Technology, Inc. (95)
Exactech, Inc. (8)
Extended Stay America (50)
Galileo Technology Ltd. (31)
Gehl Company (86)
Genesis Microchip, Inc. (58)
Gentner Communications (20)
Global Imaging Systems, Inc. (38)
Hauppauge Digital, Inc. (28)
Hello Direct, Inc. (69)
InnerDyne, Inc. (13)
InSilicon Corp. (82)
Integral Systems, Inc. (11)
InterCept Group, Inc., The (33)
Interliant, Inc. (81)
International FiberCom (35)
International Home Foods, Inc.
    (76)
Kensey Nash Corp. (29)
Kewaunee Scientific Corp. (84)

LaserVision Centers, Inc. (39)
Mail-Well, Inc. (75)
Manatron, Inc. (49)
Mitek Systems, Inc. (85)
Moldflow Corp. (59)
Monterey Pasta Company (55)
NetScout Systems, Inc. (48)
NETsilicon, Inc. (45)
Network Access Solutions (92)
North American Scientific, Inc. (1)
Novidigm, Inc. (25)
Opinion Research Corp. (27)
Optibase, Ltd. (3)
PFF Bancorp, Inc. (78)
PW Eagle, Inc. (21)
Radyne ComStream, Inc. (30)
Richton International Corp. (4)
Rubio's Restaurants, Inc. (65)
Sage, Inc. (93)
Semitool, Inc. (94)
Sevenson Environmental Services,
    Inc. (100)

Somera Communications (47)
Sonic Automotive, Inc. (40)
Sound Advice, Inc. (74)
Southwest Water Company (57)
SpectraLink Corp. (22)
Spectrum Control, Inc. (60)
Standard Pacific Corp. (44)
STV Group, Inc. (56)
Summa Industries (26)
Take-Two Interactive Software,
    Inc. (37)
Taro Pharmaceuticals Industries
    Ltd. (53)
TD Waterhouse Group, Inc. (34)
Tidel Technologies, Inc. (10)
Trend Micro, Inc. (32)
V3 Semiconductor, Inc. (18)
Wabash National Corp. (99)
White Electronic Designs Corp.
    (79)
Xicor, Inc. (98)

Preface

In this second edition of *The 100 Best Stocks to Own for Under $25,* I've tried to serve up a new list of dynamic young companies. A few of the stocks on the list also appeared in the first edition, but the vast majority are new to the book. I dropped most of the stocks from the first edition for one of three reasons: their price rose too high, they were acquired by another company, or their performance was subpar.

For the new list, I've tried to learn from the experience of the first edition. I've included more technology stocks and more manufacturers—because those were the stocks that performed best in the first edition—and fewer service companies, distributors, financial companies, and retailers. If I've done my job well, by the time you read this, there will be some stocks on the list that are already trading at well over $25 a share. That's one of the hazards of this work: good stocks in a strong market won't stay under $25 forever. In fact, over time, I hope they all grow to over $25. But even at a higher price, many of these stocks should continue to be solid investments with a bright future.

It is also likely that some of the stocks on the list will suddenly disappear as a result of a merger or acquisition. Many of the best small stocks ultimately become buyout targets for larger companies. Fortunately, with a list of 100 stocks, there will still be plenty of other picks from which to choose. (We'll try to keep track of the major changes at our investment research Web site <www.allstarstocks.com>.) The world of small stocks is constantly in flux. That's part of the draw of the small stock segment. They're exciting young companies in transition. Get them while they're hot.

Acknowledgments

A lot of people have contributed to the success of this book. Ed Lawler and Larry Nelson played a major role in the project. Ed, who is an accomplished author in his own right, helped on this book by writing many of the company profiles—as he has done for several other *100 Best Stocks* books. Larry, who, has helped with nearly every book I've written since 1990, worked from start to finish on this project, assisting with the research and fact-gathering, the graphs, the tables, and other key elements of the book.

I would also like to again thank Randy Royals and Paul Mallon, who initially came up with the idea for this book. And I want to thank my editors at Dearborn Trade, including Cynthia Zigmund, Jack Kiburz, and Sandy Thomas, who have helped shape the book into an attractive, professional, user-friendly format.

Introduction

There are a lot of good reasons to like small stocks. The best, of course, is that for the past century, small stocks have outperformed every other conventional form of investment.

In other words, if you want to get rich, small stocks are your best shot.

That's not to say, however, that *all* small stocks make good investments. Most are cheap for a reason—their growth prospects are suspect, their track history is checkered, and their economic business model is as yet unproved.

By their very nature, small stocks tend to be little-known companies with short histories and uncertain futures. Just a handful are followed by the major Wall Street brokerage houses. Many are involved in technologies or services that we don't understand. There are no household names among the small stock universe.

But, in a sense, that's exactly what is so appealing about small stocks. They are young, up-and-coming companies that have not yet been discovered by the rest of the investing world. And when you hit the right stock at the right time, small stocks have the kind of home run potential that larger blue chips could never deliver.

The purpose of this book is to identify some of the best fast-growing, unknown, and under-appreciated small stocks available today on the U.S. stock market. Not all will flourish, and certainly few, if any, will perform as well as Newport Corp., a stock from the first edition that grew more than 1,000 percent in the first nine months. But many of these stocks could enjoy growth of 25 to 100 percent over the next few months.

WHY SMALL STOCKS?

It's no secret to anyone who follows the market that small stocks are prone to wild swings in price. But that short-term volatility belies the extraordinary performance small stocks have enjoyed over the long term. The clearest indication recently has been the performance of the Nasdaq market, which comprises primarily smaller, newer companies.

Over the past five years, the Nasdaq has soared more than 500 percent. That's more than three times the rate of the Dow Jones Industrial Average, which comprises primarily larger, older blue chip stocks.

The recent success of small stocks is part of a well-established trend. Since 1925, small stocks have provided an average annual return of about 13 percent, compared with a return of about 11 percent return for large stocks.

Growth of Small Stocks versus Large Stocks, 1925–2000

	Avg. Annual Growth	Current Value of $1,000 Invested in 1925
Large Stocks	11%	$2.52 million
Small Stocks	13	9.56 million

The difference has been even more dramatic in recent decades, particularly among stocks with market capitalizations of under $25 million. A $10,000 investment in small stocks at the end of 1951, if held through 1994, would have grown to $29 million, according to a study by James P. O'Shaughnessy, author of *What Works on Wall Street.* That's an annual average return of 20 percent.

Another study by Mark Reinganum of the University of Southern California also showed a dramatic difference in the performance of small stocks versus large stocks during a 17-year period from 1963 through 1980. Reinganum divided all stocks of the New York Stock Exchange into eight categories from smallest to largest and reassembled the list anew each of the 17 years. As the following chart demonstrates, there was a clear and dramatic correlation between the size of the stock and the rate of growth.

Small Stocks versus Large Stocks, 1963–1980*
(Listed from largest to smallest stocks)

Avg. Annual Return	1980 Value of $10,000 Invested in 1963
1. 11.8%	$ 75,000
2. 12.9	88,200
3. 15.1	126,800
4. 15.2	127,000
5. 16.2	139,500
6. 18.5	201,000
7. 17.9	185,000
8. 23.7	452,000

* Based on a study of the stocks of the New York Stock Exchange by Mark Reinganum of the University of Southern California

As the chart demonstrates, for investors interested in explosive growth, smaller stocks clearly offered more potential. But great performance of small stocks *as a group* doesn't necessarily translate into great performance of small stocks on an individual basis. The challenge is finding the stocks that are most likely to live up to that potential.

THE SELECTION PROCESS

With more than 8,000 stocks selling for under $25, paring the list to the "best" 100 was clearly a daunting undertaking.

My first step was to study the stocks from the first edition of this book to see which types of stocks fared well, and which didn't. The stocks that did the best were manufacturers of technology-related products—primarily in the computer, telecommunications, and medical sectors. Manufacturers tended to do better than distributors or service-oriented companies, and technology stocks tended to do better than stocks from other areas of the economy.

Since the best stocks seemed to be technology-related companies, those were the areas I focused on most in selecting stocks for this book. My assistant, Larry Nelson, and I scrutinized hundreds of technology stocks—every one we could find selling for under $25—including computer and software makers, semiconductor manufacturers, video components and storage device makers, telecommunications and fiber-optics operations, and medical products manufacturers. We also did a broad-sweeping screen of all stocks under $25 to find the fastest-growing companies of every industry.

The selections were based on earnings and revenue growth, momentum, industry prospects, and simple gut reaction. Ultimately, all our in-depth analysis boiled down to one final test—Would I be interested in adding the stock to my own portfolio? If so, it made the list. If not, I moved on to other prospects. The final list is a technology-laden compilation of 100 dynamic, young companies that should stir the speculative juices of investors large and small.

There are no guarantees, of course. Some of these stocks will prosper; others will fade. They all show promise, but they all have flaws. That's why you can buy them now for under $25. If they were industry leaders with years of consistent earnings and revenue growth, their prices would be much higher. But at these prices, most of the 100 stocks appear to be well worth the gamble. The vast majority are very inexpensive relative to the rest of the market, with price-earnings ratios and price-to-sales ratios well below many of the larger blue chip stocks. The stocks that can continue to rack up record earnings and revenue should see their stock prices sky-rocket well into the future.

RANKING THE STOCKS

The stocks are ranked from 1 through 100 based on a 16-point rating system, with four key factors:

1. Four-year earnings growth
2. Four-year revenue growth
3. Three-year stock growth
4. Four-year consistency of earnings and revenue growth

I also took some extenuating circumstances into consideration. For instance, a company with strong earnings growth in the current year might receive an extra point, whereas a stock whose earnings had weakened during the current year might lose a point. But for the most part, the stocks were rated based on the following 16-point system:

Earnings Growth (Based on Four-Year Returns)

Avg. Annual Return	Points Awarded
10–14%	★
15–19%	★ ★
20–29%	★ ★ ★
30% and above	★ ★ ★ ★

Revenue Growth (Based on Four-Year Returns)

Avg. Annual Return	Points Awarded
15–19%	★
20–24%	★ ★
25–34%	★ ★ ★
35% and above	★ ★ ★ ★

Stock Growth (Based on Three-Year Returns)

Avg. Annual Return	Points Awarded
10–14%	★
15–19%	★ ★
20–29%	★ ★ ★
30% and above	★ ★ ★ ★

Consistency

A stock that has had four consecutive years of increased revenue and earnings per share would earn the maximum of four points. One point is deducted for every time the company did not post an increase in earnings or revenue. For instance, a company with earnings gains three of the past four years and revenue gains all four years would score a three out of four. A company with earnings gains three of the past four years and revenue gains three of the past four years would score just two out of four. A company with earnings gains and revenue gains just two of the past four years would have all four points deducted for a score of zero.

BREAKING TIES

The higher the score, the higher the rank. I evaluated several factors in breaking ties. First I looked at growth momentum. Companies whose revenue and earnings were still growing at a strong clip got the nod over companies that seemed to be losing speed. I also looked at the size of the company, the type of products or services it offered, and its consistency in terms of revenue and earnings growth. The ones that looked to be the better bets for the long run got the higher ranking.

INVESTING IN SMALL STOCKS

Every stock has its risks, and small stocks are no exception. But you can increase your odds by playing the averages. Rather than invest in 1 or 2 small stocks, select 5 to 10 stocks that look promising (or even up to 20 stocks if you can afford to put at least $1,000 into each stock), and invest a little in each. Small stock investing is like a home run derby: the more swings you take, the better your chances of hitting a home run. Two or three big winners could keep your entire portfolio on the upswing.

Here's an example: Let's say you buy six stocks, investing $1,000 in each stock. Four stocks remain about the same, and two triple in price. Suddenly your initial $6,000 investment is worth $10,000—a 67 percent increase. That's the way to play the small stock market. Play the averages by picking several stocks that look attractive.

SEVEN MYTHS OF SMALL STOCK INVESTING

Investors have some unusual ideas about small stock investing. Here are some common misconceptions:

1. You can't lose big money on small stocks.   Fact: You can lose as much on small stocks as you can on any other stocks. Whatever you invest, you can lose. Whether it's a $3 stock or $300, if a stock drops 95 percent, you're taking a bath.

2. Low-priced stocks are cheap.   To the eyes of a Wall Street analyst, stock price really has no bearing on whether a stock is cheap or expensive. What matters is the price-earnings ratio (stock price divided by earnings per share), which is the leading ratio analysts use to determine the fair value of a stock. For example, a $5 stock with a price-earnings ratio (PE) of 50 is much more expensive, in value terms, than a $50 stock with a PE of 5. For a stock with a 50 PE, you are paying $50 for every $1 of earnings versus $5 for every $1 of earnings with a 5 PE stock. So in terms of value per dollar, the $5 stock with a 50 PE is 10 times more expensive than a $50 stock with a 5 PE—even though, on the surface, it would seem to be just the opposite.

3. Buying a small stock mutual fund is the same as buying small stocks.   Most small stock mutual funds are so broadly diversified—with investments in dozens or hundreds of different stocks—that the performance of one or two stocks within the fund would have very little discernible impact on the overall performance of the fund. Small stock funds tend to be less volatile than individual stocks, but they have no home run potential. Good funds may beat the market by a few percentage points, offering returns in a good year of 25 to 40 percent. But a great small stock can grow 500 percent or more in a good year.

4. You can't buy big stocks with small dollars.   Some investors are drawn to small stocks, because they don't think they can afford big stocks.

There's really no difference between buying 100 shares of a $10 stock or 10 shares of $100 stock. The brokerage fee is about the same, and if either stock grows 10 percent, that's a $100 gain. The number of shares you own is irrelevant. Buy the best stocks regardless of price.

5. Double down on small stocks if they drop in price. The practice of buying a stock down, which is to buy more shares as the price drops, may be a sound policy for investing in established blue chips, such as Merck or General Electric, but it's not always wise with small stocks. When small stocks run into trouble, they can drop fast and far—and then drop some more. Most recover slowly, if at all. A friend of mine bought the stock of a company called Statosphere that operated a hotel at the edge of Las Vegas. The stock reached a high of $14 and started dropping. The more it dropped, the more shares my friend bought. Ultimately, the company went into bankruptcy, and the stock fell to under $1 a share. My friend lost thousands of dollars throwing good money after bad. If a small, speculative stock starts drifting south, don't chase it. Move on.

6. Always sell stocks after a big run-up in price. Some investors love to take a profit on their winners. They're often the same investors who like to hold onto their losers in hopes of a turnaround. Those investors take the expression "buy low and sell high" too literally. If you always sell your winners and hold your losers, you'll end up with a portfolio of losers. What you want is a portfolio of winners, so keep your winners and dump your losers. Imagine, for instance, the investor who sold Microsoft in 1987 after watching the stock jump 30 percent. A $10,000 investment would have netted a nice $3,000 short-term gain. But if the investor had held the stock instead of selling, it would now be worth over $1 million. Don't settle for chump change. Swing for the home run. That's why you're investing in the world of small stocks.

7. Always buy and hold for the long term. Buying stocks you *hope* to hold for the long term is a good policy, but that doesn't mean you should always *hold* every stock for the long term. Some small stocks aren't worth holding.

If you buy a stock because the company is growing quickly, then be prepared to sell if the growth starts to level off. Review your portfolio periodically to see which stocks are doing well and which ones are going nowhere. When appropriate, weed out the ones that aren't moving. But don't sell a stock if its revenue and earnings are still rising quickly—even if its stock price has been stagnant. Be patient. Sometimes it takes a while for the market to react. But if a company's earnings and revenue continue to rise, ultimately the stock price must follow.

Because small stocks have proven to be wildly volatile, you may also want to sell some shares if your stock gets caught up in a momentum rally. Sometimes market traders can push a stock price up 300 to 400 percent in a relatively short period of time. If that happens, you might consider taking some gains.

For example, you buy 100 shares of a $10 stock ($1,000 total). If that stock suddenly rockets up to $40—and your investment grows to $4,000—you might want to sell $1,000 worth to recoup your initial investment. That way, no matter what the stock does—whether it goes up, down, or stays the same—it's all gravy to you. You've already recovered your entire initial investment.

The world of small stock investing can range from heart-wrenching to unbridled exuberance—but it's never dull. If you do the best you can in selecting promising stocks for your portfolio and give them time to grow; if you add regularly to your holdings and keep the faith, over time good things will come from those small packages.

Here's hoping you can cull from this list some of the great growth stocks of the 21st century.

North American Scientific, Inc.

20200 Sunburst Street
Chatsworth, CA 91311
818-734-8600
Nasdaq: NASI
www.nasi.net

Chairman:
Irwin J. Gruverman
President and CEO:
L. Michael Cutrer

Earnings Growth	★ ★ ★ ★
Revenue Growth	★ ★ ★ ★
Stock Growth	★ ★ ★ ★
Consistency	★ ★ ★
Total	**15 Points**

North American Scientific is attacking one of the leading killers of American men—prostate cancer. The biotechnology company makes a line of radioactive pellets that when implanted in the prostate gland are designed to kill the cancer.

The treatment is known as brachytherapy, derived from the Greek word *brachy,* meaning a short distance. Implanting rice-sized radioactive "seeds" into the prostate via thin, hollow needles treats the prostate cancer. It's most effective in the cancer's early stages. The seeds remain permanently in the prostate in order to deliver enough radiation to arrest the cancer while minimizing exposure to surrounding tissue and organs.

Brachytherapy has produced survival success rates similar to those of other prostate cancer treatments such as the surgical removal of the prostate. The invasive surgical procedure costs between $20,000 and $30,000, requires several weeks of recovery time, and often results in such side effects as impotence and incontinence.

By contrast, a brachytherapy procedure costs about $10,000 to $15,000 and has a shorter recovery period, because it is performed on an outpatient basis under local anesthesia. The side effects are less pronounced. The procedure has been gaining wider acceptance among physicians and patients. About 179,000 cases of prostate cancer are diagnosed annually in the United States. The disease that has no known cure causes about 37,000 deaths.

As a leader in the brachytherapy sector, North American is the only company that makes both longer half-life iodine and the shorter half-life palladium brachytherapy seeds (the most common pellets for prostate brachytherapy procedures).

The California-based operation is also a leader in applying radioisotope technology to the development of products for use in nuclear medicine, biotechnology, environmental safety, and industrial research. For example, the company is developing a product to help doctors visualize, with unprecedented sensitivity and speed, the body's response to cancer treatments, heart disease, and the body's immune response to an organ transplant.

North American also has a wide range of related treatments in the pipeline that should add to the bottom line in the years ahead.

Founded in 1995, North American Scientific has about 50 employees and a market capitalization of about $130 million.

EARNINGS PER SHARE PROGRESSION ★ ★ ★ ★

Past 4 years: 1,467 percent (99 percent per year)

REVENUE GROWTH ★ ★ ★ ★

Past 4 years: 596 percent (63 percent per year)

STOCK GROWTH ★ ★ ★ ★

Past 3 years: 423 percent (75 percent per year)
Dollar growth: $10,000 over 3 years would have grown to about $52,000.

CONSISTENCY

Increased earnings per share: 3 of the past 4 years
Increased sales: 4 consecutive years

NORTH AMERICAN SCIENTIFIC AT A GLANCE

Fiscal year ended: Oct. 31
Revenue and net income in $ millions

						4-Year Growth	
						Avg. Annual (%)	Total (%)
	1995	**1996**	**1997**	**1998**	**1999**		
Revenue ($)	1.84	3.06	3.38	5.84	12.8	63	596
Net income ($)	0.131	0.413	0.276	1.10	3.37	120	2,472
Earnings/share ($)	0.03	0.09	0.05	0.16	0.47	99	1,467
PE range	—	—	21–336	23–203	11–24		

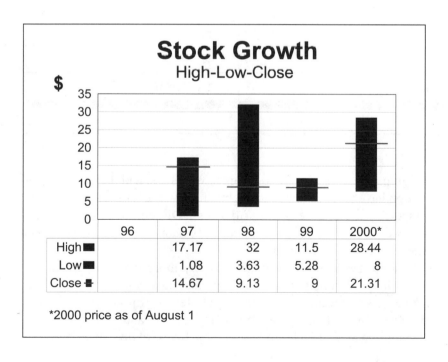

Stock Growth
High-Low-Close

	96	97	98	99	2000*
High■		17.17	32	11.5	28.44
Low■		1.08	3.63	5.28	8
Close ■		14.67	9.13	9	21.31

*2000 price as of August 1

2
Advanced Digital Information Corp.

11431 Willows Road, NE
P.O. Box 97057
Redmond, WA 98073
425-881-8004
Nasdaq: ADIC
www.adic.com

Chairman and CEO:
Peter van Oppen
President:
Charles Stonecipher

Earnings Growth	★ ★ ★ ★
Revenue Growth	★ ★ ★ ★
Stock Growth	★ ★ ★ ★
Consistency	★ ★ ★
Total	**15 Points**

Sharper graphics, smoother videos, bigger Web sites, and the explosion of information have all contributed to the business world's insatiable appetite for computer data storage space. Advanced Digital Information Corp. (ADIC) has developed a line of high-capacity data storage devices to help meet the sky-rocketing demand.

Disk storage sales have been growing by more than 80 percent per year, according to International Data Corp., an industry research company. Storage space sales went from 10,000 terabytes (a trillion bytes) in 1994 to 116,000 terabytes in 1998—a 1,000 percent rise—and it is projected to reach 1.5 million terabytes (1.5 million-trillion bytes) of disk space by 2002.

ADIC makes hardware and software-based data storage systems for the open systems marketplace. Its storage systems are used to capture, protect, manage, and archive the increasingly complex stream of computer data. Most of its storage devices are used as part of a computer network operated by a business or organization.

The Redmond, Washington operation incorporates its hardware, software, and connectivity products with hardware and software from other manufacturers to tailor its systems to the requirements of each customer.

ADIC offers a broad range of automated storage "libraries" priced from about $2,000 to nearly $2 million, depending on the size and speed of the storage systems. Its largest mixed media systems hold up to 70,000 data tape cartridges.

The core component of ADIC's storage system is its automated tape library. The system can be programmed to automatically back up a network's data, using specific tapes at predetermined times. The company is also developing libraries that use optical technology.

ADIC sells its products through a worldwide network of independent distributors and original manufacturers, such as Dell Computer, IBM, and Fujitsu.

Founded in 1983, ADIC has about 500 employees and a market capitalization of about $700 million.

EARNINGS PER SHARE PROGRESSION ★ ★ ★ ★

Past 3 years: 260 percent (53 percent per year)

REVENUE GROWTH ★ ★ ★ ★

Past 4 years: 605 percent (63 percent per year)

STOCK GROWTH ★ ★ ★ ★

Past 3 years: 300 percent (60 percent per year)
Dollar growth: $10,000 over 3 years would have grown to $40,000.

CONSISTENCY ★ ★ ★

Increased earnings per share: 3 of the past 4 years
Increased sales: 4 consecutive years

ADVANCED DIGITAL AT A GLANCE

Fiscal year ended: Oct. 31
Revenue and net income in $ millions

	1995	1996	1997	1998	1999	4-Year Growth Avg. Annual (%)	Total (%)
Revenue ($)	31.7	58.9	93.2	114.6	223.4	63	605
Net income ($)	.294	3.43	8.49	1.56	15.5	162	5,172
Earnings/share ($)	0.01	0.10	0.23	0.04	0.36	144	3,500
PE range	—	23–41	13–25	39–131	9–80		

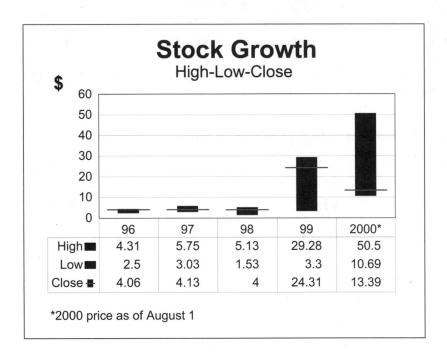

Stock Growth
High-Low-Close

	96	97	98	99	2000*
High	4.31	5.75	5.13	29.28	50.5
Low	2.5	3.03	1.53	3.3	10.69
Close	4.06	4.13	4	24.31	13.39

*2000 price as of August 1

3
Optibase, Ltd.

7 Shenkar Street
Herzliya, Israel 46120
408-260-6760 (U.S.)
Nasdaq: OBAS
www.optibase.com

Chairman:
Mordechai Gorfung
President:
Amir Aharoni
CEO:
Ran Eisenberg

Earnings Growth	★ ★ ★ ★
Revenue Growth	★ ★ ★
Stock Growth	★ ★ ★ ★
Consistency	★ ★ ★ ★
Total	**15 Points**

The Internet is moving rapidly toward high-quality digital video, and Optibase is leading the charge.

The Israeli operation makes systems for handling digital video, which is the key component of the booming computer multimedia arena. Optibase combines high-powered software applications with specialized hardware platforms to provide a suite of products that produce video streaming for video commerce, online education, and business TV.

Because of infrastructure technology shortcomings, Internet videos tend to be short in length, suffer from poor resolution, and are painfully slow and unreliable. Optibase provides the "video infrastructure" needed to upgrade hardware in order to facilitate high-end multimedia applications. Its products include:

- **Video publishing tools.** These are full-blown environments used by professionals to produce digital videos. Optibase makes composing tools to create content in both the MPEG (moving pictures experts group) and DVD (digital video disc) formats.
- **Digital video hardware.** Optibase manufactures special computer boards that are installed in computers and networking devices. Some products are used to create DVDs and CD-ROMs. Others are used for video projection, digital broadcasting over cable TV networks, and even to play back digital video at point-of-sale kiosks.
- **Digital video networking.** The company also makes hardware and software to deploy streaming video applications for such uses as video-conferencing, Internet news and entertainment videocasting, security video surveillance, and computer-based training.

Optibase is at the cutting edge of digital video. It has applied for several patents for proprietary technologies to make MPEG work better and has recently focused on creating video networking technology to make the Internet handle video faster and more reliably.

The company sells mainly through distributors and systems integrators. Major customers include Time Warner, the Bloomberg financial news service, and NEC.

Optibase went public with its initial stock offering in 1999. The company has about 105 employees and a market capitalization of about $230 million.

EARNINGS PER SHARE PROGRESSION   ★ ★ ★ ★

Past 2 years: 5,200 percent (620 percent per year)

REVENUE GROWTH   ★ ★ ★

Past 4 years: 150 percent (26 percent per year)

STOCK GROWTH   ★ ★ ★ ★

Past year: 157 percent
Dollar growth: $10,000 over 1 year would have grown to about $26,000.

CONSISTENCY   ★ ★ ★ ★

Positive earnings progression: 4 consecutive years
Increased sales: 4 consecutive years

OPTIBASE AT A GLANCE

Fiscal year ended: Dec. 31
Revenue and net income in $ millions

	1995	1996	1997	1998	1999	4-Year Growth Avg. Annual (%)	4-Year Growth Total (%)
Revenue ($)	10.4	12.8	14.4	20.4	26.0	26	150
Net income ($)	−0.81	−0.53	0.06	1.62	4.35	760*	7,400*
Earnings/share ($)	−0.22	−0.14	0.01	0.26	0.53	620*	5,200*
PE range	—	—	—	—	9–67		

*Net income and earnings per share growth figures are based on 2-year performance.

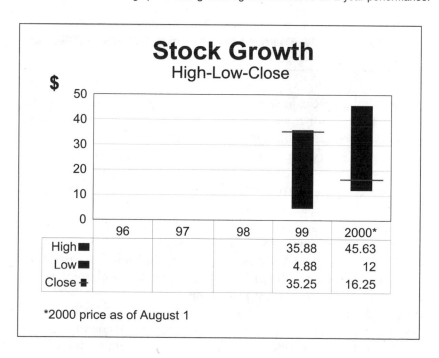

Stock Growth
High-Low-Close

$	96	97	98	99	2000*
High ■				35.88	45.63
Low ■				4.88	12
Close ■				35.25	16.25

*2000 price as of August 1

4
Richton International Corp.

767 Fifth Avenue
New York, NY 10153
212-751-1445
NYSE: RHT
www.richton.com

Chairman and President:
Fred R. Sullivan

Earnings Growth	★ ★ ★ ★
Revenue Growth	★ ★ ★
Stock Growth	★ ★ ★ ★
Consistency	★ ★ ★ ★
Total	**15 Points**

Bring on the drought. Richton's ready. The company is a leading supplier of sprinkler systems for a wide range of applications, including farms, golf courses, and residential and commercial lots.

Through its Century Supply subsidiary, Richton is the nation's largest wholesale distributor of sprinkler irrigation systems. It sells systems and related products from more than 60 suppliers, including Rain Bird, Hunter, Irritrol, and Legacy. Century is a distributor for all of the leading manufacturers of turf irrigation equipment in the United States.

The company has about 128 branch offices in about 33 states, primarily in the East, South, and Midwest. Its primary customers are irrigation and landscape contractors who install irrigation systems for commercial, residential, and golf course watering systems.

In all, Richton sells to a customer base of more than 20,000 contractors. The firm has begun to expand to other regions of the country through strategic acquisitions of smaller regional irrigation system suppliers.

Richton supplements its sales business with some related services, including design assistance, training seminars, and incentive programs.

The bulk of Richton's revenue is derived from irrigation sales. The company also sells outdoor lighting and decorative fountain equipment through its Century Supply subsidiary, although sprinklers account for about 93 percent of Century's total revenue.

In addition to its irrigation distribution business, Richton recently acquired CBE Technologies, which is a systems integrator providing network consulting, design, and installation; network management and related support; technical services outsourcing; comprehensive hardware maintenance; and equipment sales.

CBE serves as an authorized service and warranty center for most leading PC and printer manufacturers, including IBM, Compaq, Hewlett-Packard, Apple, and many others. The company has offices in Boston, New York, Los Angeles, and Portland, Maine.

Richton International has about 700 employees and a market capitalization of about $45 million.

EARNINGS PER SHARE PROGRESSION ★ ★ ★ ★

Past 4 years: 393 percent (49 percent per year)

REVENUE GROWTH ★ ★ ★

Past 4 years: 228 percent (33 percent per year)

STOCK GROWTH ★ ★ ★ ★

Past 3 years: 342 percent (65 percent per year)
Dollar growth: $10,000 over 3 years would have grown to about $44,000.

CONSISTENCY ★ ★ ★ ★

Increased earnings per share: 4 consecutive years
Increased sales: 4 consecutive years

RICHTON INTERNATIONAL AT A GLANCE

Fiscal year ended: Dec. 31
Revenue and net income in $ millions

	1995	1996	1997	1998	1999	4-Year Growth Avg. Annual (%)	Total (%)
Revenue ($)	66.6	87.7	106.5	147.9	218.2	33	228
Net income ($)	1.37	1.76	2.29	3.53	7.16	52	423
Earnings/share ($)	0.43	0.54	0.68	1.06	2.12	49	393
PE range	5–9	5–9	5–10	5–10	4–8		

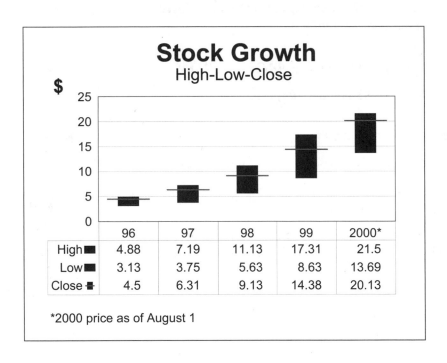

Stock Growth
High-Low-Close

$

	96	97	98	99	2000*
High■	4.88	7.19	11.13	17.31	21.5
Low■	3.13	3.75	5.63	8.63	13.69
Close ■	4.5	6.31	9.13	14.38	20.13

*2000 price as of August 1

5

Concord Camera Corp.

4000 Hollywood Boulevard,
Suite 650N
Hollywood, FL 33021
954-331-4200
Nasdaq: LENS
www.concordcam.com

Chairman, President, and CEO:
Ira B. Lampert

Earnings Growth	★ ★ ★ ★
Revenue Growth	★ ★ ★
Stock Growth	★ ★ ★ ★
Consistency	★ ★ ★
Total	**14 Points**

Picture this: Failing camera maker gives up on old-fashioned cameras and goes high tech. New focus brings picture-perfect rebound.

Traditional camera manufacturer Concord Camera saw its fortunes fall steadily when consumer interest in its old line of cameras began to fade. But in 1995, the company changed directions, updated its offerings, adjusted its marketing strategy, and reversed its fortunes. Concord's earnings and revenue have been growing rapidly ever since.

The three key changes the Hollywood, Florida operation implemented include:

1. **One-time-use cameras.** Concord began making the increasingly popular one-time-use cameras, which now account for more than 80 percent of all new cameras sold in the United States. The company manufactures its own line of disposable cameras, as well as private label cam-

eras for Kodak, Polaroid (PopShots), and Wal-Mart (Easy Shot). The single-use-camera market is growing at about 20 percent per year.

2. **Digital cameras.** The company began selling its first digital camera in 2000. Its cameras are smaller, lighter, and less expensive than most other digital cameras.

3. **New marketing strategy.** In the past, Concord generated most of its revenue through retail sales. Now about two-thirds of its revenue comes from leading camera companies, such as Kodak and Polaroid, that contract with Concord to manufacture cameras for them.

Concord is also setting up alliances to develop and manufacture wireless image-capture devices that will be able to take pictures and send them over the Internet or to a wireless phone. The company markets its cameras under the trade names Concord, Keystone, LeClic, Apex, and Crayola.

Concord Camera is global in scope, with international offices in Canada, France, China, Germany, and England. The company has about 160 employees and a market capitalization of about $375 million.

EARNINGS PER SHARE PROGRESSION   ★ ★ ★ ★

Past 2 years: 146 percent (57 percent per year)

REVENUE GROWTH   ★ ★ ★

Past 4 years: 159 percent (27 percent per year)

STOCK GROWTH   ★ ★ ★ ★

Past 3 years: 1,580 percent (150 percent per year)
Dollar growth: $10,000 over 3 years would have grown to about $170,000.

CONSISTENCY   ★ ★ ★

Positive earnings progression: 4 consecutive years
Increased sales: 3 of the past 4 years

CONCORD CAMERA AT A GLANCE

Fiscal year ended: June 30
Revenue and net income in $ millions

	1996	1997	1998	1999	2000	4-Year Growth Avg. Annual (%)	Total (%)
Revenue ($)	66.8	65.7	102.7	118.4	173.2	27	159
Net income ($)	−1.7	−0.83	6.0	7.7	15.4	60*	157*
Earnings/share ($)	−0.08	−0.04	0.26	0.33	0.64	57*	146*
PE range	—	—	4–14	5–36			

*Net income and earnings per share growth figures are based on 2-year performance.

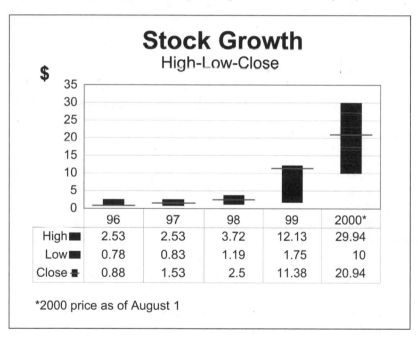

Stock Growth
High-Low-Close

$	96	97	98	99	2000*
High■	2.53	2.53	3.72	12.13	29.94
Low■	0.78	0.83	1.19	1.75	10
Close ■	0.88	1.53	2.5	11.38	20.94

*2000 price as of August 1

6
AstroPower, Inc.

Solar Park
Newark, DE 19716
302-366-0400
Nasdaq: APWR
www.astropower.com

President and CEO:
Allen M. Barnett

Earnings Growth	★ ★ ★ ★
Revenue Growth	★ ★ ★ ★
Stock Growth	★ ★ ★ ★
Consistency	★ ★
Total	**14 Points**

As the supply of conventional fuels declines, and prices climb, the world will look to the sun for more of its energy. That's where AstroPower makes its mark.

The Delaware-based operation is a leading manufacturer of solar electric power products, including solar cells, modules, and panels. Its solar cells are semiconductor devices that convert sunlight into electricity and form the building blocks for all solar electric power products.

The development of solar power products still leaves a lot to be desired, but AstroPower is making progress. Its products are used in three types of applications: The fastest growing is on-grid, in which solar power is used as an environmentally preferred source or supplemental source for customers already connected to a power grid. It is also used for minimal electrification applications in rural areas of underdeveloped countries where standard electric service is not available. And third, it is used for a wide range of applications related to the telecommunications and transportation industries, such as cellular phone base stations, fiber-optic and radio repeaters, traffic information, and warning displays.

The company sells several categories of products, including:

- **Solar cells.** These semiconductor devices convert sunlight directly into electricity through a process known as the photovoltaic effect.
- **Modules.** These assemblies of solar cells are connected together and encapsulated in a weatherproof package.
- **Panels.** These are made of several modules wired together at the factory and mounted on a common support structure.
- **Systems.** These groups of panels and system controls are designed primarily for residential rooftops.

The company has continued to improve its products through research and development contracts with government research laboratories and alliances with corporate partners and strategic customers.

AstroPower has about 350 employees and a market capitalization of about $200 million.

EARNINGS PER SHARE PROGRESSION   ★ ★ ★ ★

Past 4 years: 1,100 percent (87 percent per year)

REVENUE GROWTH   ★ ★ ★ ★

Past 4 years: 249 percent (38 percent per year)

STOCK GROWTH   ★ ★ ★ ★

Past 3 years: 286 percent (57 percent per year)
Dollar growth: $10,000 over 3 years would have grown to about $39,000.

CONSISTENCY   ★ ★

Increased earnings per share: 2 of the past 4 years
Increased sales: 4 consecutive years

ASTROPOWER AT A GLANCE

Fiscal year ended: Dec. 31
Revenue and net income in $ millions

	1995	1996	1997	1998	1999	Avg. Annual (%)	Total (%)
						4-Year Growth	
Revenue ($)	9.9	10.6	16.6	23.1	34.6	38	249
Net income ($)	0.098	−2.36	0.65	2.41	2.27	120	2,216
Earnings/share ($)	0.02	−0.40	0.11	0.27	0.24	87	1,100
PE range	—	—	—	21–39	38–83		

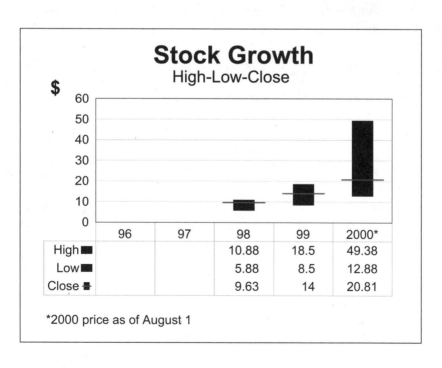

Stock Growth
High-Low-Close

$

	96	97	98	99	2000*
High			10.88	18.5	49.38
Low			5.88	8.5	12.88
Close			9.63	14	20.81

*2000 price as of August 1

Akorn, Inc.

Akorn inc.

2500 Millbrook Drive
Buffalo Grove, IL 60089
847-279-6100
Nasdaq: AKRN
www.akorn.com

Chairman:
John N. Kooper
President and CEO:
Floyd Benjamin

Earnings Growth	★ ★ ★ ★
Revenue Growth	★ ★ ★
Stock Growth	★ ★ ★ ★
Consistency	★ ★ ★
Total	**14 Points**

Akorn is intensely focused on improving the vision of older Americans.

Widely known among U.S. optometrists and ophthalmologists, Akorn is developing a pharmaceutical product to help eye doctors diagnose Age-Related Macular Degeneration, or ARMD, which attacks the macula of the eye. The macula is the light-sensing area of the central retina that provides vision for fine work and reading, and where the sharpest central vision and color perception occurs.

A cruel disease that afflicts more than 10 million Americans, ARMD reduces the clear central vision needed for reading, driving, identifying faces, watching TV, and performing other daily tasks. It's estimated that 11 percent of Americans aged 65 to 74 and 28 percent of Americans 75 or older have the disease. Akorn estimates the market for this product is about $350 million.

On May 2, 2000, the company announced it had entered into a worldwide exclusive license agreement with Johns Hopkins University's Applied Physics Laboratory. The agreement grants Akorn the exclusive rights to two patents covering the methodology and instrumentation for the treatment of ARMD.

In addition to developing, manufacturing, and marketing pharmaceutical products to the ophthalmological niche, the company also targets markets for rheumatology, anesthesia, antidotes, and hospital products. Akorn makes surgical products, too, including surgical knives, surgical tapes, and anti-ultraviolet goggles. The company's sales and marketing efforts are directed at the traditional doctors offices and hospital pharmacies, as well as drug wholesalers, hospital groups, and mail-order pharmacies.

Akorn has been fueling its sales growth through the acquisition or licensing of branded specialty products. In 1999, it acquired the specialty ophthalmic diagnostic product Paredine, which diagnoses Horner's Syndrome, a neurological disorder that prevents the pupil of the eye from dilating.

Founded in 1971, Akorn has about 350 employees and a market capitalization of about $140 million.

EARNINGS PER SHARE PROGRESSION ★ ★ ★ ★

Past 4 years: 620 percent (64 percent per year)

REVENUE GROWTH ★ ★ ★

Past 4 years: 291 percent (41 percent per year, but slowing)

STOCK GROWTH ★ ★ ★ ★

Past 3 years: 259 percent (53 percent per year)
Dollar growth: $10,000 over 3 years would have grown to $36,000.

CONSISTENCY ★ ★ ★

Increased earnings per share: 3 of the past 4 years
Increased sales: 4 consecutive years

AKORN AT A GLANCE

Fiscal year ended: Dec. 31
Revenue and net income in $ millions

	1995	1996	1997	1998	1999	4-Year Growth Avg. Annual (%)	Total (%)
Revenue ($)	16.5	33.9	42.3	56.7	64.6	41	291
Net income ($)	0.79	0.44	1.79	4.65	6.67	71	746
Earnings/share ($)	0.05	0.00	0.11	0.25	0.36	64	620
PE range	13–24	33–74	17–42	10–37	9–15		

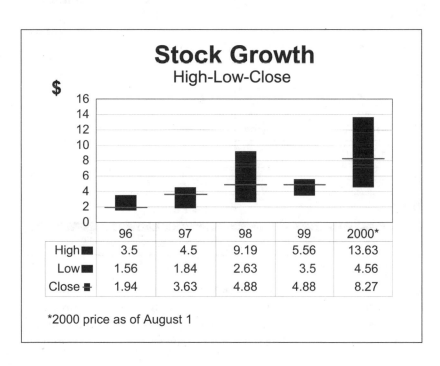

Stock Growth
High-Low-Close

$	96	97	98	99	2000*
High	3.5	4.5	9.19	5.56	13.63
Low	1.56	1.84	2.63	3.5	4.56
Close	1.94	3.63	4.88	4.88	8.27

*2000 price as of August 1

Exactech, Inc.

2320 N.W. 66th Court
Gainesville, FL 32653
352-377-1140
Nasdaq: EXAC
www.exac.com

Chairman and CEO:
William Petty, M.D.
President:
Timothy J. Seese

Earnings Growth	★ ★ ★
Revenue Growth	★ ★ ★ ★
Stock Growth	★ ★ ★ ★
Consistency	★ ★ ★
Total	**14 Points**

Exactech wants to keep aging baby boomers on their feet. With the generation's leading edge now into their mid-50s, there's no shortage of aching knees and hips that have been damaged through arthritis or injury. More than a million joint replacement operations are performed each year worldwide.

Exactech makes and markets orthopedic implants, such as knee and hip replacements, specialized surgical tools, and a bone grafting material called Opteform. Made from a biologic substance that helps surgeons repair damaged bones, Opteform is puttylike when heated but firm when it cools to body temperature. An Opteform "bone" implant spares a patient the discomfort of having doctors harvest a section of bone from another part of the body.

About two-thirds of the company's revenues are generated by the sale of its knee replacement devices. The Optetrak knee system, introduced in 1995, offers patients a better range of motion, while reducing the stress level on the joint by using precision manufacturing techniques. The less stress, the better the chance that the replacement will be long lasting.

The Gainesville, Florida operation competes with much larger health care concerns like Johnson & Johnson and Biomet, but it sells its products to doctors and hospitals at a lower price. The company has about 2 percent of the market for knee replacements and about 1 percent for hip replacements. Its international sales are approaching 25 percent of its total revenues.

In 1997, the company introduced its AuRA hip, an implant system that was updated in 1999. The company has an active new-product pipeline. Its recent innovations include a new socket system to improve the longevity of hip replacements and an improved type of polyethylene to increase the longevity of knee replacements.

Exactech was founded in 1985 and went public with its initial stock offering in 1996. It has about 80 employees and a market capitalization of about $70 million.

EARNINGS PER SHARE PROGRESSION ★ ★ ★

Past 4 years: 126 percent (23 percent per year)

REVENUE GROWTH ★ ★ ★ ★

Past 4 years: 261 percent (38 percent per year)

STOCK GROWTH ★ ★ ★ ★

Past 3 years: 138 percent (34 percent per year)
Dollar growth: $10,000 over 3 years would have grown to about $24,000.

CONSISTENCY ★ ★ ★

Increased earnings per share: 3 of the past 4 years
Increased sales: 4 consecutive years

EXACTECH AT A GLANCE

Fiscal year ended: Dec. 31
Revenue and net income in $ millions

	1995	1996	1997	1998	1999	Avg. Annual (%)	Total (%)
						4-Year Growth	
Revenue ($)	9.1	13.8	17.6	24.0	32.9	38	261
Net income ($)	.828	1.55	1.58	2.13	3.17	40	283
Earnings/share ($)	0.27	0.37	0.32	0.43	0.61	23	126
PE range	—	13–32	12–31	11–31	14–26		

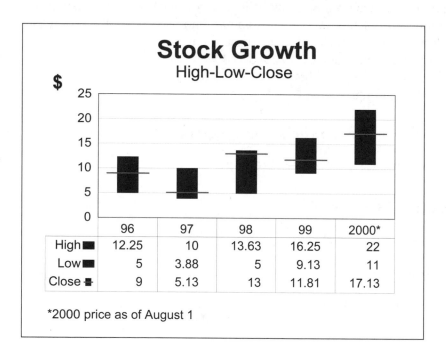

Stock Growth
High-Low-Close

	96	97	98	99	2000*
High■	12.25	10	13.63	16.25	22
Low■	5	3.88	5	9.13	11
Close⬛	9	5.13	13	11.81	17.13

*2000 price as of August 1

Actrade International, Ltd.

7 Penn Plaza, Suite 422
New York, NY 10001
212-563-1036
Nasdaq: ACRT
www.actrade.com

Chairman and CEO:
Amos Aharoni
President:
Alexander C. Stonkus

Earnings Growth	★ ★ ★ ★
Revenue Growth	★ ★ ★ ★
Stock Growth	★ ★
Consistency	★ ★ ★ ★
Total	**14 Points**

International trade is safer and easier thanks to a payment system devised by Actrade International. The New York operation offers a "Trade Acceptance Draft" (TAD), which allows U.S. companies to buy and sell their goods and services in the international market without risk of getting short-changed in the deal.

The TAD is a negotiable note signed by the buyer and made payable to the seller. Once the buyer signs the TAD agreement, it confirms that the goods or services were delivered by the seller and accepted by the buyer. The receivable is converted to an insured financial instrument purchased by Actrade.

TADs are used by small and large companies alike. They eliminate the problem of aging receivables and the cost and personnel time of pursuing collection of past due accounts. They have become an increasingly popular option for companies, as reflected in Actrade's balance sheet. Actrade's sales have doubled every year, and earnings have grown at nearly 50 percent per year.

In addition to TADs, Actrade has created a similar instrument for Internet transactions. The "E-TAD" is designed to appeal to businesses buying and selling through Web sites. It allows suppliers to receive payment within 48 hours, while buyers may receive extended terms of up to six months. Actrade assumes the credit risk, handles the collection, and provides the financing—collecting a percentage for its services.

Actrade also has an international trading arm that exports products to the Middle East, South America, Europe, and the Pacific Rim. Actrade delivers foreign buyers for products of U.S. companies through its network of buyers, wholesalers, and distributors. The company can also arrange required export services, including air or sea shipping, inland freight arrangements, and other shipping arrangements.

Founded in 1987, Actrade went public with its initial stock offering in 1992. The company has about 50 employees and a market capitalization of about $185 million.

EARNINGS PER SHARE PROGRESSION ★ ★ ★ ★

Past 4 years: 914 percent (80 percent per year)

REVENUE GROWTH ★ ★ ★ ★

Past 4 years: 1,169 percent (90 percent per year)

STOCK GROWTH ★ ★

Past 3 years: 50 percent (15 percent per year)
Dollar growth: $10,000 over 3 years would have grown to $15,000.

CONSISTENCY ★ ★ ★ ★

Increased earnings per share: 4 consecutive years
Increased sales: 4 consecutive years

ACTRADE INTERNATIONAL AT A GLANCE

Fiscal year ended: June 30
Revenue and net income in $ millions

	1995	1996	1997	1998	1999	4-Year Growth Avg. Annual (%)	Total (%)
Revenue ($)	16.4	23.8	43.5	98.5	208.2	90	1,169
Net income ($)	.408	.758	1.9	4.42	6.23	97	1,427
Earnings/share ($)	0.07	0.14	0.24	0.50	0.71	80	914
PE range	16–27	12–58	30–121	19–54	14–34		

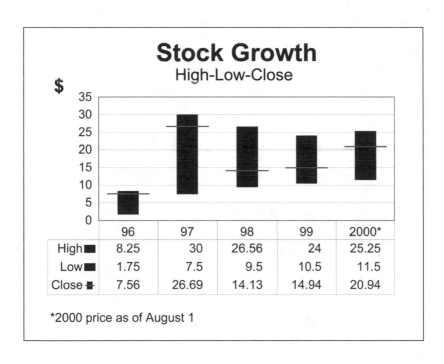

Stock Growth
High-Low-Close

$	96	97	98	99	2000*
High	8.25	30	26.56	24	25.25
Low	1.75	7.5	9.5	10.5	11.5
Close	7.56	26.69	14.13	14.94	20.94

*2000 price as of August 1

Tidel Technologies, Inc.

5847 San Felipe, Suite 900
Houston, TX 77057
713-783-8200
Nasdaq: ATMS
www.tidel.com

Chairman and CEO:
James T. Rash
President:
Mark K. Levenick

Earnings Growth	★ ★ ★
Revenue Growth	★ ★ ★ ★
Stock Growth	★ ★ ★ ★
Consistency	★ ★ ★
Total	**14 Points**

It's definitely not your father's ATM. Tidel Technologies's next-generation automated teller machine is an interactive, multimedia kiosk with stereo speakers that can do a whole lot more than spit out cash.

Known as the Chameleon, Tidel's Internet-enabled machine puts the world of e-commerce at a user's fingertips. Using a simplified touchscreen interface on its 15-inch color screen, a person can book an airline ticket, buy movie tickets, or even sample the view from a seat in an arena before buying a concert ticket. And yes, it can also dispense cash.

The machine is versatile. Retailers can configure the Chameleon to be a point-of-information terminal at one moment and a point-of-sale terminal next, selling tickets and prepaid phone cards and dispensing coupons. The machine can also present streaming media advertising. Behind the scenes, the machine runs on a Windows NT platform with a Pentium III processor.

While the Chameleon represents Tidel's future, the bulk of its revenues are generated by the sale of the more traditional ATM to retailers. Tidel makes cash-dispensing ATMs that are used in retail locations, such as convenience stores and gas stations.

Tidel's ATMs, particularly its new IS-6000 unit, are smarter than ever. It has six storage bins that allow it to dispense various items, such as postage stamps, general admission tickets, and multiple denominations of currency. The market for new ATM machines is expected to be bullish, as new retail sites are launched and established sites upgrade their older ATMs.

Tidel's other leading product is its original offering, the Timed Access Cash Controller, or TACC, which functions as both drop safe and cash dispenser. It is designed to discourage robberies in retail locations and other locations that handle large volumes of cash.

Founded in 1987, the Houston-based operation has about 150 employees and a market capitalization of about $130 million.

EARNINGS PER SHARE PROGRESSION ★ ★ ★

Past 3 years: 89 percent (23 percent per year)

REVENUE GROWTH ★ ★ ★ ★

Past 4 years: 321 percent (43 percent per year)

STOCK GROWTH ★ ★ ★ ★

Past 3 years: 270 percent (55 percent per year)
Dollar growth: $10,000 over 3 years would have grown to about $37,000.

CONSISTENCY ★ ★ ★

Increased earnings per share: 3 of the past 4 years
Increased sales: 4 consecutive years

TIDEL TECHNOLOGIES AT A GLANCE

Fiscal year ended: Sept. 30
Revenue and net income in $ millions

	1995	1996	1997	1998	1999	4-Year Growth Avg. Annual (%)	Total (%)
Revenue ($)	10.9	20.1	30.1	33.6	45.9	43	321
Net income ($)	−3.42	1.21	2.11	4.24	2.94	34*	143*
Earnings/share ($)	−0.29	0.09	0.14	0.25	0.17	23*	89*
PE range	—	10–37	9–32	3–16	7–19		

*Net income and earnings per share growth figures are based on 3-year performance.

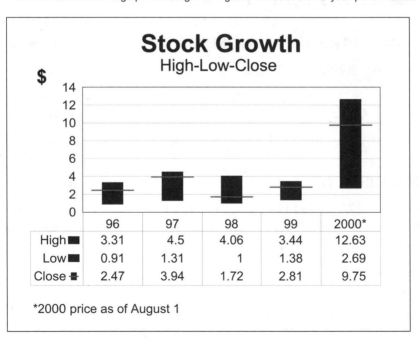

Stock Growth
High-Low-Close

	96	97	98	99	2000*
High	3.31	4.5	4.06	3.44	12.63
Low	0.91	1.31	1	1.38	2.69
Close	2.47	3.94	1.72	2.81	9.75

*2000 price as of August 1

11
Integral Systems, Inc.

5000 Philadelphia Way, Suite A
Lanham, MD 20706
301-731-4233
Nasdaq: ISYS
www.integ.com

Chairman and CEO:
Steven R. Chamberlain
President:
Thomas L. Gough

Earnings Growth	★ ★ ★ ★
Revenue Growth	★ ★ ★
Stock Growth	★ ★ ★ ★
Consistency	★ ★ ★
Total	**14 Points**

Off-the-shelf ground control—that's what software maker Integral Systems offers for satellite system operators. The Lanham, Maryland operation sells the world's only off-the-shelf satellite command and control software capable of controlling any satellite from any manufacturer.

Integral has provided the software for more than 100 satellite missions. Its customers include NASA, the U.S. Air Force, and the National Oceanic and Atmospheric Administration, which is Integral's biggest customer, accounting for more than 40 percent of the company's revenue. Integral also sells products to a number of commercial satellite operators in the United States and abroad, which accounts for about one-third of its total revenue.

Traditionally, satellite operators had to develop their own ground control systems, a process that could take many years and up to $100 million to accomplish. Controllers with several satellites had to set up and use several different computer control programs to keep their satellites on course. In fact, Integral Systems was originally in the business of building some of those custom ground control systems. But with the universal acceptance of the personal computer, Integral began to develop software for PCs that could control any satellite.

Integral's software systems are not only practical because of their ability to control a whole fleet of different satellites from the same PC, they are also considerably cheaper than the old custom controllers and much faster to install. The company's Epoch 2000 software takes just six months to implement and reduces ground control costs by more than 90 percent.

The company's software controllers are used on missions for scientific research, remote sensing, meteorology, and communications applications. The firm also offers ground control system software for real-time environmental monitoring by satellite, as well as systems for satellite payload processing, spacecraft integration and test, simulation, and environmental monitoring.

Incorporated in 1982, Integral Systems has about 225 employees and a market capitalization of about $130 million.

EARNINGS PER SHARE PROGRESSION   ★ ★ ★ ★

Past 4 years: 686 percent (67 percent per year)

REVENUE GROWTH   ★ ★ ★

Past 4 years: 267 percent (38 percent per year, but slowing in 2000)

STOCK GROWTH   ★ ★ ★ ★

Past 3 years: 211 percent (45 percent per year)
Dollar growth: $10,000 over 3 years would have grown to about $31,000.

CONSISTENCY   ★ ★ ★

Increased earnings per share: 3 of the past 4 years
Increased sales: 4 consecutive years

INTEGRAL SYSTEMS AT A GLANCE

Fiscal year ended: Sept. 30
Revenue and net income in $ millions

	1995	1996	1997	1998	1999	4-Year Growth Avg. Annual (%)	Total (%)
Revenue ($)	10.8	11.2	20.1	28.0	39.6	38	267
Net income ($)	0.380	0.324	0.628	1.91	3.72	78	879
Earnings/share ($)	0.07	0.06	0.11	0.31	0.55	67	686
PE range	43–78	55–90	33–66	21–97	20–82		

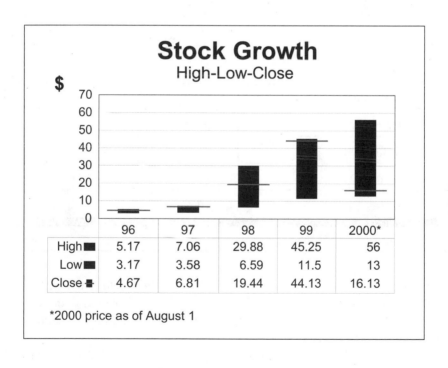

Stock Growth
High-Low-Close

	96	97	98	99	2000*
High	5.17	7.06	29.88	45.25	56
Low	3.17	3.58	6.59	11.5	13
Close	4.67	6.81	19.44	44.13	16.13

*2000 price as of August 1

12
Embrex, Inc.

1035 Swabia Court
Durham, NC 27703
919-941-5185
Nasdaq: EMBX
www.embex.com

Chairman:
Charles E. Austin
President and CEO:
Randall L. Marcuson

Earnings Growth	★ ★ ★ ★
Revenue Growth	★ ★ ★
Stock Growth	★ ★ ★
Consistency	★ ★ ★ ★
Total	**14 Points**

The poultry population is growing quickly around the world, and Embrex is helping keep the birds healty. The Durham, North Carolina operation has developed an automated in-the-egg injection system that can inoculate 20,000 to 50,000 eggs per hour.

The company's Inovoject system eliminates the need for manual, post-hatch injection of certain vaccines. Inovoject is now used to vaccinate more than 80 percent of the poultry raised in North America against Marek's disease. Embrex has installed more than 300 Inovoject systems in the United States and Canada, and it is expanding aggressively overseas.

Inovoject systems are now being used in 29 countries in Europe, the Middle East, Asia, Latin America, Australia, and Africa.

The Inovoject system is designed to inject vaccines and other compounds in precisely calibrated volumes into targeted compartments within the egg. Embrex markets the system to commercial poultry producers, charging a fee for each egg injected. The systems were designed by Embrex, but are produced by a specialty manufacturer under contract with Embrex.

In addition to the Inovoject system, Embrex has developed a viral neutralizing factor antibody, which permits single-dose immunization of the avian embryo effective for the life of the bird. Embrex also makes Bursaplex, a vaccine for protection against avian bursal disease, a condition that weakens the bird's immune system.

Embrex is actively researching and developing other related pharmaceutical and biological products to improve bird health, reduce production costs, and provide other economic benefits to poultry producers. Products in the pipeline include vaccines, immune enhancers, performance modifiers, and genetic materials designed to increase poultry productivity.

Embrex was first incorporated in 1985. It went public with its initial stock offering in 1991. Embrex has 170 employees and a market capitalization of about $130 million.

EARNINGS PER SHARE PROGRESSION ★ ★ ★ ★

Past 3 years: 1,260 percent (142 percent per year)

REVENUE GROWTH ★ ★ ★

Past 4 years: 146 percent (25 percent per year)

STOCK GROWTH ★ ★ ★

Past 3 years: 96 percent (25 percent per year)
Dollar growth: $10,000 over 3 years would have grown to about $20,000.

CONSISTENCY ★ ★ ★ ★

Increased earnings per share: 4 consecutive years
Increased sales: 4 consecutive years

EMBREX AT A GLANCE

Fiscal year ended: Dec. 31
Revenue and net income in $ millions

	1995	1996	1997	1998	1999	4-Year Growth Avg. Annual (%)	Total (%)
Revenue ($)	13.7	20.6	24.8	28.6	33.7	25	146
Net income ($)	−4.5	0.34	1.8	2.9	5.7	151*	1,576*
Earnings/share ($)	−0.73	0.05	0.22	0.35	0.68	142*	1,260*
PE range	—	122–183	24–37	11–20	6–19		

*Net income and earnings per share growth figures are based on 3-year performance.

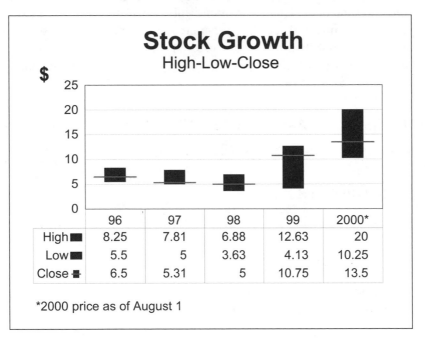

Stock Growth
High-Low-Close

$	96	97	98	99	2000*
High	8.25	7.81	6.88	12.63	20
Low	5.5	5	3.63	4.13	10.25
Close	6.5	5.31	5	10.75	13.5

*2000 price as of August 1

InnerDyne, Inc.

InnerDyne, Inc.

1244 Reamwood Avenue
Sunnyvale, CA 94089
408-745-6570
Nasdaq: IDYN
www.innerdyne.com

President and CEO:
William G. Mavity

Earnings Growth	★ ★ ★
Revenue Growth	★ ★ ★ ★
Stock Growth	★ ★ ★
Consistency	★ ★ ★ ★
Total	**14 Points**

InnerDyne has carved out a small niche in the medical market by designing an instrument capable of carving out a small—but precise—opening in the human body.

The InnerDyne "Step" is an instrument originally designed for use in punching holes through the abdomen in laparoscopic surgery, and other procedures. It is currently used for a variety of minimally invasive general, gynecological, and pediatric surgical procedures.

The Step uses a special needle that inserts a woven plastic sleeve when it's inserted into the abdomen. The surgeon dilates the sleeve to part the layers of tissue prior to operating. After the operation, the sleeve is removed, and the tissue closes up with a much smaller wound than was possible under traditional methods. It greatly reduces the risk of a hernia or of severing the arteries or puncturing the bowel.

In one recent clinical study, the Step reduced device-related complications during surgery by more than 90 percent and resulted in a 22 percent savings in surgery time, as compared with the conventional trocar incision instrument.

The Sunnyvale, California operation makes several types of Steps, including a "Short Step" used for children and smaller adults, and several other specialized Steps. The company spends about $3 million a year for research and development to expand its product line.

InnerDyne sells its products both domestically and internationally through a network of independent sales representatives and a few company employees. Although the company currently faces stiff competition from larger companies that sell the conventional trocar devices, its Step has been slowly making headway. And with ongoing studies that continue to show major benefits of the Step, the company expects to see solid sales growth in the future.

The company, which introduced its first Step in 1994, has about 130 employees and a market capitalization of about $100 million.

EARNINGS PER SHARE PROGRESSION ★ ★ ★

Past year: 299 percent

REVENUE GROWTH ★ ★ ★ ★

Past 4 years: 285 percent (40 percent per year)

STOCK GROWTH ★ ★ ★

Past 3 years: 115 percent (29 percent per year)
Dollar growth: $10,000 over 3 years would have grown to about $21,000.

CONSISTENCY ★ ★ ★ ★

Positive earnings progression: 4 consecutive years
Increased sales: 4 consecutive years

INNERDYNE AT A GLANCE

Fiscal year ended: Dec. 31
Revenue and net income in $ millions

	1995	1996	1997	1998	1999	4-Year Growth Avg. Annual (%)	Total (%)
Revenue ($)	5.3	9.1	15.7	17.6	20.4	40	285
Net income ($)	−5.6	−4.6	−0.907	0.425	1.48	NA	248*
Earnings/share ($)	−0.32	−0.23	−0.04	0.02	0.06	NA	299*
PE range	—	—	—	46–197	17–66		

*Net income and earnings per share growth figures are for 1-year performance.

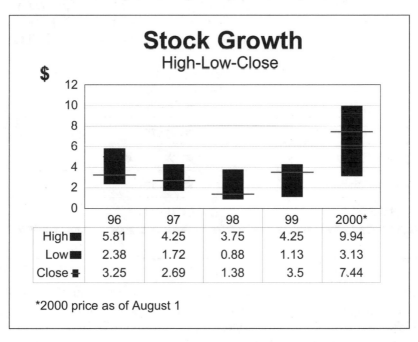

Stock Growth
High-Low-Close

	96	97	98	99	2000*
High■	5.81	4.25	3.75	4.25	9.94
Low■	2.38	1.72	0.88	1.13	3.13
Close ■	3.25	2.69	1.38	3.5	7.44

*2000 price as of August 1

Candela Corp.

530 Boston Post Road
Wayland, MA 01778
508-358-7400
Nasdaq: CLZR
www.clzr.com

Chairman:
Kenneth D. Roberts
President and CEO:
Gerard E. Puorro

Earnings Growth	★ ★ ★ ★
Revenue Growth	★ ★ ★
Stock Growth	★ ★ ★ ★
Consistency	★ ★ ★
Total	**14 Points**

Image-conscious baby boomers who place a premium on good health and personal appearance have kept Candela's bottom line growing.

Unwanted hair, unsightly varicose veins, and scarred facial skin are among the cosmetic and medical conditions that can be treated with Candela's laser systems. Most of the treatments aren't covered by an employer's health plan, but many aging baby boomers have demonstrated a willingness to pay for the laser treatments out of their own pockets. In fact, American women spend an estimated $2 billion a year on hair removal products and services.

Candela's laser systems are used by specialists, such as dermatologists and plastic surgeons, who offer aesthetic treatments on a private, fee-for-service basis. The systems are used in a doctor's office rather than in a hospital's operating room.

Increasingly, lasers such as Candela's GentleLASE system have been used to perform the cosmetic procedure. The GentleLASE system uses a proprietary cooling device to minimize discomfort to the patient undergoing hair removal or leg vein treatment. Called the Dynamic Cooling Device, or DCD, it cools the upper layers of a patient's skin prior to the laser pulse, minimizing pain.

Another Candela laser system, ScleroPLUS, which is also equipped with the DCD cooling system, is used to treat the so-called spider veins in a patient's leg. It's estimated that 80 million men and women in the United States are affected by the condition. Other Candela lasers include Gentle-Peel, which is a skin exfoliation system, and CFK/Skintonic, which massages the face and body.

Candela's laser system can also be used to treat or remove pigmented lesions and tattoos. Candela has sold more than 4,000 laser systems to doctors in the United States and more than 40 countries.

The company was founded in 1970 and went public with its initial stock offering in 1986. It has about 285 employees and a market capitalization of about $150 million.

EARNINGS PER SHARE PROGRESSION ★ ★ ★ ★

Past 4 years: 644 percent (64 percent per year)

REVENUE GROWTH ★ ★ ★

Past 4 years: 148 percent (26 percent per year)

STOCK GROWTH ★ ★ ★ ★

Past 3 years: 131 percent (32 percent per year)
Dollar growth: $10,000 over 3 years would have grown to about $23,000.

CONSISTENCY ★ ★ ★

Increased earnings per share: 3 of the past 4 years
Increased sales: 4 consecutive years

CANDELA AT A GLANCE

Fiscal year ended: June 30
Revenue and net income in $ millions

	1996	1997	1998	1999	2000	4-Year Growth Avg. Annual (%)	Total (%)
Revenue ($)	30.4	35.5	37.0	58.6	75.4	26	148
Net income ($)	1.2	0.238	−4.4	7.5	14.6	85	1,117
Earnings/share ($)	0.16	0.03	−0.54	0.91	1.19	64	644
PE range	21–51	95–215	—	4–17	—		

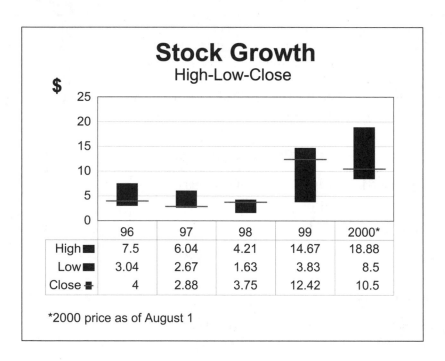

Stock Growth
High-Low-Close

	96	97	98	99	2000*
High ■	7.5	6.04	4.21	14.67	18.88
Low ■	3.04	2.67	1.63	3.83	8.5
Close ▬	4	2.88	3.75	12.42	10.5

*2000 price as of August 1

15
CompuDyne Corp.

7249 National Drive
Hanover, MD 21076
410-712-0275
Nasdaq: CDCY
www.compudyne.com

Chairman, President, and CEO:
Martin A. Roenigk

Earnings Growth	★ ★ ★
Revenue Growth	★ ★ ★ ★
Stock Growth	★ ★ ★ ★
Consistency	★ ★ ★
Total	**14 Points**

It may have the ring of a high-tech computer operation, but CompuDyne is nothing of the kind. The company makes and installs detention hardware and security systems, and manufactures "embassy grade" attack windows and doors.

CompuDyne, through its subsidiaries, is the country's largest supplier of physical and electronic security products, integration services and maintenance for jails, prisons, and courthouses. It is also involved in security maintenance outsourcing, providing for routine maintenance and emergency repair of sophisticated security control systems and related equipment.

The company operates through several subsidiaries, including:

- **Norment Security Group** provides physical and electronic security prod-ucts and services primarily to the corrections industry (jails and prisons) and secondarily to the courthouse, municipal, and commercial markets.
- **TrenTech** is an electronic security systems designer, manufacturer, and integrator. The firm integrates security products and software as well as designs proprietary security systems.
- **Airteq** offers a complete line of locks and locking devices to the cor-rections industry.
- **CorrLogic** develops, installs, and maintains the most extensive soft-ware in the industry for the management of inmates and other person-nel and processes within the courthouse, jail, and prison environment. Its software is used in some of the country's largest jails, including Wayne County (Detroit), Shelby County (Memphis), and Hennepin County (Minneapolis).
- **Norshield** is the country's largest manufacturer of bullet, blast, and at-tack resistant windows and doors designed for high security applica-tions, such as embassies, courthouses, Federal Reserve buildings, and banks. Its biggest customer is the U.S. Department of State.
- **Quanta Systems** has been assisting the government's intelligence op-erations (such as the FBI and CIA) since 1950 in classified projects in-volving physical and electronic security.

The Maryland operation has about 650 employees and a market capi-talization of about $40 million.

EARNINGS PER SHARE PROGRESSION   ★ ★ ★

Past 4 years: 148 percent (25 percent per year)

REVENUE GROWTH   ★ ★ ★ ★

Past 4 years: 913 percent (82 percent per year)

STOCK GROWTH   ★ ★ ★ ★

Past 3 years: 284 percent (57 percent per year)
Dollar growth: $10,000 over 3 years would have grown to about $38,000.

CONSISTENCY   ★ ★ ★

Increased earnings per share: 4 consecutive years
Increased sales: 3 of the past 4 years

COMPUDYNE CORP. AT A GLANCE

Fiscal year ended: Dec. 31
Revenue and net income in $ millions

	1995	1996	1997	1998	1999	4-Year Growth Avg. Annual (%)	Total (%)
Revenue ($)	10.3	22.1	20.0	31.9	111.4	82	981
Net income ($)	−.210	.391	.696	.847	2.67	90	583*
Earnings/share ($)	−0.40	0.09	0.16	0.19	0.45	70	400*
PE range	—	7–19	5–18	9–28	9–20		

*Net income and earnings per share growth figures are based on 3-year performance.

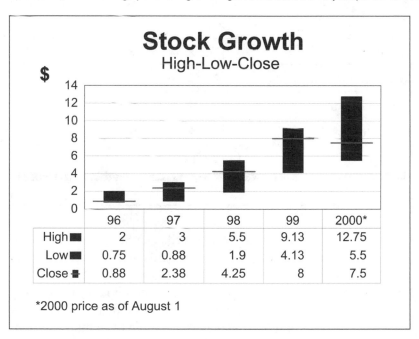

Stock Growth
High-Low-Close

	96	97	98	99	2000*
High■	2	3	5.5	9.13	12.75
Low■	0.75	0.88	1.9	4.13	5.5
Close ■	0.88	2.38	4.25	8	7.5

*2000 price as of August 1

16
Daktronics, Inc.

331 32nd Avenue
Brookings, SD 57006-5128
605-697-4000
Nasdaq: DAKT
www.daktronics.com

President and CEO:
Aelred J. Kurtenbach

Earnings Growth	★ ★ ★ ★
Revenue Growth	★ ★
Stock Growth	★ ★ ★ ★
Consistency	★ ★ ★ ★
Total	**14 Points**

What's the score? Daktronics has you covered. The South Dakota operation has installed tens of thousands of scoreboards and electronic display systems in more than 65 countries.

Daktronics offers the most complete line of scoreboards and display systems in the industry, from the smaller indoor scoreboards to highway and airport electronic information display signs to the huge multi-million-dollar outdoor video display systems. Prices of its products range from less than $1,000 to more than $7 million.

The firm also sells scoreboards and message centers to elementary, middle, and high schools and to park and recreation departments. It manufactures display boards for motor racing venues, swimming pools, and track and field stadiums, and it makes the giant electronic scoreboards used at major stadiums and arenas.

But Daktronics does more than just keep score. The company also sells indoor and outdoor programmable signs for businesses, including information and advertising panels, time and temperature and price display signs, and spectacular multi-million-dollar video display advertising signs.

In addition to its sports and corporate business, Daktronics manufactures signs for government agencies, including transportation terminal signs, over-the-road systems for motorist information, and legislative voting systems.

Most of its signs can be reprogrammed through Windows-based control systems. Daktronics not only designs and manufactures the displays it sells, it also provides the installation and servicing for most of its products.

Daktronics sells its products through both its own sales staff and a network of independent resellers throughout the world.

Founded in 1968, Daktronics went public with its initial stock offering in 1994. It has about 640 employees and a market capitalization of about $80 million.

EARNINGS PER SHARE PROGRESSION   ★ ★ ★ ★

Past 3 years: 278 percent (55 percent per year)

REVENUE GROWTH   ★ ★

Past 4 years: 135 percent (24 percent per year)

STOCK GROWTH   ★ ★ ★ ★

Past 3 years: 290 percent (57 percent per year)
Dollar growth: $10,000 over 3 years would have grown to about $40,000.

CONSISTENCY   ★ ★ ★ ★

Increased earnings per share: 4 consecutive years
Increased sales: 4 consecutive years

DAKTRONICS AT A GLANCE

Fiscal year ended: April 31
Revenue and net income in $ millions

	1996	1997	1998	1999	2000	4-Year Growth Avg. Annual (%)	Total (%)
Revenue ($)	52.5	62.6	69.9	95.9	123.4	24	135
Net income ($)	−215	1.5	3.4	4.2	6.2	61*	313*
Earnings/share ($)	−0.03	0.18	0.39	0.48	0.68	55*	278*
PE range	—	9–19	6–21	6–22			

*Net income and earnings per share growth figures are based on 3-year peformance.

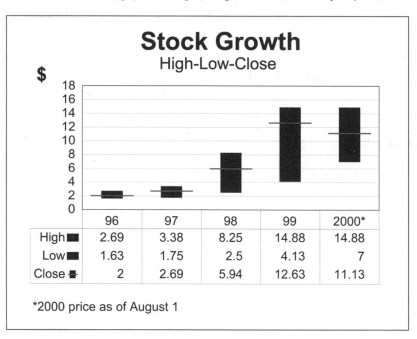

Stock Growth
High-Low-Close

$	96	97	98	99	2000*
High	2.69	3.38	8.25	14.88	14.88
Low	1.63	1.75	2.5	4.13	7
Close	2	2.69	5.94	12.63	11.13

*2000 price as of August 1

17

ePresence, Inc.

120 Flanders Road
P.O. Box 5013
Westboro, MA 01581-5013
508-898-1000
Nasdaq: EPRE
www.epresence.com

Chairman, President, and CEO:
William P. Ferry

Earnings Growth	★ ★ ★
Revenue Growth	★ ★ ★ ★
Stock Growth	★ ★ ★ ★
Consistency	★ ★ ★
Total	**14 Points**

EPresence helps businesses strike a more intimate online relationship with their customers, business partners, and employees.

The company's consultants and designers have helped such Fortune 500 companies as DaimlerChrysler, Ericcson, and Sony reach their customers via the Web on a secure and cost-effective basis. Services include Web site design and Web portal design, as well as the development of Web-based databases, including directories, image banks, course catalogs, archives, and document libraries.

The company had been known as Banyan Worldwide, a maker and marketer of networking software. That business diminished, and the company recognized the wealth of opportunities the Internet presented. In early 2000, the company bought a privately held e-business services company called ePresence, which specialized in Web design and development, and took the name as its own.

The company has exited the software business to concentrate on e-services, which it calls its ePresence Solutions Division. The company believes it's well positioned to seize on the rapidly growing demand for Internet services worldwide.

The mission of a second division, called ePresence Ventures, is to make investments in Internet businesses that add value to its e-services division. Initial holdings include Software.com and Corechange. The company also operates a subsidiary, Switchboard, that offers an electronic directory at its Web site that includes the listings of about 100 million individuals, 12 million businesses, and 4 million e-mail addresses. Switchboard.com is an online version of the traditional White and Yellow Pages.

One of Switchboard's key investors is CBS. In 1999, the network agreed to place up to $95 million of promotion over seven years across the full range of CBS properties. The agreement allows Switchboard to use the familiar CBS logo for up to ten years.

The company was founded in 1982 and went public with its initial stock offering in 1992. It has 350 employees and a market capitalization of about $300 million.

EARNINGS PER SHARE PROGRESSION ★ ★ ★

Past year: 1,750 percent (losses previous 3 years)

REVENUE GROWTH ★ ★ ★ ★

Past 4 years: 594 percent (62 percent per year)

STOCK GROWTH ★ ★ ★ ★

Past 3 years: 223 percent (49 percent per year)
Dollar growth: $10,000 over 3 years would have grown to about $32,000.

CONSISTENCY ★ ★ ★

Positive earnings progression: 3 of the past 4 years
Increased sales: 4 consecutive years

EPRESENCE AT A GLANCE

Fiscal year ended: Dec. 31
Revenue and net income in $ millions

	1995	1996	1997	1998	1999	4-Year Growth Avg. Annual (%)	Total (%)
Revenue ($)	6.6	7.4	10.5	27.8	45.8	62	594
Net income ($)	−21.4	−27.0	−16.9	1.11	28.1	2,431	NA
Earnings/share ($)	−1.27	−1.59	−0.97	0.06	1.11	1,750	NA
PE range	—	—	—	—	6–23		

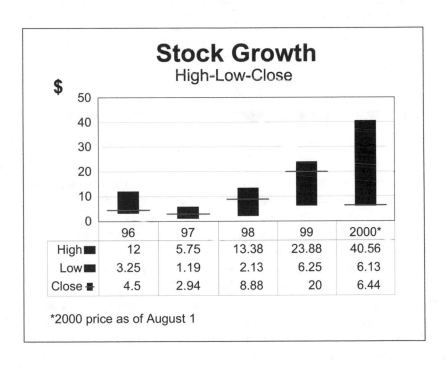

Stock Growth
High-Low-Close

	96	97	98	99	2000*
High	12	5.75	13.38	23.88	40.56
Low	3.25	1.19	2.13	6.25	6.13
Close	4.5	2.94	8.88	20	6.44

*2000 price as of August 1

V3 Semiconductor, Inc.

250 Consumers Road, Suite 901
North York, ON, Canada M2J 4V6
416-497-8884
Nasdaq: VVVI
www.vcubed.com

President and CEO:
John Zambakkides

Earnings Growth	★ ★
Revenue Growth	★ ★ ★ ★
Stock Growth	★ ★ ★ ★
Consistency	★ ★ ★
Total	**13 Points**

Unless you're fond of prying apart an electronic device's microprocessor—the brain of the operation—you'll never actually see one of V3 Semiconductor's products.

V3 designs and markets high-performance silicon chips and chipsets that boost the speed and improve the performance of microprocessors embedded in electronic devices such as modems, network servers, consumer appliances, and telecommunication devices. While V3's chips are not seen by the consumer, they're top of mind with design engineers, who use the company's products to get their own gadgets quickly to market.

Worldwide demand for semiconductors is projected by analysts to grow rapidly over the next several years, driven by the quest for greater speed and functionality of the server, PC, storage, networking, and telecommunications industries.

The Canadian operation's client roster is strictly blue chip: Cisco, Compaq, Hewlett-Packard, Xerox, IBM, Lucent Technologies, and Nortel Networks. Ironically, V3 doesn't make any of the products it designs or sells, because it's a "fabless" semiconductor company. Rather than assume the enormous overhead of owning and operating chip fabrication facilities, which can cost from $500 million to $1 billion, V3 contracts the work out to companies like Hyundai, Samsung, and KLSI to do the manufacturing.

The company carefully inspects the work of its contractors to ensure that it meets the high-quality standards that V3 is known for. To better manage its complex supply chain, V3 in early 2000 handed over its logistics, fulfillment, and inventory-management functions to Virtual Integration Associates in Toronto. V3 customers are now saving about 20 percent of their supply-chain related costs.

By outsourcing those functions, V3 can concentrate on what it does best—designing and marketing its advanced chips to the world's leading electronics companies.

Founded in 1985, V3 has about 60 employees and a market capitalization of about $115 million.

EARNINGS PER SHARE PROGRESSION ★ ★

V3 has gone steadily from losses to gains the past 3 years.

REVENUE GROWTH ★ ★ ★ ★

Past 3 years: 663 percent (98 percent per year)

STOCK GROWTH ★ ★ ★ ★

Past 3 years: 344 percent (65 percent per year)
Dollar growth: $10,000 over 3 years would have grown to about $44,000.

CONSISTENCY ★ ★ ★

Positive earnings progression: 3 consecutive years
Increased sales: 3 consecutive years

V3 SEMICONDUCTOR AT A GLANCE

Fiscal year ended: Sept. 30
Revenue and net income in $ millions

	1995	1996	1997	1998	1999	3-Year Growth Avg. Annual (%)	Total (%)
Revenue ($)	—	.882	1.95	3.82	6.82	98	663
Net income ($)	—	−0.551	−0.125	0.167	0.229	37	NA
Earnings/share ($)	—	−0.13	−0.03	0.03	0.04	33	NA
PE range	—	—	—	78–221	92–337		

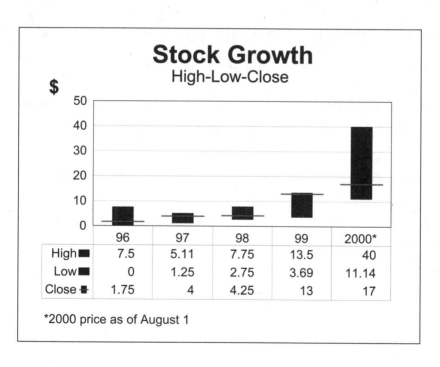

Stock Growth
High-Low-Close

$

	96	97	98	99	2000*
High ■	7.5	5.11	7.75	13.5	40
Low ■	0	1.25	2.75	3.69	11.14
Close ■	1.75	4	4.25	13	17

*2000 price as of August 1

Comtech Telecommunications Corp.

105 Baylis Road
Melville, NY 11747
631-777-8900
Nasdaq: CMTL
www.comtech.com

Chairman, President, and CEO:
Fred Kornberg

Earnings Growth	★ ★ ★ ★
Revenue Growth	★
Stock Growth	★ ★ ★ ★
Consistency	★ ★ ★ ★
Total	**13 Points**

Whether it's traveling by land, sea, or air, Comtech Telecommunications can track it down anytime, anywhere. Defense agencies, government units, and transportation companies rely on Comtech's Mobile Data Communications Services to tell them exactly where their trains, boats, or planes are at any given moment.

Comtech's Web-enabled, satellite-based data communication system also allows a customer to communicate with its fixed or mobile assets, like trucks and ships, via two-way messaging, e-mail, and automated reading of sensors. Comtech routes signals through its earthstation gateway in Germantown, Maryland.

Impressed with the system's operational and cost advantages, the U.S. Army in 1999 awarded Comtech an eight-year, $418 million contract to provide a global system for its Logistics Command to help track mobile assets. The system will also allow the Army to communicate in near real time with its various units from fixed and mobile command centers around the world.

⚫ The company believes that the global expansion of telecommunications, particularly in the developing countries of Asia, South America, the Middle East, and Eastern Europe, represents an enormous opportunity. More than 250 of its sophisticated products and systems are being used in more than 100 countries.

In addition to its rapidly growing mobile data communications services division, Comtech operates two other divisions. Its Telecommunications Transmission Division provides modems, high-power amplifiers, microwave radios, and other products to defense contractors, communication companies, and oil companies. Customers include DirecTV, BP Amoco, and Hughes Network Systems.

Its RF (radio frequency) Division offers high-power broadband amplifier products to test cellular and wireless instruments and to jam signals for defense purposes. Customers include Motorola, the U.S. government, Lucent Technologies, and Raytheon Systems.

Comtech Telecommunications has about 270 employees and a market capitalization of about $80 million.

EARNINGS PER SHARE PROGRESSION   ★ ★ ★ ★

Past 3 years: 5,749 percent (288 percent per year)

REVENUE GROWTH   ★

Past 4 years: 131 percent (19 percent per year)

STOCK GROWTH   ★ ★ ★ ★

Past 3 years: 1,373 percent (145 percent per year)
Dollar growth: $10,000 over 3 years would have grown to $147,000.

CONSISTENCY   ★ ★ ★ ★

Positive earnings progression: 4 consecutive years
Increased sales: 4 consecutive years

COMTECH TELECOMMUNICATIONS AT A GLANCE

Fiscal year ended: July 31
Revenue and net income in $ millions

	1995	1996	1997	1998	1999	4-Year Growth Avg. Annual (%)	Total (%)
Revenue ($)	16.4	20.9	24.7	30.1	37.9	19	131
Net income ($)	−1.5	0.072	0.484	1.1	6.5	348*	8,903*
Earnings/share ($)	−0.39	0.02	0.12	0.26	1.15	288*	5,749*
PE range	—	81–236	14–30	10–28	2–21		

*Net income and earnings per share growth figures are based on 3-year performance.

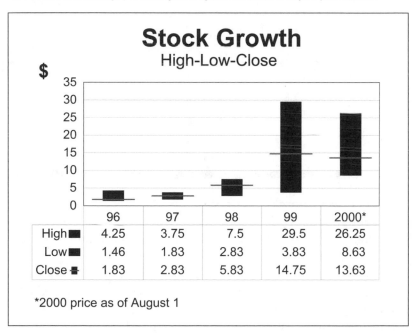

Stock Growth
High-Low-Close

	96	97	98	99	2000*
High	4.25	3.75	7.5	29.5	26.25
Low	1.46	1.83	2.83	3.83	8.63
Close	1.83	2.83	5.83	14.75	13.63

*2000 price as of August 1

Gentner Communications

Gentner®

1825 Research Way
Salt Lake City, UT 84119
801-975-7200
Nasdaq: GTNR
www.gentner.com

President and CEO:
Frances M. Flood

Earnings Growth	★ ★ ★ ★
Revenue Growth	★ ★
Stock Growth	★ ★ ★ ★
Consistency	★ ★ ★
Total	**13 Points**

Talk is anything but cheap as far as Gentner Communications is concerned. In fact, it's the lifeblood of the company's business.

Gentner makes easy-to-use audio room-conferencing systems used in corporate boardrooms, distance learning classrooms, courtrooms, and telemedicine facilities. Its Audio Perfect line of conferencing systems provides high-quality transmission of exactly what's being said, not the indecipherable noise from a squawk box.

In early 2000, Gentner introduced its first video-based conferencing system to complement its more-established audio products. The company has also introduced what it calls the TheDataPort.com, a conferencing service that can link up to 2,000 participants in a multimedia presentation over the Internet. Participants from around the world can share documents, view streaming video, and hear live audio from their desktop computers.

The Salt Lake City operation is eager to seize on the U.S. audio-, video-, and data-conferencing market that analysts predict will grow more than threefold to about $3 billion per year over the next several years.

Gentner's other division focuses on the broadcast market. Its most familiar product in that industry is the so-called Gentner box, a telephone system that queues up talk-show callers and keeps station personnel apprised of incoming calls. The system converts the telephonic voice into audio-quality sound.

Gentner's other major product in this division is a remote control system, so radio and TV stations can monitor and control multiple remote transmitter facilities from a single location. The Federal Communications Commission requires broadcast outlets to monitor their transmitter facilities around the clock. The system can alert a station to problems and then issue the appropriate corrective commands.

The company was founded in 1983 and went public in 1985 by way of a reverse purchase when Insular Inc. bought Gentner Engineering and changed it to Gentner Electronics. The name was changed again in 1991 to Gentner Communications. It has about 155 employees and a market capitalization of about $135 million.

EARNINGS PER SHARE PROGRESSION ★ ★ ★ ★

Past 3 years: 650 percent (94 percent per year)

REVENUE GROWTH ★ ★

Past 4 years: 107 percent (20 percent per year)

STOCK GROWTH ★ ★ ★ ★

Past 3 years: 1,767 percent
Dollar growth: $10,000 over 3 years would have grown to about $187,000.

CONSISTENCY ★ ★ ★

Increased earnings per share: 3 of the past 4 years
Increased sales: 4 consecutive years

GENTNER COMMUNICATIONS AT A GLANCE

Fiscal year ended: June 30
Revenue and net income in $ millions

	1995	1996	1997	1998	1999	4-Year Growth Avg. Annual (%)	Total (%)
Revenue ($)	11.1	11.5	13.4	17.3	23.0	20	107
Net income ($)	−.116	.282	−.372	1.4	2.5	73*	786*
Earnings/share ($)	−0.02	0.04	−0.05	0.18	0.30	94*	650*
PE range	—	19–36	—	5–24	9–59		

*Net income and earnings per share growth figures are based on 3-year performance.

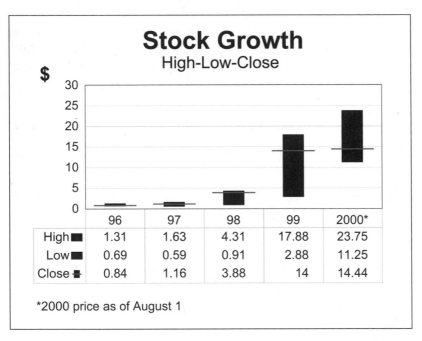

Stock Growth
High-Low-Close

$	96	97	98	99	2000*
High ■	1.31	1.63	4.31	17.88	23.75
Low ■	0.69	0.59	0.91	2.88	11.25
Close ▪	0.84	1.16	3.88	14	14.44

*2000 price as of August 1

PW Eagle, Inc.

PW Eagle

333 South Seventh Street,
Suite 2430
Minneapolis, MN 55402
612-305-0339
Nasdaq: PWEI
www.pwpipe.com

Chairman:
Harry W. Spell
CEO:
William H. Spell
President:
James Rash

Earnings Growth	★ ★ ★ ★	
Revenue Growth	★ ★ ★	
Stock Growth	★ ★ ★ ★	
Consistency	★ ★	
Total	**13 Points**	

Will it be copper or plastic? The answer for homebuilders, highway builders, municipalities, and appliance makers has increasingly been plastic, as in polyvinyl chloride (PVC) pipes.

That trend bodes well for a company like PW Eagle, one of the nation's leading manufacturers of PVC pipe and fittings and polyethylene (PE) pipe and tubing products. In the commercial and residential construction segment, plastic pipes, tubes, and fittings are increasingly replacing materials made of copper, clay, cast iron, or aluminum. Customers appreciate the plastic products' competitive price, its light weight, its resistance to corrosion, and the relative ease with which it can be installed.

The steady growth of the U.S. economy has been a boon to companies like PW Eagle, which must produce to meet the demands of builders of residential and commercial projects. More than ever, government agencies responsible for the infrastructure are using PVC pipes to provide services to new developments and upgrade aging sewer, drinking water, and drainage systems.

Makers of refrigerators, freezers, and air conditioners also use PW Eagle's plastic tubing. Other big users of the products include natural gas pipeline companies, turf and agricultural irrigation concerns, and telecommunications companies, which use the tubing to protect their fiber-optic networks. Each day, PW Eagle makes about 750 miles of PVC and PE pipe, or the rough distance between Denver and Phoenix.

The Minneapolis operation took a great leap forward in September 1999 when it purchased Pacific Western Extruded Plastics Company, or PW Pipe, from Mitsubishi Chemical America. The deal nearly quadrupled its existing pipe business and transformed PW Eagle into the nation's second-largest pipe and tubing manufacturer and the largest of its kind in the Western United States.

The company has about 835 employees and a market capitalization of about $130 million.

EARNINGS PER SHARE PROGRESSION ★ ★ ★ ★

Past 3 years: 492 percent (58 percent per year)

REVENUE GROWTH ★ ★ ★

Past 4 years: 200 percent (32 percent per year)

STOCK GROWTH ★ ★ ★ ★

Past 3 years: 700 percent (100 percent per year)
Dollar growth: $10,000 over 3 years would have grown to about $80,000.

CONSISTENCY ★ ★

Increased earnings per share: 2 of the past 4 years
Increased sales: 4 consecutive years

PW EAGLE AT A GLANCE

Fiscal year ended: Dec. 31
Revenue and net income in $ millions

	1995	1996	1997	1998	1999	4-Year Growth Avg. Annual (%)	4-Year Growth Total (%)
Revenue ($)	51.3	65.3	71.7	74.0	153.9	32	200
Net income ($)	−0.87	3.48	0.93	1.79	14.5	61*	316*
Earnings/share ($)	−0.27	0.25	0.05	0.05	1.48	58*	492*
PE range	—	2–8	40–75	9–18	1–3		

*Net income and earnings per share growth figures are based on 3-year performance.

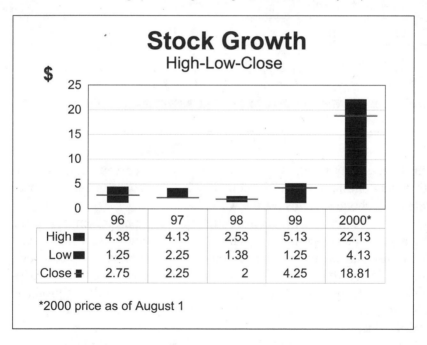

Stock Growth
High-Low-Close

$

	96	97	98	99	2000*
High■	4.38	4.13	2.53	5.13	22.13
Low■	1.25	2.25	1.38	1.25	4.13
Close ▪	2.75	2.25	2	4.25	18.81

*2000 price as of August 1

22
SpectraLink Corp.

5755 Central Avenue
Boulder, CO 80301
303-440-5330
Nasdaq: SLNK
www.spectralink.com

President and CEO:
Bruce Holland

Earnings Growth	★ ★ ★ ★
Revenue Growth	★ ★ ★
Stock Growth	★ ★ ★ ★
Consistency	★ ★
Total	**13 Points**

In this increasingly wireless world, SpectraLink has carved out its own lucrative and dominant niche. The company is the leading manufacturer of wireless telephone systems for the workplace.

SpectraLink sells its products through marketing arrangements with a wide range of major operations, such as Norstan, Panasonic, Siemens, and GTE. It also has an impressive customer base, including Amazon.com, Arthur Andersen, AT&T, Barnes & Noble, Cisco Systems, General Motors, Microsoft, and MCI WorldCom. The company also sells its products to colleges, such as UCLA, and government agencies, such as the U.S. Postal Service.

The company has about a 30 percent share of the workplace wireless market in the United States. Its phone systems are designed to integrate with a facility's existing phone system to provide telephone access anywhere in the workplace.

The SpectraLink wireless telephone systems increase the efficiency of employees by enabling users to walk throughout a building and maintain telephone contact, or make and receive phone calls. The system uses a microcellular design and interfaces directly with a PBX, Centrex, or key/hybrid system. And because all calls are routed through the corporate phone system, there are no airtime charges incurred.

The systems are marketed to organizations that require certain employees to have a high degree of mobility yet remain readily accessible by telephone to customers or coworkers. For instance, retailers may need them so they can obtain information from employees dispersed throughout the store, and manufacturers and distributors may be able to operate more efficiently by maintaining ongoing communications with workers in the factory or distribution center who can solve problems or answer questions quickly.

SpectraLink markets its products through its direct sales force and through about 130 dealers in 270 locations.

Founded in 1990, SpectraLink has about 260 employees and a market capitalization of about $225 million.

EARNINGS PER SHARE PROGRESSION ★ ★ ★ ★

Past 4 years: 486 percent (56 percent per year)

REVENUE GROWTH ★ ★ ★

Past 4 years: 147 percent (25 percent per year)

STOCK GROWTH ★ ★ ★ ★

Past 3 years: 160 percent (38 percent per year)
Dollar growth: $10,000 over 3 years would have grown to $26,000.

CONSISTENCY ★ ★

Increased earnings per share: 3 of the past 4 years (but down through the first half of 2000)
Increased sales: 4 consecutive years

SPECTRALINK AT A GLANCE

Fiscal year ended: Dec. 31
Revenue and net income in $ millions

	1995	1996	1997	1998	1999	4-Year Growth Avg. Annual (%)	Total (%)
Revenue ($)	16.7	21.5	27.8	35.1	41.2	25	147
Net income ($)	1.18	2.55	−.560	2.07	7.93	62	572
Earnings/share ($)	0.07	0.14	−0.03	0.11	0.41	56	486
PE range	—	18–93	—	20–53	7–43		

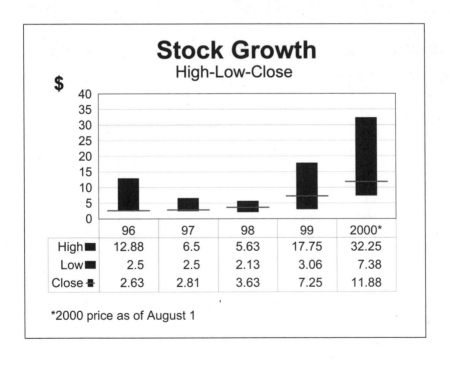

Stock Growth
High-Low-Close

$

	96	97	98	99	2000*
High	12.88	6.5	5.63	17.75	32.25
Low	2.5	2.5	2.13	3.06	7.38
Close	2.63	2.81	3.63	7.25	11.88

*2000 price as of August 1

23
Abaxis, Inc.

1320 Chesapeake Terrace
Sunnyvale, CA 94089
408-734-0200
Nasdaq: ABAX
www.abaxis.com

Chairman, President, and CEO:
Clinton H. Severson

Earnings Growth	★ ★
Revenue Growth	★ ★ ★ ★
Stock Growth	★ ★ ★ ★
Consistency	★ ★ ★
Total	**13 Points**

Want to know what's ailing your pet? Ask Abaxis. The company makes portable blood analysis systems called VetScan, which are becoming increasingly popular in veterinarians' offices.

Abaxis also makes a portable blood analyzer for the human medical market called Piccolo. Results from either of the automated systems are available in less than 15 minutes, and the cost is far less than shipping blood off-site to a contract laboratory. Armed with the results, the veterinarian or doctor is able to provide a complete diagnosis based on clinically accurate information.

The VetScan system was launched in 1994, and the Piccolo system was introduced the following year. Although VetScan is enjoying increasing acceptance in the veterinary community, Piccolo is only now beginning to make headway with the medical professionals.

The Sunnyvale, California operation is also developing technology to allow the Piccolo system to perform a broader array of tests, including one to measure the level of chloride in the blood, an indicator of dehydration.

The U.S. military has been a big customer for the Piccolo line, and demand is expected to increase once the dehydration test has won government approval. In addition to military installations, Abaxis believes its Piccolo system can gain acceptance in urgent care and walk-in clinics, nursing homes, acute care hospitals, and with home care providers and ambulance companies.

With the health care industry under continuing pressure to reduce costs, Abaxis's portable blood analyzer is well positioned to take advantage of the trend toward taking blood testing out of central laboratories and into patient care settings. Because using the Piccolo system requires no special training or full-time attention, analyzing a patient's blood will become as easy as measuring blood pressure, temperature, and heart rate.

The company was founded in 1989 and went public with its initial stock offering in 1992. It has about 100 employees and a market capitalization of about $100 million.

EARNINGS PER SHARE PROGRESSION   ★ ★

Losses have declined past 3 years.

REVENUE GROWTH   ★ ★ ★ ★

Past 4 years: 686 percent (67 percent per year)

STOCK GROWTH   ★ ★ ★ ★

Past 3 years: 155 percent (36 percent per year)
Dollar growth: $10,000 over 3 years would have grown to about $25,500.

CONSISTENCY   ★ ★ ★

Positive earnings progression: 3 consecutive years
Increased sales: 4 consecutive years

ABAXIS AT A GLANCE

Fiscal year ended: March 31
Revenue and net income in $ millions

	1996	1997	1998	1999	2000	4-Year Growth Avg. Annual (%)	Total (%)
Revenue ($)	2.95	7.29	12.2	13.3	23.2	67	686
Net income ($)	–6.2	–6.1	–4.3	–4.2	–.58	NA	NA
Earnings/share ($)	–0.65	–0.74	–0.44	–0.31	–0.05	NA	NA
PE range	—	—	—	—	—		

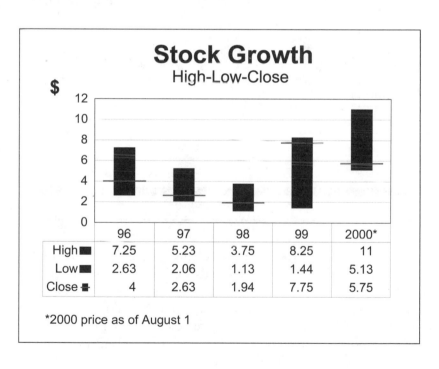

Stock Growth
High-Low-Close

$

	96	97	98	99	2000*
High	7.25	5.23	3.75	8.25	11
Low	2.63	2.06	1.13	1.44	5.13
Close	4	2.63	1.94	7.75	5.75

*2000 price as of August 1

Abercrombie & Fitch Co.

Four Limited Parkway East
Reynoldsburg, OH 43068
614-577-6500
NYSE: ANF
www.abercrombie.com

Chairman and CEO:
Michael S. Jeffries

Earnings Growth	★ ★ ★ ★
Revenue Growth	★ ★ ★ ★
Stock Growth	★
Consistency	★ ★ ★ ★
Total	**13 Points**

Abercrombie & Fitch is a youth-oriented clothing store chain, so cool that rock stars sing about it on MTV. And kids from kindergarten to college pay premium prices for shirts bearing the Abercrombie & Fitch name.

A&F is an old chain that's growing like a new start-up. The company was founded in 1892 as a supplier of rugged outdoor gear. In 1988, after years of operation as a small independent retailer, the company—and its 25 stores—was acquired by The Limited.

The Limited brought the company public in 1996, but retained 84 percent of its stock. In 1998, The Limited disposed of its shares in the market, essentially spinning off A&F as an independent operation. A&F still has certain service agreements with The Limited that include transportation and logistics as well as home office and distribution space.

The Columbus, Ohio operation has expanded rapidly in recent years, from 67 stores in 1995 to nearly 300 in 2000. It opens about 50 new stores each years. Most of its stores are located in upscale areas in shopping centers throughout the United States.

It also sells its products through a catalog, Web site, and Abercrombie & Fitch magazine.

A&F sells men's, women's, and kids casual apparel and personal care products. Its apparel is targeted to men and women ages 15 to 50 and kids ages 7 to 14. Its main emphasis recently has been on the younger set—kids from elementary school through college.

The company acquires its merchandise from about 100 suppliers and factories throughout the world.

Abercrombie has about 11,000 employees, including about 9,600 part-time employees. It has a market capitalization of about $1 billion.

EARNINGS PER SHARE PROGRESSION ★ ★ ★ ★

Past 4 years: 718 percent (69 percent per year)

REVENUE GROWTH ★ ★ ★ ★

Past 4 years: 342 percent (45 percent per year)

STOCK GROWTH ★

Past 3 years: 34 percent (10 percent per year)
Dollar growth: $10,000 over 3 years would have grown to about $13,400.

CONSISTENCY ★ ★ ★ ★

Increased earnings per share: 4 consecutive years
Increased sales: 4 consecutive years

ABERCROMBIE & FITCH AT A GLANCE

Fiscal year ended: Jan. 31
Revenue and net income in $ millions

	1996	1997	1998	1999	2000	4-Year Growth Avg. Annual (%)	Total (%)
Revenue ($)	235.6	335.4	521.6	815.8	1,042	45	342
Net income ($)	14.3	24.7	48.3	102.1	149.6	80	946
Earnings/share ($)	0.17	0.27	0.47	0.96	1.39	69	718
PE range	47–81	23–66	30–77	21–52			

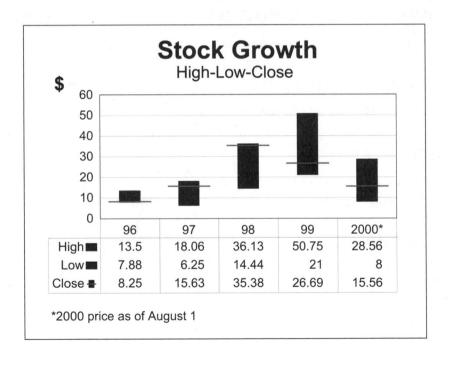

Stock Growth
High-Low-Close

$	96	97	98	99	2000*
High	13.5	18.06	36.13	50.75	28.56
Low	7.88	6.25	14.44	21	8
Close	8.25	15.63	35.38	26.69	15.56

*2000 price as of August 1

Novadigm, Inc.

One International Boulevard,
Suite 200
Mahwah, NJ 07495
201-512-1000
Nasdaq: NVDM
www.novadigm.com

Chairman and CEO:
Albion J. Fitzgerald
President:
Michael R. Carabetta

Earnings Growth	★ ★
Revenue Growth	★ ★ ★ ★
Stock Growth	★ ★ ★ ★
Consistency	★ ★ ★
Total	**13 Points**

Be it ever so humble, a single networked PC at a business actually costs the company anywhere from $8,000 to $12,000 a year to operate. Multiply that cost by hundreds or even thousands and it's no wonder why organizations are so eager to reduce the cost of owning PCs.

Riding to the rescue is Novadigm, whose stock in trade is helping companies buy, deploy, update, and automatically manage their software and content. Its roster of blue chip clients includes Viacom, Beyond.com, Motorola, Wells Fargo, and British Telecom.

About half the total cost of owning a networked computer is tied up in the management, installation, upgrading, troubleshooting, and repair of the software. Most companies can't afford to manually update and maintain programs across their networks, because the software industry continues to produce new products and upgrades.

Also driving demand for Novadigm's software products is the increasing use of e-commerce and the nation's growing mobile workforce, who do their jobs on the road or from home. Solving corporate America's enterprisewide software problems is a big and growing business. The market is expected to soar to nearly $7 billion a year from about $1.5 billion in 1997.

Novadigm's e-wrap technology enables companies to reduce software ownership costs by more than 80 percent, and it can help companies deploy software and content 70 percent faster than other technologies. Speed, of course, is of the essence in e-commerce, where Novadigm is establishing a name for itself.

InformationWeek recently named Novadigm to its "E-business 100," a ranking of the most innovative companies in electronic commerce. The magazine lauded Novadigm for its level of business and technology integration and its ability to execute its e-business strategy.

The New Jersey–based operation was founded in 1990 and went public with its initial stock offering in 1992. It has about 160 employees and a market capitalization of about $287 million.

EARNINGS PER SHARE PROGRESSION ★ ★

The company has had a positive earnings progression the past 3 years.

REVENUE GROWTH ★ ★ ★ ★

Past 4 years: 913 percent (79 percent per year)

STOCK GROWTH ★ ★ ★ ★

Past 3 years: 498 percent (81 percent per year)
Dollar growth: $10,000 over 3 years would have grown to about $60,000.

CONSISTENCY ★ ★ ★

Increased earnings per share: 3 consecutive years
Increased sales: 4 consecutive years

NOVADIGM AT A GLANCE

Fiscal year ended: March 31
Revenue and net income in $ millions

	1996	1997	1998	1999	2000	4-Year Growth Avg. Annual (%)	Total (%)
Revenue ($)	25.0	22.4	23.4	32.1	44.7	913	79
Net income ($)	5.04	−12.5	−9.0	1.8	5.14	NA	2
Earnings/share ($)	0.28	−0.72	−0.52	0.10	0.25	NA	−11
PE range	17–106	—	—	65–255			

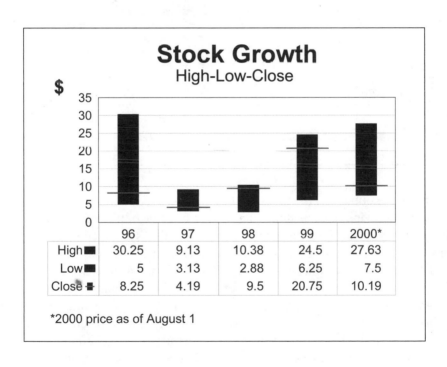

Stock Growth
High-Low-Close

$

	96	97	98	99	2000*
High ■	30.25	9.13	10.38	24.5	27.63
Low ■	5	3.13	2.88	6.25	7.5
Close ■	8.25	4.19	9.5	20.75	10.19

*2000 price as of August 1

Summa Industries

21250 Hawthorne Boulevard,
Suite 500
Torrance, CA 90503
310-792-7024
Nasdaq: SUMX
www.summaindustries.com

Chairman, President, and CEO:
James R. Swartwout

Earnings Growth	★ ★ ★ ★
Revenue Growth	★ ★ ★ ★
Stock Growth	★ ★ ★
Consistency	★ ★
Total	**13 Points**

Plastics may not be the growth industry it once was, but Summa Industries has posted growing revenue through its expanding line of plastics products. The company makes lighting fixture lenses, irrigation system components, conveyor belt parts, and other specialty plastic items.

In addition to its expanding product line, Summa has also been growing through an aggressive series of acquisitions. The Torrance, California company focuses on profitable companies in the plastics manufacturing business. Typically, Summa holds onto the management of the companies it acquires, letting them continue to run the operations while Summa takes care of the financing, purchasing, employee benefits, marketing, and business development.

Summa recently acquired manufacturers Plastron Industries, Broadview Injection Molding, Canyon Mold, GST Industries, Falcon Belting, and Calnetics.

Summa manufactures products in several broad categories, including:

- **Optical components.** Summa makes injection-molded plastic prismatic lenses, refractors, and reflectors for commercial and industrial lighting fixtures, such as street lights and traffic signals.
- **Irrigation components.** The firm makes engineered fittings, valves, filters, and accessories for irrigation systems.
- **Conveyor components.** The company makes engineered plastic components for conveyer belts and chains in the food processing industry that are lightweight and require no lubrication, which helps keep the equipment free of contaminants that could taint the food.
- **Winding cores.** These coiled components are used in transformers, relays, switches, power supplies, and electronic motors.

Summa also makes plastic tubing and extruded plastic sheets.

Most of Summa's products are sold to manufacturers for use as components in their products. Summa has thousands of active customers, including many Fortune 1,000 companies and large privately held businesses.

The company does most of its own manufacturing, although some of its products are made by third-party manufacturers.

Summa Industries was founded in 1942 and went public with its initial stock offering in 1993. The company has about 760 employees and a market capitalization of about $55 million.

EARNINGS PER SHARE PROGRESSION   ★ ★ ★ ★

Past 4 years: 248 percent (36 percent per year)

REVENUE GROWTH   ★ ★ ★ ★

Past 4 years: 483 percent (56 percent per year)

STOCK GROWTH   ★ ★ ★

Past 3 years: 111 percent (28 percent per year)
Dollar growth: $10,000 over 3 years would have grown to about $21,000.

CONSISTENCY   ★ ★

Increased earnings per share: 3 of the past 4 years
Increased sales: 3 of the past 4 years

SUMMA INDUSTRIES AT A GLANCE

Fiscal year ended: Aug. 31
Revenue and net income in $ millions

	1995	1996	1997	1998	1999	4-Year Growth Avg. Annual (%)	Total (%)
Revenue ($)	18.3	12.7	43.2	85.7	106.7	56	483
Net income ($)	0.65	0.57	2.25	4.87	6.55	78	908
Earnings/share ($)	0.42	0.35	0.41	1.10	1.46	36	248
PE range	14–22	16–27	10–25	6–14	5–11		

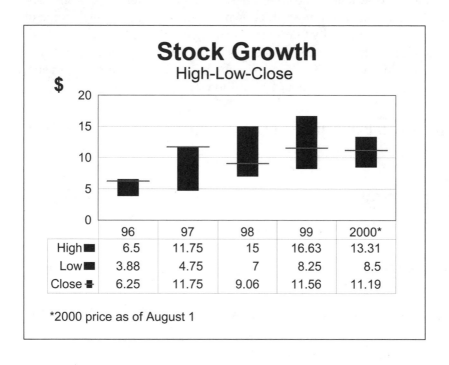

Stock Growth
High-Low-Close

	96	97	98	99	2000*
High■	6.5	11.75	15	16.63	13.31
Low■	3.88	4.75	7	8.25	8.5
Close ■	6.25	11.75	9.06	11.56	11.19

*2000 price as of August 1

27

Opinion Research Corp.

OPINION RESEARCH CORPORATION^{SM}

23 Orchard Road
Skillman, NJ 08558
908-281-5100
AMEX: OPI
www.opinionresearch.com

Chairman, President, and CEO:
John F. Short

Earnings Growth	★ ★ ★ ★
Revenue Growth	★ ★ ★
Stock Growth	★ ★ ★
Consistency	★ ★ ★
Total	**13 Points**

Is your marketing plan hitting its mark? Opinion Research helps companies analyze the effectiveness of their marketing and advertising programs through customer satisfaction surveys, market demand analysis and forecasting, corporate image consulting, and competitive positioning.

The Skillman, New Jersey operation collects customer and market information through computer-assisted telephone interviews, personal interviews, mail questionnaires, and specialized techniques such as business panels.

The company is global in scope, with about one-third of its revenue coming from foreign markets. It does business in more than 100 countries on six continents.

Opinion Research serves both government and industry. Its major focus is on the automotive, financial services, telecommunications, retail and trade, and health care industries.

About half of the company's revenues come from projects that require periodic updating and tracking of information, offering the potential for recurring revenues.

The firm offers assistance to its customers on a wide range of issues, including:

- **Customer loyalty and retention.** The company assists clients in quantifying customer loyalty, assessing customer satisfaction with products and services, and increasing customer retention.
- **Corporate reputation and branding.** The firm works with clients to manage their corporate and brand images and to identify and achieve optimal positioning in the marketplace.
- **Market demand analysis and forecasting.** The company helps customers gauge the market demand for new products and services.
- **Advanced analytical and data modeling.** Opinion Research uses advanced market research techniques and predictive segmentation learning models to help client companies improve their teleservices success rates.

Founded in 1938, Opinion Research went public with its initial stock offering in 1993. The company has about 1,500 employees and a market capitalization of about $30 million.

EARNINGS PER SHARE PROGRESSION   ★ ★ ★ ★

Past 3 years: 205 percent (45 percent per year)

REVENUE GROWTH   ★ ★ ★

Past 4 years: 169 percent (28 percent per year)

STOCK GROWTH   ★ ★ ★

Past 3 years: 86 percent (23 percent per year)
Dollar growth: $10,000 over 3 years would have grown to $18,600.

CONSISTENCY   ★ ★ ★

Increased earnings per share: 3 of the past 4 years
Increased sales: 4 consecutive years

OPINION RESEARCH AT A GLANCE

Fiscal year ended: Dec. 31
Revenue and net income in $ millions

	1995	1996	1997	1998	1999	4-Year Growth Avg. Annual (%)	4-Year Growth Total (%)
Revenue ($)	44.1	47.3	56.7	73.2	118.6	28	169
Net income ($)	−1.67	.808	1.15	−.020	2.51	47*	211*
Earnings/share ($)	−0.39	0.19	0.28	−.01	0.58	45*	205*
PE range	—	16–38	11–20	—	5–17		

*Net income and earnings per share growth figures are based on 3-year performance.

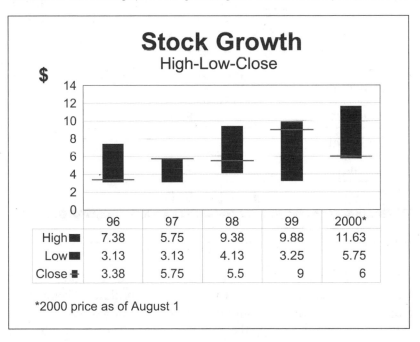

Stock Growth
High-Low-Close

$

	96	97	98	99	2000*
High	7.38	5.75	9.38	9.88	11.63
Low	3.13	3.13	4.13	3.25	5.75
Close	3.38	5.75	5.5	9	6

*2000 price as of August 1

28
Hauppauge Digital, Inc.

91 Cabot Court
Hauppauge, NY 11788
516-434-1600
Nasdaq: HAUP
www.hauppauge.com

Chairman and CEO:
Kenneth Plotkin
President:
Kenneth R. Aupperle

Earnings Growth	★ ★
Revenue Growth	★ ★ ★ ★
Stock Growth	★ ★ ★ ★
Consistency	★ ★ ★
Total	**13 Points**

Not only does Hauppauge Digital offer TV on your PC, the company has also been known to take investors on a roller-coaster thrill ride. Hauppauge, which makes a special video card for computers that allows users to watch TV while typing reports, surfing the Web, or setting up spread sheets, was the number-one stock in the first edition of this book.

The stock climbed quickly from about $10 in early 1999, then split 2-for-1 and surged again to $48 a share—a return of more than 800 percent in less than a year. But after reporting disappointing sales in early 2000, the stock crashed back down to under $10 a share.

Hauppauge still has potential because its products have a market-leading position in some exciting PC-to-TV convergence technologies. But the big sales have not come as quickly as the company anticipated.

Based in Hauppauge, New York, the company has a whole line of video-related products designed to be used with computers. Its leading product is the WinTV card, which allows computer users to connect their computers to an antenna, satellite TV, or cable TV line, and watch television in an adjustable window on their monitor. Hauppauge also makes the VideoWizard product line to capture and edit videotapes digitally on a PC; the Impact VCB boards used by manufacturers to add video display and Internet video conferencing applications to computers; and the VideoTalk product line used by consumers to video-conference over the Internet.

Hauppauge recently introduced a new video card that can turn your computer into a high-definition TV for under $200.

The company markets its products through distributors, computer retailers, and computer manufacturers. Distributors and retailers account for about 85 percent of total sales.

The basic WinTV computer card retails for about $79. The boards were first developed in 1992, and have been refined and expanded a couple of times since. Hauppauge's most advanced TV board is the WinCast/TV model, which has a 125-channel cable-ready TV tuner with automatic channel scan and a video digitizer. The digitizer allows users to capture still and motion video images to hard disk in order to create presentations and to video-conference over the Internet.

The company's ImpactVCB boards offer a low-cost alternative to digitized video. Designed for PC-based video-conferencing and industrial applications, the boards provide live video in a window on the monitor, still image capture, and AVI capture driver.

Hauppauge went public with its initial stock offering in 1995. It has about 100 employees and a market capitalization of about $65 million.

EARNINGS PER SHARE PROGRESSION ★ ★

Past 3 years: 633 percent (95 percent per year, but dropping in 2000)

REVENUE GROWTH ★ ★ ★ ★

Past 4 years: 409 percent (50 percent per year)

STOCK GROWTH ★ ★ ★ ★

Past 3 years: 366 percent (67 percent per year)
Dollar growth: $10,000 over 3 years would have grown to about $47,000.

CONSISTENCY   ★ ★ ★

Increased earnings per share: 4 consecutive years (but dropping in 2000)
Increased sales: 4 consecutive years

HAUPPAUGE DIGITAL AT A GLANCE

Fiscal year ended: Sept. 30
Revenue and net income in $ millions

	1995	1996	1997	1998	1999	4-Year Growth Avg. Annual (%)	Total (%)
Revenue ($)	11.6	14.7	25.6	38.8	58.6	50	409
Net income ($)	−1.5	0.309	1.04	2.48	4.59	140*	1,385*
Earnings/share ($)	−0.32	0.05	0.11	0.21	0.33	95*	633*
PE range	—	31–93	10–28	10–38	11–57		

*Net income and earnings per share growth figures are based on 3-year performance.

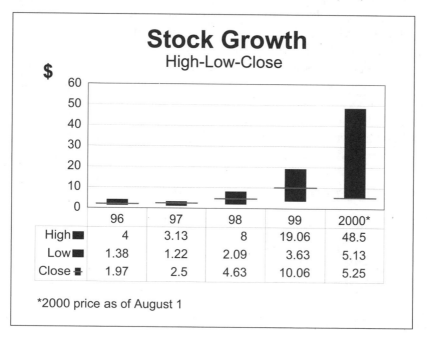

Stock Growth
High-Low-Close

$	96	97	98	99	2000*
High	4	3.13	8	19.06	48.5
Low	1.38	1.22	2.09	3.63	5.13
Close	1.97	2.5	4.63	10.06	5.25

*2000 price as of August 1

Kensey Nash Corp.

Kensey Nash

55 East Uwchlan Avenue,
Suite 204
Marsh Creek Corporate Center
Exton, PA 19341
610-524-0188
Nasdaq: KNSY
www.kenseynash.com

President and CEO:
Joseph W. Kaufmann

Earnings Growth	★ ★ ★ ★
Revenue Growth	★ ★ ★ ★
Stock Growth	
Consistency	★ ★ ★ ★
Total	**12 Points**

Think of it as an absorbable band-aid to quicken the recovery time of patients who have undergone a heart procedure. Kensey Nash's Angio-Seal is designed to close artery punctures of patients who have had cardiac catheterizations, such as an angiogram or balloon angioplasty.

Prior to the development of and government approval of Angio-Seal, heart patients would have to lie in bed for up to 40 minutes while manual pressure was painfully applied to the femoral artery in the groin area to stop the bleeding. The Angio-Seal, a sort of anchor on the punctured artery's wall, is inserted through a tube.

The Angio-Seal biodegrades in the patient's body in about 60 to 90 days. A clinical study found that patients being treated with the Angio-Seal were back on their feet less than an hour and half after the catheter was removed, versus more than six and a half hours for patients who were treated with manual pressure.

Kensey Nash's market for this product appears to have enormous potential. Worldwide, there are some seven million cardiac catheterizations performed each year. However, less than 15 percent of the catheterizations are completed with a sealing device. Kensey Nash reports that there is growing acceptance in the U.S. and European medical communities for sealing devices like the Angio-Seal.

The Pennsylvania-based operation also manufactures bio-absorbable polymers, such as staples, sutures, pins, and screws used for orthopedic purposes. In clinical trials in both the United States and international markets, Kensey Nash's new technology was successful in opening revascularizing coronary arteries. The company believes it can carve out a significant share of the market for that procedure.

Kensey Nash was founded in 1984 and went public with its initial stock offering in 1995. It has about 100 employees and a market capitalization of about $78 million.

EARNINGS PER SHARE PROGRESSION ★ ★ ★ ★

Past 2 years: 1,400 percent (275 percent per year)

REVENUE GROWTH ★ ★ ★ ★

Past 4 years: 332 percent (44 percent per year)

STOCK GROWTH

Past 3 years: 3 percent (1 percent per year)
Dollar growth: $10,000 over 3 years would have grown to $10,300.

CONSISTENCY ★ ★ ★ ★

Positive earnings progression: 4 consecutive years
Increased sales: 4 consecutive years

KENSEY NASH AT A GLANCE

Fiscal year ended: June 30
Revenue and net income in $ millions

	1996	1997	1998	1999	2000	4-Year Growth Avg. Annual (%)	Total (%)
Revenue ($)	2.97	7.9	11.3	16.2	19.8	44	332
Net income ($)	−5.9	−0.3	0.34	3.2	4.7	NA	NA
Earnings/share ($)	−1.00	−0.04	0.04	0.42	0.60	275*	1,400*
PE range	—	—	104–550	15–41			

*Earnings per share growth figures are based on 2-year performance.

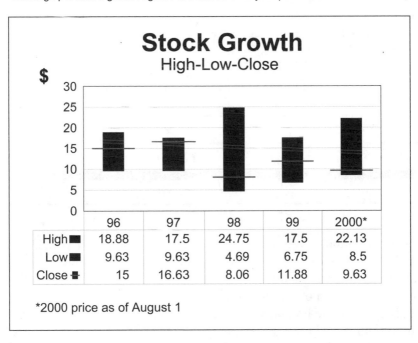

Stock Growth
High-Low-Close

$	96	97	98	99	2000*
High ■	18.88	17.5	24.75	17.5	22.13
Low ■	9.63	9.63	4.69	6.75	8.5
Close ■	15	16.63	8.06	11.88	9.63

*2000 price as of August 1

Radyne ComStream, Inc.

3138 East Elwood Street
Phoenix, AZ 85034
605-697-4000
Nasdaq: RADN
www.radynecomstream.com

Chairman:
Ming Seong Lim
President:
Brian Duggan
CEO:
Robert C. Fitting

Earnings Growth	★ ★
Revenue Growth	★ ★ ★ ★
Stock Growth	★ ★ ★ ★
Consistency	★ ★
Total	**12 Points**

The communications revolution has been very, very good to Radyne Com-Stream. The explosive growth of both the Internet and the wireless industry is presenting a wealth of opportunities to the maker of the ground-based portion of satellite communication systems.

Radyne's satellite ground station equipment is used for Internet, data, telephone, and digital transmission. Its products are used for Reuters' private satellite broadcast networks, the largest of its kind in the world. Italy's first digital telephone/data network relies on Radyne equipment, and the world's highest-capacity domestic digital satellite telephone network, operated by PT Telkom in Indonesia, uses the company's state-of-the-art equipment.

The company is continually seeking innovative, high-growth markets for its products—and it seems to be finding them. In a single month in 2000, Radyne landed three significant contracts, each very different from the other.

The first order was from an international common carrier for high-speed broadband equipment to transmit Olympic programming from Sydney. The second order was for communications equipment for the U.S. government, and the third was the first part of an Internet-based multicasting system to provide satellite-delivered financial information for the Chinese stock exchange.

Two-thirds of the company's revenues are generated in 80 international markets. The company estimates that the global market for ground-based satellite equipment is about $800 million a year and growing rapidly as the world improves its communication infrastructure.

Satellite communication systems provide an advantage in international markets for several reasons, including the fact that it's not cost effective to land-based networks and because satellite can be deployed more quickly to offer international services in remote or sparsely populated areas.

Radyne ComStream was founded in 1980. It has about 185 employees and a market capitalization of about $207 million.

EARNINGS PER SHARE PROGRESSION ★ ★

Radyne has gone from losses to positive earnings the past 4 years.

REVENUE GROWTH ★ ★ ★ ★

Past 4 years: 2,900 percent (138 percent per year)

STOCK GROWTH ★ ★ ★ ★

Past 3 years: 263 percent (54 percent per year)
Dollar growth: $10,000 over 3 years would have grown to about $36,000.

CONSISTENCY ★ ★

Positive earnings progression: 2 of the past 4 years
Increased sales: 4 consecutive years

RADYNE COMSTREAM AT A GLANCE

Fiscal year ended: Dec. 31
Revenue and net income in $ millions

	1995	1996	1997	1998	1999	4-Year Growth Avg. Annual (%)	Total (%)
Revenue ($)	4.2	11.6	14.7	25.6	38.8	75	830
Net income ($)	-1.3	-1.5	0.28	0.986	1.9	60*	578*
Earnings/share ($)	-1.03	-0.64	0.09	0.22	0.44	70*	388*
Avg. PE ratio	—	—	63	20	23	—	—

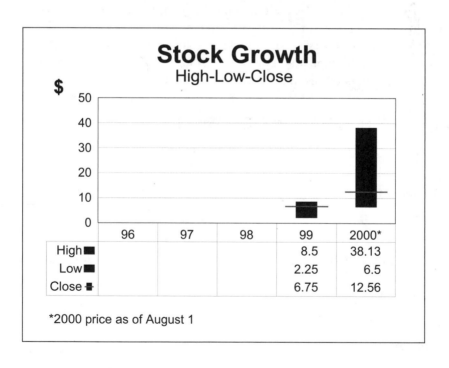

Stock Growth
High-Low-Close

$	96	97	98	99	2000*
High				8.5	38.13
Low				2.25	6.5
Close				6.75	12.56

*2000 price as of August 1

31

Galileo Technology Ltd.

142 Charcot Avenue
San Jose, CA 95131-1101
408-367-1400
Nasdaq: GALT
www.galileot.com

Chairman and CEO:
Avigdor Willenz
President:
Manuel Alba

Earnings Growth	★ ★ ★ ★
Revenue Growth	★ ★ ★ ★
Stock Growth	
Consistency	★ ★ ★ ★
Total	**12 Points**

Although Galileo Technology was named for famed Italian astronomer Galileo Galilei, the company's mission isn't to explore the heavens but to drive communication here on earth.

Galileo Technology designs and markets complex semiconductor devices that are used principally for data communications. Its chips are used to power microcontrollers embedded in cellular base stations, laser printers, routers, switches, and digital video distribution equipment. Its largest customer is Cisco Systems, which is responsible for about 20 percent of the company's business. Other large customers include Hewlett-Packard, D-Link, and Bay Networks/NETGEAR. The company also makes Ethernet switches and chips that serve as the building blocks for wide area networks, or WANs.

Galileo is a "fabless" semiconductor company, meaning it specializes in designing and marketing its chips but leaves the manufacturing to contract fabrication plants. Its chips are produced at plants that meet the highest international quality of standards, including Samsung's fab in Korea, TSMC's in Taiwan, and Matra MHS's in France.

Galileo's marketing and business development functions are housed at its San Jose, California headquarters, while the architecture and design of its semiconductor devices is done in Karmiel, Israel, where the company was first established. Galileo does all its product engineering, test engineering, and quality control in Israel.

Galileo prides itself on the close relationship it strikes with its customers. Because it is not preoccupied with the manufacturing process, it can focus on designing semiconductor devices that allow original equipment manufacturer customers to get their own products to market more quickly. The company also aims to reduce the cost and risk of integrating its chips into a customer's highly technical data communication or imaging system.

The company was founded in 1993 and went public with its initial stock offering in 1997. It has about 100 employees and a market capitalization of about $760 million.

EARNINGS PER SHARE PROGRESSION ★ ★ ★ ★

Past 2 years: 115 percent (46 percent per year)

REVENUE GROWTH ★ ★ ★ ★

Past 3 years: 1,134 percent (225 percent per year)

STOCK GROWTH

Past year: Even
Dollar growth: $10,000 over 1 year would have stayed at $10,000.

CONSISTENCY ★ ★ ★ ★

Positive earnings progression: 4 consecutive years
Increased sales: 4 consecutive years

GALILEO TECHNOLOGY AT A GLANCE

Fiscal year ended: Dec. 31
Revenue and net income in $ millions

	1995	1996	1997	1998	1999	3-Year Growth Avg. Annual (%)	Total (%)
Revenue ($)	0.843	6.46	36.5	51.6	79.7	225	1,134
Net income ($)	−1.6	−.934	10.5	16.2	27.5	64*	162*
Earnings/share ($)	−0.08	−0.04	0.27	0.36	0.58	46*	115*
PE range	—	—	41–85	9–57	15–59		

*Net income and earnings per share growth figures are based on 2-year performance.

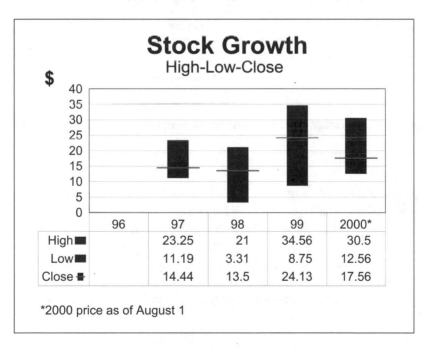

Stock Growth
High-Low-Close

	96	97	98	99	2000*
High ■		23.25	21	34.56	30.5
Low ■		11.19	3.31	8.75	12.56
Close ■		14.44	13.5	24.13	17.56

*2000 price as of August 1

32

Trend Micro, Inc.

Odakyu Southern Tower, 10th Floor
2-1, Yoyogi 2 chome
Shibuya-ku
Tokyo, Japan
212-815-2042 (U.S.)
Nasdaq: TMIC
www.trendmicro.com

Chairman, President, and CEO:
Steve Chang

Earnings Growth	★ ★ ★ ★
Revenue Growth	★ ★ ★ ★
Stock Growth	★
Consistency	★ ★ ★
Total	**12 Points**

In a Web world fraught with hackers and viruses, Trend Micro offers some sense of security. The Japanese-based operation makes products that protect the flow of information on PCs, file servers, e-mail servers, and the Internet gateway.

Trend's combination of products provides a complete centrally controlled virus protection system for enterprise computer networks. Headquartered in Tokyo, the company does business in 15 countries, including the United States.

Gartner Group, a business research company, has named Trend Micro as the most visionary malicious code management supplier for three consecutive years.

Trend develops its products through a network of strategic alliances with such market leaders as Cisco Systems, Compaq, Hewlett-Packard, and Lucent. Customers include GTE, Coca-Cola, MCI WorldCom, and Bank of America.

The company also offers a range of Web-based services for consumer and corporate users, including e-mail and Web content filtering and the remote management of network antivirus protection.

One of the company's biggest projects is its eDoctor Global Network, an Internet security service for Net users that involves many of the leading Internet service providers and related companies, such as Sprint and British Telecom.

Trend's product line includes:

- **InterScan VirusWall** scans Internet traffic for computer viruses.
- **ScanMail** scans e-mail messages on Lotus Notes, Microsoft Exchange, and other servers.
- **ServerProtect** provides antivirus protection for Windows NT and Novell NetWare.
- **OfficeScan** provides antivirus scanning on workstations throughout a company, with central management and reporting.
- **PC-cillin** is an antivirus scanning program for home computers that protects against a wide range of viruses.

The company has also launched a new subsidiary named ipTrend to develop Linux based e-commerce software.

Founded in 1988, Trend Micro went public with its initial stock offering in Japan in 1998 and was first listed on the Nasdaq in 1999. The company has about 850 employees and a market capitalization of about $8 billion.

EARNINGS PER SHARE PROGRESSION ★ ★ ★ ★

Past 2 years: 107 percent (45 percent per year)

REVENUE GROWTH ★ ★ ★

Past 2 years: 84 percent (35 percent per year)

STOCK GROWTH ★ ★ ★

Past year: 221 percent
Dollar growth: $10,000 over 1 year would have grown to about $32,000.

CONSISTENCY ★ ★

Increased earnings per share: 1 year
Increased sales: 2 consecutive years

TREND MICRO AT A GLANCE

Fiscal year ended: Dec. 31
Revenue and net income in billions of yen
Earnings per share in thousands of yen

	1995	1996	1997	1998	1999	2-Year Growth Avg. Annual (%)	Total (%)
Revenue ($)	—	—	7.39	9.74	13.63	35	84
Net income ($)	—	—	0.85	0.40	2.15	58	153
Earnings/share ($)	—	—	15.8	6.9	32.8	45	107
PE range	—	—	—	—	NA		

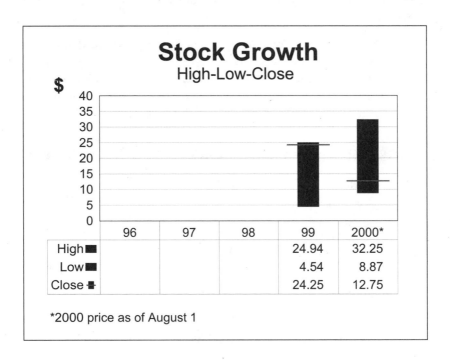

Stock Growth
High-Low-Close

$	96	97	98	99	2000*
High ■				24.94	32.25
Low ■				4.54	8.87
Close ■				24.25	12.75

*2000 price as of August 1

The InterCept Group, Inc.

3150 Holcomb Bridge Road,
Suite 200
Norcross, GA 30071-1370
770-248-9600
Nasdaq: ICPT
www.intercept.com

Chairman and CEO:
John W. Collins
President:
Donny R. Jackson

Earnings Growth	★ ★ ★ ★
Revenue Growth	★ ★ ★ ★
Stock Growth	★
Consistency	★ ★ ★
Total	**12 Points**

Small community banks now have access to the same type of electronic transaction services as the big institutions, thanks to the InterCept Group. The company offers electronic funds transfer services, data communication management, check imaging, Internet banking, client/server enterprise software, and other processing solutions for more than a thousand community banks and savings institutions.

The Georgia-based operation has grown quickly through a series of acquisitions. It has become the largest third-party processor of automatic teller machine transactions in the southeastern United States. InterCept offers a wide range of services for savings institutions, including:

- **Electronic funds transfer.** The firm offers automatic funds transfer services for banks, including transactions for money machines, point

of sale, debit card and scrip debit transactions, funds transfers, and re
mote banking transactions.

- **BancAccess Internet banking.** InterCept helps community banks establish an Internet presence, offering electronic banking functions that
  help small banks set up online banking services for their customers.
- **Data communications management.** Through its InterCept Frame
  Relay Network, the company manages data communications and voice-
  over-frame communications, which eliminate certain long-distance
  charges for its customers. It also designs and manages local and wide
  area data communications networks for its customers and offers them
  certain Internet services, including managed firewall and e-mail service.
- **Client/server enterprise software and services.** InterCept offers ledger
  and financial management, customer information file maintenance,
  loan and deposit processing, financial accounting and reporting, and
  automated clearing house interfaces using its InterCept Frame Relay
  Network.

Most of the company's customers are located in the southeastern
United States and Colorado. Typically, InterCept's customer banks have
assets of under $500 million.

The InterCept Group went public with its initial stock offering in 1998.
The company has about 320 employees and a market capitalization of about
$280 million.

EARNINGS PER SHARE PROGRESSION   ★ ★ ★ ★

Past 4 years: 308 percent (42 percent per year)

REVENUE GROWTH   ★ ★ ★ ★

Past 4 years: 476 percent (55 percent per year)

STOCK GROWTH   ★

Past year: 16 percent
Dollar growth: $10,000 over 1 year would have grown to about $11,600.

CONSISTENCY   ★ ★ ★

Increased earnings per share: 3 of the past 4 years
Increased sales: 4 consecutive years

THE INTERCEPT GROUP AT A GLANCE

Fiscal year ended: Dec. 31
Revenue and net income in $ millions

	1995	1996	1997	1998	1999	4-Year Growth Avg. Annual (%)	Total (%)
Revenue ($)	8.2	14.5	23.3	28.9	47.2	55	476
Net income ($)	0.681	−1.42	−0.395	2.47	5.0	65	634
Earnings/share ($)	0.12	−0.24	−0.06	0.30	0.49	42	308
PE range	—	—	—	15–29	7–32		

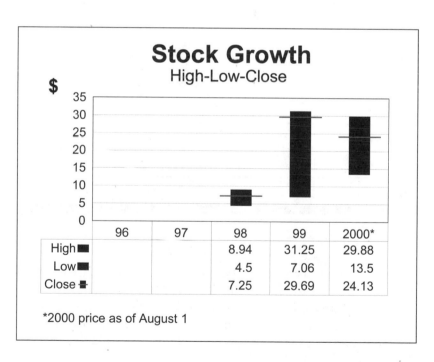

Stock Growth
High-Low-Close

	96	97	98	99	2000*
High			8.94	31.25	29.88
Low			4.5	7.06	13.5
Close			7.25	29.69	24.13

*2000 price as of August 1

34
TD Waterhouse Group, Inc.

100 Wall Street
New York, NY 10005
212-806-3500
NYSE: TWE
www.tdwaterhouse.com

Chairman:
A. C. Baillie
President:
F. J. Petrilli
CEO:
Stephen D. McDonald

Earnings Growth	★ ★ ★ ★
Revenue Growth	★ ★ ★ ★
Stock Growth	
Consistency	★ ★ ★ ★
Total	**12 Points**

TD Waterhouse Group is an old-school discount broker that has found new life in the online brokerage world. The company has been in business for more than 20 years, providing discount brokerage services for investors throughout North America, Australia, the United Kingdom, and Hong Kong.

With more than four million customers, TD Waterhouse is the world's second-largest discount broker.

Its customer base has been growing at about 50 percent per year recently, thanks to the boom in online investing. About half of its customers now execute some of their transactions through the firm's online site.

Despite its growing Internet presence, TD Waterhouse has continued to add to its brick-and-mortar infrastructure. The firm has more than 220 customer retail outlets worldwide and has been adding about 25 new outlets each year. It was the first online discount broker to have retail outlets in all 50 states.

TD Waterhouse sells a wide range of financial instruments, including stocks, bonds, mutual funds, and CDs. It also offers some banking services.

The company offers customers a broad range of investment news, third-party research reports, and investment management tools, such as portfolio tracking and stock and mutual fund screening programs.

TD Waterhouse began operations in the United States in 1979 as Waterhouse Securities. In 1996, it was acquired by TD Bank, Canada's largest discount broker. The company has continued its growth through additional acquisitions of discount brokerage companies, as well as through aggressive advertising and marketing.

The company, which has its headquarters on Wall Street in New York City, still has a very strong presence in Canada, where it has more than one million customers. But the United States remains its leading market with more than two million customers.

TD Waterhouse Group went public with its initial stock offering in 1999. It has about 6,200 employees and a market capitalization of about $7.5 billion.

EARNINGS PER SHARE PROGRESSION ★ ★ ★ ★

Past 3 years: 250 percent (51 percent per year)

REVENUE GROWTH ★ ★ ★ ★

Past 3 years: 473 percent (79 percent per year)

STOCK GROWTH

Past year: −29 percent
Dollar growth: $10,000 over 1 year would have declined to about $7,000.

CONSISTENCY ★ ★ ★ ★

Increased earnings per share: 3 consecutive years
Increased sales: 3 consecutive years

TD WATERHOUSE GROUP AT A GLANCE

Fiscal year ended: Oct. 31
Revenue and net income in $ millions

	1995	1996	1997	1998	1999	3-Year Growth Avg. Annual (%)	Total (%)
Revenue ($)	—	167.4	446.6	614.4	960.1	79	473
Net income ($)	—	29.6	36.2	48.7	97.3	47	229
Earnings/share ($)	—	0.08	0.10	0.13	0.28	51	250
PE range	—	—	—	—	41–97		

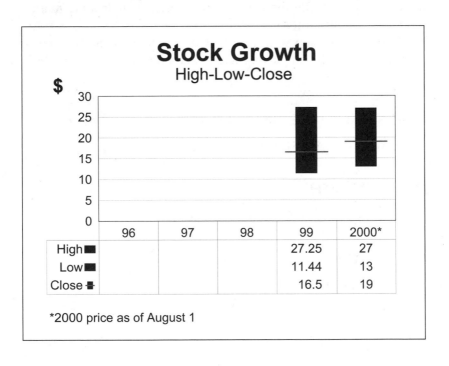

Stock Growth
High-Low-Close

$	96	97	98	99	2000*
High ■				27.25	27
Low ■				11.44	13
Close ■				16.5	19

*2000 price as of August 1

International FiberCom

International FiberCom, Inc.

3410 East University Drive,
Suite 180
Phoenix, AZ 85034
602-387-4000
Nasdaq: IFCI
www.ifci.net

Chairman and President:
Joseph P. Kealy

Earnings Growth	★ ★
Revenue Growth	★ ★ ★ ★
Stock Growth	★ ★ ★ ★
Consistency	★ ★
Total	**12 Points**

International FiberCom isn't above getting a little dirt beneath its finger-nails as it helps to build America's new broadband communications network.

The company tears up streets and buildings to install optical fiber and coaxial cable to pave the way for broadband transmission of audio, video, or data services. International FiberCom does much more than the heavy lifting. It designs, develops, tests, and maintains networks for Internet service providers, or ISPs; telephone companies; and cable TV operators. AT&T Broadband, SBC, Time Warner Telecom, Adelphia, and Cox Communications are among the company's major customers.

America has developed an insatiable appetite for greater bandwidth and the raft of services that race along the new high-speed networks that

International FiberCom is helping to install. A single strand of optical fiber can carry tens of thousands of times the information that traditional copper telephone wires could.

The Phoenix-based operation has a reputation for tackling some of the toughest installation challenges. It can engineer and install systems to allow the transmission of cellular, AM, or FM signals where connectivity is a problem. It also lays networks in such challenging environments as tunnels and subways.

The company's Systems Integration Group plans, designs, and installs local area and wide area networks, installs Internet equipment such as routers and switches, and develops on-premises voice and data networks. It is also a major distributor of telecommunications equipment. Its Wireless Division designs communication solutions for customers who no longer want to rely on copper-wire connectivity.

The company reports receiving contracts at record levels in 2000. One of its newest is an engineering project in New Zealand, underscoring its claim that it can engineer and install a broadband network anywhere in the world.

Founded in 1972, International FiberCom has about 2,500 employees and a market capitalization of about $550 million.

EARNINGS PER SHARE PROGRESSION   ★ ★

The company has gone from losses to gains the past 4 years.

REVENUE GROWTH   ★ ★ ★ ★

Past 4 years: 1,320 percent (92 percent per year)

STOCK GROWTH   ★ ★ ★ ★

Past 3 years: 900 percent (116 percent per year)
Dollar growth: $10,000 over 3 years would have grown to $100,000.

CONSISTENCY

Increased earnings per share: 2 of the past 4 years
Increased sales: 4 consecutive years

INTERNATIONAL FIBERCOM AT A GLANCE

Fiscal year ended: Dec. 31
Revenue and net income in $ millions

	1995	1996	1997	1998	1999	4-Year Growth Avg. Annual (%)	4-Year Growth Total (%)
Revenue ($)	12.0	19.2	57.3	105.0	170.4	92	1,320
Net income ($)	−2.2	−3.8	6.4	11.4	7.7	3*	20*
Earnings/share ($)	−0.50	−0.64	0.33	0.42	0.26	NA	−21*
PE range	—	—	2–25	11–23	17–35		

*Net income and earnings per share growth figures are based on 2-year performance.

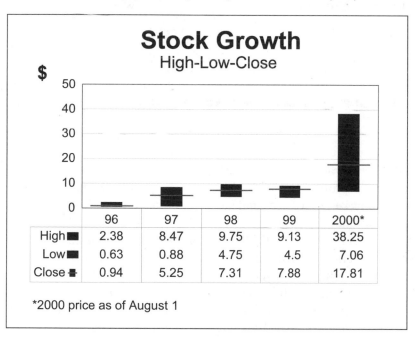

Stock Growth
High-Low-Close

	96	97	98	99	2000*
High■	2.38	8.47	9.75	9.13	38.25
Low■	0.63	0.88	4.75	4.5	7.06
Close■	0.94	5.25	7.31	7.88	17.81

*2000 price as of August 1

36

Ameritrade Holding Corp.

4211 South 102nd Street
Omaha, NE 68127
402-331-7856
NYSE: AMTD
www.ameritrade.com

Chairman and CEO:
J. Joe Ricketts

Earnings Growth	★
Revenue Growth	★ ★ ★ ★
Stock Growth	★ ★ ★ ★
Consistency	★ ★ ★
Total	**12 Points**

The online brokerage business is booming, but you won't see Ameritrade racking up big profits these days. The company has been spending all it can now to market its services and attract new customers while the industry is in its infancy.

Ameritrade believes that this is a crucial stage of the online brokerage battle. Customers it attracts now could be with them for years to come. That's why Ameritrade budgeted $200 million for advertising in 2000. The strategy is working. The company was on pace to add nearly a million new customers in its fiscal 2000—more than doubling its total client base.

A pioneer in the online brokerage business, Ameritrade has helped change the way Americans buy and sell stocks. But while its online trading concept is relatively new, Ameritrade founder Joe Ricketts has been breaking new ground in the brokerage industry for more than a quarter of a century.

Ricketts opened his first discount brokerage company in 1975. The firm, First Omaha Securities (later changed to Accutrade), was one of the first companies to offer discount commissions. In 1995, Ricketts purchased K. Aufhauser & Company and its WealthWeb service, which had been the first firm to offer securities trading over the Internet in 1994.

Ameritrade, which was officially launched in 1997, has attracted a growing customer base thanks to its relentless marketing and its flat rate commissions of just $8 per trade. Ameritrade Holdings consolidates all of the services of Ricketts's companies, including Accutrade, Ameritrade, AmeriVest (which offers discount services to banks, savings and loans, and credit unions), Advanced Clearing, a securities clearing and financial services firm, and OnMoney, a financial portal.

The Omaha-based operation went public with its initial stock offering in 1997. It has about 2,500 employees and a market capitalization of about $2.5 billion.

EARNINGS PER SHARE PROGRESSION   ★

Past 4 years: 56 percent (12 percent per year)

REVENUE GROWTH   ★ ★ ★ ★

Past 4 years: 635 percent (64 percent per year)

STOCK GROWTH   ★ ★ ★ ★

Past 3 years: 795 percent (105 percent per year)
Dollar growth: $10,000 over 3 years would have grown to about $90,000.

CONSISTENCY   ★ ★ ★

Increased earnings per share: 3 of the past 4 years
Increased sales: 4 consecutive years

AMERITRADE HOLDING AT A GLANCE

Fiscal year ended: Sept. 30
Revenue and net income in $ millions

	1995	1996	1997	1998	1999	4-Year Growth Avg. Annual (%)	Total (%)
Revenue ($)	42.9	65.3	95.7	164.2	315.2	64	635
Net income ($)	7.03	11.1	13.8	.209	11.5	13	64
Earnings/share ($)	0.045	0.07	0.08	0.00	0.07	12	56
PE range	—	—	11–38	—	75–951		

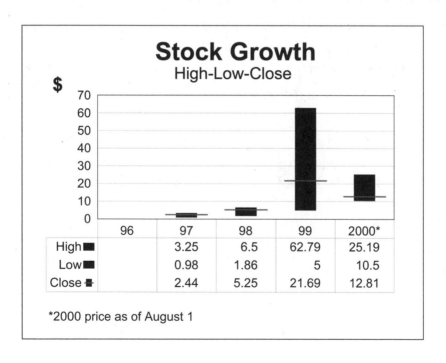

Stock Growth
High-Low-Close

$	96	97	98	99	2000*
High		3.25	6.5	62.79	25.19
Low		0.98	1.86	5	10.5
Close		2.44	5.25	21.69	12.81

*2000 price as of August 1

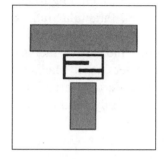

37

Take-Two Interactive Software, Inc.

575 Broadway
New York, NY 10012
212-334-6633
Nasdaq: TTWO
www.take2games.com

Co-Chairmen:
Barry Rutcofsky and Anthony Williams
President:
Paul Eibeler
CEO:
Ryan Brant

Earnings Growth	★ ★ ★ ★
Revenue Growth	★ ★ ★ ★
Stock Growth	★
Consistency	★ ★ ★
Total	**12 Points**

You can crash, smash, steal, and reel with Take Two Interactive video games. And coming soon—Oh baby, groovy—international superspy Austin Powers will work his magic on a series of Take-Two Interactive home video games.

Take-Two has developed a line of video games and accessories for PCs, Sony PlayStation, Nintendo 64, Nintendo Game Boy, and Sega Dreamcast.

The New York operation markets its games through more than 20,000 retail outlets in the United States, including Wal-Mart, Toys R Us, Best Buy, Ames Department Stores, and other supermarkets, drug stores, and discount stores. Its games are also sold throughout Europe and Asia.

The company produces games under several studios, including Rockstar Games, Mission Studios, GearHead Entertainment, Tarantula Studios, Alternative Reality Technologies, and TalonSoft.

Some of its leading games include: Midnight Club (street racing), Grand Theft Auto, Black Bass Lure Fishing, Monster Truck Madness, Smugglers Run, Thrasher, Bass Hunter 64, Monkey Hero, International Soccer, The Operational Art of War, Battle of Britain, Hollywood Pinball, and Las Vegas Cool Hand.

Take-Two has several games in the pipeline, including a series of secret agent titles based on the box office smash, *Austin Powers,* and some new releases of the popular Duke Nukem video game series. The company has been ratcheting up its research and development expenses to keep the new hits coming. It spent $5.2 million on R&D in 1999, up from $1.7 million in 1998.

In addition to its video game development business, Take-Two operates Jack of All Games, which is a distributor of entertainment software with offices worldwide. Take-Two also recently launched Broadband Studios to develop online broadband game delivery technologies.

Take-Two Interactive has about 540 employees and a market capitalization of about $330 million.

EARNINGS PER SHARE PROGRESSION ★ ★ ★ ★

The company has gone from losses to positive earnings the past 4 years.

REVENUE GROWTH ★ ★ ★ ★

Past 4 years: 5,015 percent (160 percent per year)

STOCK GROWTH ★

Past 3 years: 46 percent (14 percent per year)
Dollar growth: $10,000 over 3 years would have grown to $14,600.

CONSISTENCY ★ ★ ★

Positive earnings progression: 3 of the past 4 years
Increased sales: 4 consecutive years

TAKE-TWO INTERACTIVE SOFTWARE AT A GLANCE

Fiscal year ended: Oct. 31
Revenue and net income in $ millions

	1995	1996	1997	1998	1999	4-Year Growth Avg. Annual (%)	Total (%)
Revenue ($)	5.98	12.5	97.3	194.0	305.9	160	5,015
Net income ($)	−0.77	0.55	−2.77	7.34	16.4	NA	NA
Earnings/share ($)	−0.13	0.04	−0.25	0.42	0.76	NA	NA
PE range	—	—	—	11–20	9–23		

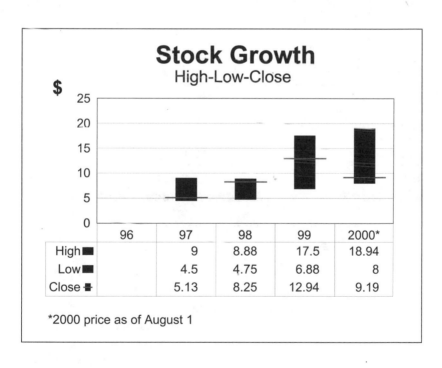

Stock Growth

High-Low-Close

	96	97	98	99	2000*
High		9	8.88	17.5	18.94
Low		4.5	4.75	6.88	8
Close		5.13	8.25	12.94	9.19

*2000 price as of August 1

38
Global Imaging Systems, Inc.

3820 Northdale Boulevard,
Suite 200-A
Tampa, FL 33624
813-960-5508
Nasdaq: GISX
www.global-imaging.com

Chairman:
Carl D. Thoma
President and CEO:
Thomas S. Johnson

Earnings Growth	★ ★ ★ ★
Revenue Growth	★ ★ ★ ★
Stock Growth	
Consistency	★ ★ ★ ★
Total	**12 Points**

Global Imaging Systems aims to be a nationwide one-stop shop for organizations in search of everything from copiers and fax machines to the design and installation of networked systems.

The Tampa operation has a growing online presence and a national network of subsidiary companies, but its name is not so widely recognized. Under Global's system, its business units retain their local names and identities.

Administration is centralized at Global's Florida headquarters, while service is dished out locally. That's just the way Global wants it—quick, responsive, and close to the ground. Since its founding in 1994, Global has acquired more than 40 companies with nearly 100 locations. Fifteen of the companies are organized into core or stand-alone companies in such growth markets as Chicago, Houston, and Atlanta. The rest serve as satellites to the 15 core companies.

Global continues to build its network. It's evaluating another 40 to 50 companies in the document imaging, network services, and automated office equipment fields. To further extend its reach, Global recently introduced a business-to-business e-commerce Web site for its 100,000 copier customers. The new site offers each user a customized entry screen that includes information on current and past quotes, existing orders, frequent searches, and standard equipment packages.

Global derives a large portion of its operating income from after-market service and supplies for the fax machines, copiers, printers, electronic presentation systems, and document imaging software and hardware it sells to corporate customers. The company expects to become more involved in the fast-growing fields of network integration, electronic presentation systems, and document imaging management.

Global Imaging Systems was founded in 1994 and went public with its initial stock offering in 1998. It has about 1,750 employees and a market capitalization of about $15 million.

EARNINGS PER SHARE PROGRESSION ★ ★ ★ ★

Past 2 years: 276 percent (91 percent per year)

REVENUE GROWTH ★ ★ ★ ★

Past 4 years: 1,180 percent (88 percent per year)

STOCK GROWTH

Past 2 years: −25 percent
Dollar growth: $10,000 over 2 years would have declined to about $7,500.

CONSISTENCY ★ ★ ★ ★

Positive earnings progression: 4 consecutive years
Increased sales: 4 consecutive years

GLOBAL IMAGING SYSTEMS AT A GLANCE

Fiscal year ended: March 31
Revenue and net income in $ millions

	1996	1997	1998	1999	2000	4-Year Growth Avg. Annual (%)	Total (%)
Revenue ($)	37.0	64.1	164.4	289.0	473.7	88	1,180
Net income ($)	−.191	1.12	4.45	13.1	15.7	136*	1,302*
Earnings/share ($)	−0.15	−0.03	0.21	0.62	0.79	91*	276*
PE range	—	—	33–128	12–34			

*Net income growth figures are based on 3 years, and earnings per share are based on 2 years.

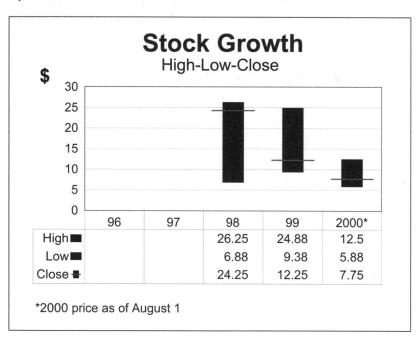

Stock Growth
High-Low-Close

$

	96	97	98	99	2000*
High■			26.25	24.88	12.5
Low■			6.88	9.38	5.88
Close ■			24.25	12.25	7.75

*2000 price as of August 1

LaserVision Centers, Inc.

540 Maryville Centre Drive,
Suite 200
St. Louis, MO 63141
314-434-6900
Nasdaq: LVCI
www.laservision.com

Chairman and CEO:
John J. Klobnak
President:
James C. Wachman

Earnings Growth	★ ★
Revenue Growth	★ ★ ★ ★
Stock Growth	★ ★ ★
Consistency	★ ★ ★
Total	**12 Points**

Who needs four eyes when two will do? With corrective laser vision surgery, Americans are abandoning their eyeglasses and contact lenses. More than a million people were expected to undergo the increasingly affordable procedure in 2000.

LaserVision Centers is one of the largest providers of the excimer lasers, which can restore a person's 20/20 vision, or close to it. The company operates more than 80 excimer lasers in the United States. More than 715 eye surgeons used LaserVision's systems on a per-procedure basis at more than 300 locations throughout the United States. Worldwide, the company has 86 excimer lasers in operation.

Eye doctors and their patients don't always need to go to LaserVision, because LaserVision will go to them. About 70 percent of the lasers the company operates are mobile systems. The company hauls the systems, accompanied by a trained technician, to eye doctors in small and medium-sized cities that often don't have access to excimer lasers. About 100,000 people a month are undergoing the procedure to correct nearsightedness, farsightedness, or astigmatism on a LaserVision system.

Most eye doctors aren't doing enough laser surgeries to justify the outright purchase of a system, which can cost as much as $500,000. Not only is the cost of an excimer laser prohibitive, but it also takes up too much room in a doctor's office.

The St. Louis operation has also entered the cataract market. In 1998, LaserVison purchased Midwest Surgical Services, which operates mobile cataract suites. The company cross-markets both its cataract services and its excimer laser services to its target audience of eye surgeons.

LaserVision Centers was founded in 1986 and went public with its initial stock offering in 1991. It has about 180 employees and a market capitalization of about $115 million.

EARNINGS PER SHARE PROGRESSION ★ ★

Losses have turned to gains over the past 3 years.

REVENUE GROWTH ★ ★ ★ ★

Past 4 years: 1,480 percent (99 percent per year)

STOCK GROWTH ★ ★ ★

Past 3 years: 115 percent (29 percent per year)
Dollar growth: $10,000 over 3 years would have grown to about $22,000.

CONSISTENCY ★ ★ ★

Positive earnings progression: 3 consecutive years
Increased revenue: 4 consecutive years

LASERVISION CENTERS AT A GLANCE

Fiscal year ended: April 30
Revenue and net income in $ millions

	1995	1996	1997	1998	1999	4-Year Growth Avg. Annual (%)	Total (%)
Revenue ($)	3.31	3.92	8.24	23.5	52.3	99	1,480
Net income ($)	−3.3	−8.8	−12.1	−3.5	6.5	NA	NA
Earnings/share ($)	−0.41	−0.88	−0.72	−0.30	0.31	NA	NA
PE range	—	—	—	—	15–77		

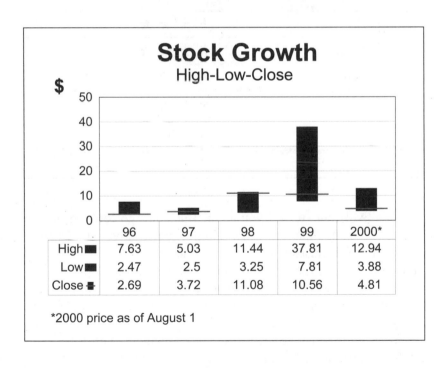

Stock Growth
High-Low-Close

	96	97	98	99	2000*
High	7.63	5.03	11.44	37.81	12.94
Low	2.47	2.5	3.25	7.81	3.88
Close	2.69	3.72	11.08	10.56	4.81

*2000 price as of August 1

Sonic Automotive, Inc.

5401 East Independence Boulevard
Charlotte, NC 28212
704-532-3320
NYSE: SAH
www.sonicautomotive.com

Chairman and CEO:
O. Bruton Smith
President:
Bryan Scott Smith

Earnings Growth	★ ★ ★ ★
Revenue Growth	★ ★ ★ ★
Stock Growth	★
Consistency	★ ★ ★
Total	**12 Points**

Sonic Automotive wants to sell you a car. But don't go looking for the Sonic sign, because the nation's second-largest automotive retailer operates all of its 173 franchises under their local names.

Sonic's dealerships are primarily in the Sunbelt, where people buy year-round—unlike the Midwest and Northeast, where harsh winters discourage auto sales. Each dealer works from essentially the same playbook. They all sell new and used cars and light trucks, and they offer parts service and collision repair services, as well as financing and vehicle insurance. Sonic operates 31 collision centers throughout the geographic markets it serves. Dealers in Sonic's three geographic regions report to a regional vice president.

Sonic dealers sell 31 different car brands, from KIAs to Cadillacs. Its best-selling brand is Ford, representing a bit more than 23 percent of the automotive dealership holding company's sales. Sonic's revenues boomed by more than 30 percent with the 1999 acquisition of FirstAmerica Automotive, a similar automotive dealership holding company. The acquisition allowed Sonic to expand into the high-growth California market.

The company continues to add new dealerships that have underperformed the industry average but have attractive product lines or good locations and would benefit from Sonic's management savvy.

While the growth of the Internet is making some auto dealers nervous, Sonic and its dealers have turned the Net into an additional sales channel. For example, Sonic has begun marketing new vehicles through Greenlight.com, a fast-growing Internet car-buying site that has a promotional agreement with Amazon.com.

Its online strategy, however, is designed to merely complement its brick-and-mortar dealerships, which Sonic believes will be the primary point of purchase for consumers in the foreseeable future.

Founded in 1997, Sonic has about 8,300 employees and a market capitalization of about $440 million.

EARNINGS PER SHARE PROGRESSION   ★ ★ ★ ★

Past 4 years: 388 percent (48 percent per year)

REVENUE GROWTH   ★ ★ ★ ★

Past 4 years: 976 percent (82 percent per year)

STOCK GROWTH   ★

Past 2 years: 30 percent (14 percent per year)
Dollar growth: $10,000 over 2 years would have grown to about $13,000.

CONSISTENCY   ★ ★ ★

Increased earnings per share: 3 of the past 4 years
Increased sales: 4 consecutive years

SONIC AUTOMOTIVE AT A GLANCE

Fiscal year ended: Dec. 31
Revenue and net income in $ millions

	1995	1996	1997	1998	1999	4-Year Growth Avg. Annual (%)	Total (%)
Revenue ($)	311.3	376.9	536.0	1,604	3,351	82	976
Net income ($)	3.3	3.1	3.7	18.6	44.6	92	1,251
Earnings/share ($)	0.26	0.24	0.27	0.74	1.27	48	388
PE range	—	—	17–23	6–24	6–14		

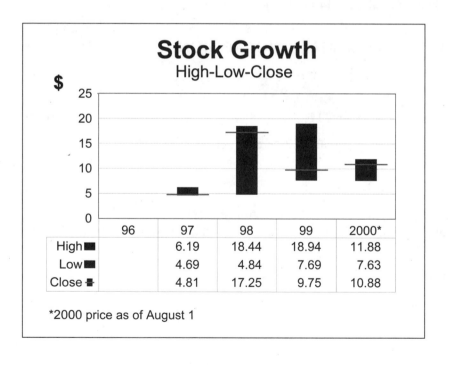

Stock Growth
High-Low-Close

$	96	97	98	99	2000*
High		6.19	18.44	18.94	11.88
Low		4.69	4.84	7.69	7.63
Close		4.81	17.25	9.75	10.88

*2000 price as of August 1

Citizens Financial Corp.

12910 Shelbyville Road
Louisville, KY 40243
502-244-2420
Nasdaq: CNFL

Chairman, President, and CEO:
Darrell R. Wells

Earnings Growth	★ ★ ★ ★
Revenue Growth	★ ★
Stock Growth	★ ★ ★
Consistency	★ ★ ★
Total	**12 Points**

Citizens Financial has the solid, established-sounding name of a bank, but its business is strictly insurance.

The company's leading products are whole life and group dental insurance sold in the District of Columbia and 29 states, primarily in the Southeast, Midwest, and mid-Atlantic. With the 1999 purchase of the Kentucky Insurance Company, Citizens Financial has begun selling fire and casualty coverage. The company is considering acquiring additional companies to help it enjoy economies-of-scale operating expense savings.

Organized as an insurance holding company, Citizens Financial operates through its principal subsidiaries—Citizens Security Life Insurance Company and Liberty Life Insurance Company.

The company's products are sold through a network of 2,400 independent insurance agents. About 350 of the agents specialize in the home service market, which consists of traditional whole life insurance. Agents for that product sell primarily small face-value policies typically ranging from $10,000 to $100,000.

Other product lines include:

- **Broker life.** This segment offers annuities, traditional whole life insurance, and universal life insurance, which provide policyholders with permanent life insurance and adjustable rates of return on cash value.
- **Preneed life.** Products in this segment are designed for individuals preplanning their funerals by providing coverage amounts of $10,000 and less. The policies are generally sold to older individuals at premium rates.
- **Dental insurance.** Policies in this segment are sold on a group basis, typically to employers with ten or more employees. All dental products have annual limits on procedures and lifetime limits on orthodontia procedures.
- **Other health insurance.** This segment includes individual accident and health insurance policies that provide coverage for such matters as monthly income during periods of hospitalization or during cancer treatment.

Founded in 1990, Citizens Financial has about 80 employees and a market capitalization of about $20 million.

EARNINGS PER SHARE PROGRESSION ★ ★ ★ ★

Past 4 years: 436 percent (53 percent per year)

REVENUE GROWTH ★ ★

Past 4 years: 123 percent (22 percent per year)

STOCK GROWTH ★ ★ ★

Past 3 years: 107 percent (27 percent per year)
Dollar growth: $10,000 over 3 years would have grown to about $21,000.

CONSISTENCY ★ ★ ★

Increased earnings per share: 3 of the past 4 years
Increased sales: 4 consecutive years

CITIZENS FINANCIAL AT A GLANCE

Fiscal year ended: Dec. 31
Revenue and net income in $ millions

	1995	1996	1997	1998	1999	4-Year Growth Avg. Annual (%)	Total (%)
Revenue ($)	16.3	23.0	23.7	27.3	36.3	22	123
Net income ($)	0.733	1.11	1.99	3.30	6.44	73	778
Earnings/share ($)	0.67	0.62	1.09	1.82	3.59	53	436
PE range	5–10	7–10	4–7	3–8	2–3		

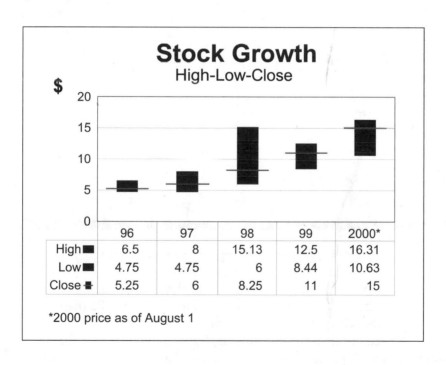

Stock Growth
High-Low-Close

	96	97	98	99	2000*
High	6.5	8	15.13	12.5	16.31
Low	4.75	4.75	6	8.44	10.63
Close	5.25	6	8.25	11	15

*2000 price as of August 1

AmeriCredit Corp.

200 Bailey Avenue
Fort Worth, TX 76102
817-332-7000
NYSE: ACF
www.americredit.com

Chairman:
Clifton H. Morris
President and CEO:
Michael R. Barrington

Earnings Growth	★ ★ ★
Revenue Growth	★ ★ ★ ★
Stock Growth	★ ★
Consistency	★ ★ ★
Total	**12 Points**

AmeriCredit specializes in putting used car buyers with big credit problems into the driver's seat. The company is the largest middle market automobile finance company in North America.

AmeriCredit is an indirect automobile finance company that purchases loans made by auto dealers to their customers. The firm focuses primarily on dealers of late model used cars, and, to a lesser extent, new car dealers. About 95 percent of its loans are originated by used car dealers. The firm purchases contracts from more than 12,000 dealerships each year.

The Ft. Worth, Texas operation targets consumers who may have trouble obtaining loans from traditional sources because of limited credit histories or prior credit difficulties. Because its customers are higher risk borrowers, the company charges a higher rate of interest on loans than traditional auto financing sources.

AmeriCredit markets its financing program to dealers through a broad network of branch offices. Branch office personnel are responsible for the solicitation, enrollment, and education of new dealers. The firm has more than 130 branch offices throughout the United States.

In selecting car dealers to solicit, AmeriCredit analyzes the dealer's operating history and reputation in the marketplace.

Once its loans are approved, the company collects and processes consumer payments, responds to consumer inquiries, and contacts consumers who are delinquent in their payments. AmeriCredit also monitors insurance coverage of the financed vehicle, and for those who fail to make their loan payments, handles the repossession and resale of the automobile.

Through its AmeriCredit Mortgage Services division, the company also originates and acquires nonprime mortgage loans through a network of mortgage brokers. The firm sells its mortgage loans and related servicing rights in the wholesale markets.

AmeriCredit was founded in 1986. It has about 2,300 employees, and a market capitalization of about $1.5 billion.

EARNINGS PER SHARE PROGRESSION ★ ★ ★

Past 4 years: 148 percent (25 percent per year)

REVENUE GROWTH ★ ★ ★ ★

Past 4 years: 913 percent (79 percent per year)

STOCK GROWTH ★ ★

Past 3 years: 62 percent (18 percent per year)
Dollar growth: $10,000 over 3 years would have grown to about $16,000.

CONSISTENCY ★ ★ ★

Increased earnings per share: 3 of the past 4 years
Increased sales: 4 consecutive years

AMERICREDIT AT A GLANCE

Fiscal year ended: June 30
Revenue and net income in $ millions

	1995	1996	1997	1998	1999	4-Year Growth Avg. Annual (%)	4-Year Growth Total (%)
Revenue ($)	33.1	80.9	123.4	209.3	335.4	79	913
Net income ($)	28.9	21.6	29.8	49.3	74.8	27	159
Earnings/share ($)	0.48	0.38	0.52	0.82	1.19	25	148
PE range	5–17	14–28	12–35	8–25	9–17		

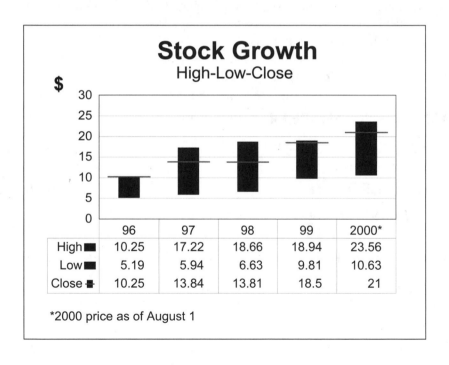

Stock Growth
High-Low-Close

$		96	97	98	99	2000*
High■		10.25	17.22	18.66	18.94	23.56
Low■		5.19	5.94	6.63	9.81	10.63
Close■		10.25	13.84	13.81	18.5	21

*2000 price as of August 1

AmeriPath, Inc.

7289 Garden Road, Suite 200
Riviera Beach, FL 33404
561-845-1850
Nasdaq: PATH
www.ameripath.com

Chairman, President, and CEO:
James C. New

Earnings Growth	★ ★ ★ ★
Revenue Growth	★ ★ ★ ★
Stock Growth	
Consistency	★ ★ ★ ★
Total	**12 Points**

Now pathologists have their own physician practice management company. AmeriPath specializes in acquiring and operating anatomic pathology practices. Pathologists analyze lab samples to help doctors diagnose diseases.

AmeriPath has practices in 14 states, with 30 outpatient laboratories, 164 hospital locations, and 43 outpatient surgery centers. Its staff of more than 300 pathologists provides medical services through outpatient pathology laboratories, hospital inpatient laboratories, and outpatient surgery centers. Most of its practices are in the South and Midwest, with the largest concentration in Florida and Texas.

The practice of pathology includes the diagnosis of diseases through examination of tissues and cells. It is a very lucrative part of the medical business.

The Riviera Beach, Florida operation manages and controls all of the nonmedical functions of its practices, including recruiting, training, and management of the technical and support staffs. The company also develops, equips, and staffs the laboratory facilities; negotiates and maintains contracts with hospitals, clinical laboratories, and managed care organizations; provides financial reporting and administration, clerical, purchasing, payroll, billing, and collection; and handles payrolls, benefits, purchasing, information systems, sales and marketing, and accounting.

In addition to the administrative functions, AmeriPath also helps drum up business for its member pathologists through increased marketing and additional contracts with hospitals. The increased business, along with the administrative cost savings brought about by the consolidation of its practices, has helped bolster the company's profit margins.

AmeriPath is the only company that focuses specifically on anatomic pathology. Its services include general surgical pathology, such as breast, prostate, and gastrointestinal pathology; cytopathology, such as Pap smears; dermatopathology; hematopathology, such as bone marrow analysis and lymph node pathology; immunopathology; neuropathology; and clinical pathology.

The company went public with its initial stock offering in 1997. AmeriPath has about 1,600 employees and a market capitalization of about $220 million.

EARNINGS PER SHARE PROGRESSION   ★ ★ ★ ★

Past 4 years: 950 percent (80 percent per year)

REVENUE GROWTH   ★ ★ ★ ★

Past 4 years: 1,354 percent (92 percent per year)

STOCK GROWTH

Past 3 years: −45 percent
Dollar growth: $10,000 over 3 years would have declined to about $5,500.

CONSISTENCY   ★ ★ ★ ★

Increased earnings per share: 4 consecutive years
Increased sales: 4 consecutive years

AMERIPATH AT A GLANCE

Fiscal year ended: Dec. 31
Revenue and net income in $ millions

	1995	1996	1997	1998	1999	4-Year Growth Avg. Annual (%)	Total (%)
Revenue ($)	16.0	42.6	108.4	177.3	232.7	92	1,354
Net income ($)	0.9	2.0	7.3	18.6	23.0	123	2,456
Earnings/share ($)	0.10	0.22	0.53	0.89	1.05	80	950
PE range	—	—	29–37	4–22	6–14		

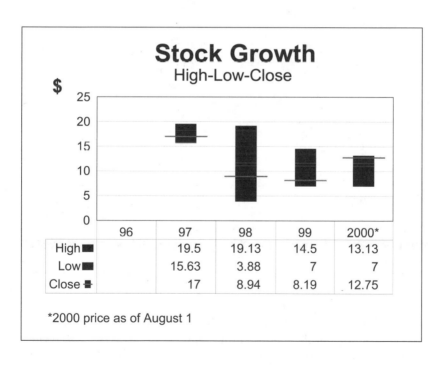

Stock Growth
High-Low-Close

$	96	97	98	99	2000*
High ■		19.5	19.13	14.5	13.13
Low ■		15.63	3.88	7	7
Close ■		17	8.94	8.19	12.75

*2000 price as of August 1

Standard Pacific Corp.

 Standard Pacific

15326 Alton Parkway
Irvine, CA 92618
949-789-1600
NYSE: SPF
www.standardpacifichomes.com

Chairman:
Arthur E. Svendsen
President and CEO:
Stephen J. Scarborough

Earnings Growth	★ ★ ★ ★
Revenue Growth	★ ★ ★ ★
Stock Growth	
Consistency	★ ★ ★ ★
Total	**12 Points**

The boom in new homes the past few years has spurred rapid growth of Standard Pacific, one of the leading homebuilders in the West. The Irvine, California builder puts up nearly 2,000 middle and high-end homes a year, a figure that has been growing about 20 percent annually.

Standard Pacific began operations in 1966 with a single tract of land in Orange County, California. Since then, it has built more than 40,000 homes in California and Texas.

Most of Standard Pacific's homes are priced in the $150,000 to $700,000 range, although in certain parts of California, higher-end models sell for as much as $1.5 million.

About 80 percent of Standard Pacific's homes are built in California. Leading areas include Orange County, which accounts for about 25 percent of all new homes; San Francisco, which accounts for about 33 percent; San Diego, 7 percent; and Ventura County, 14 percent. Most of the other 20 percent are built in Texas, mainly in the Houston, Dallas, and Austin areas. Standard Pacific also began building homes in the Phoenix area in 1999.

Standard Pacific gears its marketing effort to families who are move-up buyers—those who have owned a smaller home and are looking to move up to a larger, nicer home. Most of Standard Pacific homes are large, modern, high-quality dwellings ranging from about 1,500 to 5,000 square feet.

The company typically builds homes in groups, first acquiring unimproved or improved land zoned for residential use with enough space to build 50 to 500 homes. It generally begins a development with 10 to 30 homes, selling them almost as they build them, and then adds more homes over the years in additional increments of 10 to 30 units.

Standard Pacific has about 750 employees and a market capitalization of about $325 million.

EARNINGS PER SHARE PROGRESSION ★ ★ ★ ★

Past 4 years: 773 percent (106 percent per year)

REVENUE GROWTH ★ ★ ★ ★

Past 3 years: 246 percent (37 percent per year)

STOCK GROWTH

Past 3 years: 20 percent (including a 6 percent per year dividend)
Dollar growth: $10,000 over 3 years would have grown to about $12,000.

CONSISTENCY ★ ★ ★ ★

Increased earnings per share: 4 consecutive years
Increased sales: 4 consecutive years

STANDARD PACIFIC AT A GLANCE

Fiscal year ended: Dec. 31
Revenue and net income in $ millions

	1995	1996	1997	1998	1999	4-Year Growth Avg. Annual (%)	Total (%)
Revenue ($)	346.3	399.9	584.6	759.6	1,198	37	246
Net income ($)	−27.4	8.5	27.3	45.9	68.0	100*	700*
Earnings/share ($)	−0.73	0.26	0.81	1.58	2.27	106*	773*
PE range	—	19–28	7–20	4–13	3–6		

*Net income and earnings per share growth figures are based on 3-year performance.

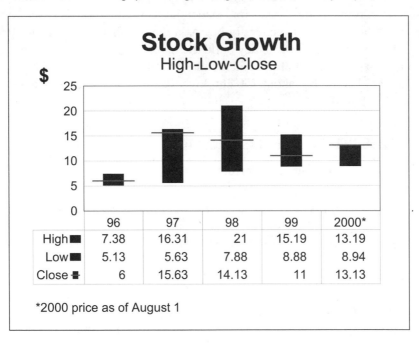

Stock Growth
High-Low-Close

$

	96	97	98	99	2000*
High■	7.38	16.31	21	15.19	13.19
Low■	5.13	5.63	7.88	8.88	8.94
Close ■	6	15.63	14.13	11	13.13

*2000 price as of August 1

45

NETsilicon, Inc.

411 Waverley Oaks Road,
Suite 227
Waltham, MA 02452
781-647-1234
Nasdaq: NSIL
www.netsilicon.com

Chairman, President, and CEO:
Cornelius Peterson

Earnings Growth	★ ★	
Revenue Growth	★ ★ ★ ★	
Stock Growth	★ ★ ★	
Consistency	★ ★	
Total	**11 Points**	

Imagine your office printer ordering repair parts or the vending machine placing a restocking order with the warehouse. That futuristic scenario, says NETsilicon chairman Cornelius Peterson, is nearly upon us. NETsilicon makes leading-edge networking systems that can tie nearly any type of electronics device into a broad network, enabling it to perform hundreds of routine tasks with minimal human intervention.

"By some estimates," says Peterson, "there will be billions of such intelligent nodes—contained in everything from microwave ovens to automobiles to printers, elevators, set-top entertainment systems, and virtually everything that runs on electricity."

NETsilicon's semiconductor-based networking devices are used in products that incorporate an "embedded system." Embedded systems are tiny computers that are inserted into larger products, such as printers, fax machines, industrial automation equipment, elevators, medical devices, vending machines, and automatic teller machines.

By inserting NETsilicon's system into those products, they can be linked to broader networks where they can be easily monitored and controlled from central locations.

The company's systems include both hardware and software. The hardware is made up of semiconductor devices that manufacturers incorporate into their embedded systems, while the software is used to set up and operate the hardware. The company sells its systems to electronics manufacturers worldwide, including such leading manufacturers as Minolta, NEC, Ricoh, Sharp, and Xerox.

NETsilicon's two leading products are NET+Embedded, which provides complete network connectivity in nearly any electronic device, including fitness equipment, medical systems, communications systems, Internet appliances, digital cameras, security devices, and building controls; and NET+Imaging, which provides networking for imaging products such as printers, copiers, faxes, and scanners.

Founded in 1984, the NETsilicon went public with its initial stock offering in October 1999. The company has about 115 employees and a market capitalization of about $360 million.

EARNINGS PER SHARE PROGRESSION   ★ ★

The company has gone from losses to positive earnings in recent years.

REVENUE GROWTH   ★ ★ ★ ★

Past 4 years: 591 percent (63 percent per year)

STOCK GROWTH   ★ ★ ★

Past year: 67 percent
Dollar growth: $10,000 over 1 year would have grown to about $17,000.

CONSISTENCY   ★ ★

Positive earnings progression: 2 of the past 4 years
Increased sales: 4 consecutive years

NETSILICON AT A GLANCE

Fiscal year ended: Jan. 31
Revenue and net income in $ millions

	1996	1997	1998	1999	2000	Avg. Annual (%)	Total (%)
						4-Year Growth	
Revenue ($)	4.6	7.4	7.9	13.4	31.8	63	591
Net income ($)	−2.4	−0.11	−0.85	−2.1	2.02	NA	NA
Earnings/share ($)	−0.34	−0.01	−0.08	−0.21	0.17	NA	NA
PE range	—	—	—	—	—		

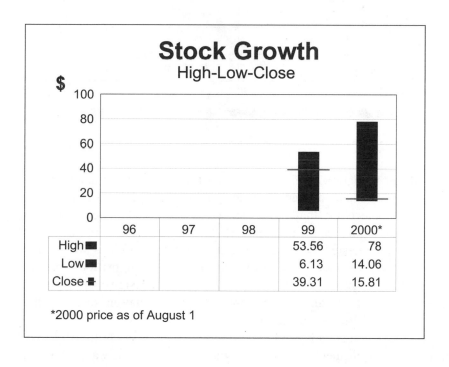

Stock Growth
High-Low-Close

$	96	97	98	99	2000*
High ■				53.56	78
Low ■				6.13	14.06
Close ■				39.31	15.81

*2000 price as of August 1

Avant! Corp.

46871 Bayside Parkway
Fremont, CA 94538
510-413-8000
Nasdaq: AVNT
www.avanticorp.com

Chairman, President, and CEO:
Gerald C. Hsu

Earnings Growth	★ ★ ★ ★
Revenue Growth	★ ★ ★ ★
Stock Growth	
Consistency	★ ★ ★
Total	**11 Points**

In an age of miniaturization, Avant! Corporation's software is an invaluable tool in the hands of electronic design engineers. They use it to craft the microscopic chips that power such devices as cell phones, digital watches, and palm-sized computers.

Electronics designers are creating the circuitry on chips with wires that are only 0.18 microns wide. A micron itself is almost too small to fathom. It's one-millionth of a meter. In order to design and test their handiwork, designers turn to electronic design automation, or EDA, the driving force of the electronics industry.

Avant!, which sounds more like a player in the fashion industry than the electronics business, is a leading maker of EDA software. Without EDA, it would be impossible to make integrated circuits, such as memory chips or microcontrollers, which serve as the brains of the futuristic, increasingly miniature devices that are becoming part of every day. Think of how small cell phones have become just in the past five years. Avant!'s software has been used on more than 7,500 designs.

Avant! generates about two-thirds of its revenues through the licensing of its software to customers. The remaining third is generated by various support services it provides customers. About 70 percent of its sales are to U.S. and Canadian customers. The company has 50 offices in 16 countries.

Much of Avant!'s services are provided through its easy-to-navigate Web site, which includes a direct link to <www.edamall.com>, the company's e-commerce site where U.S. and Canadian firms can license the company's design tools over the Web.

The company went public with its initial stock offer in 1995. It has about 1,000 employees and a market capitalization of about $327 million.

EARNINGS PER SHARE PROGRESSION ★ ★ ★ ★

Past 4 years: 306 percent (43 percent per year)

REVENUE GROWTH ★ ★ ★ ★

Past 4 years: 341 percent (45 percent per year)

STOCK GROWTH

Past 3 years: −40 percent
Dollar growth: $10,000 over 3 years would have declined to about $6,000.

CONSISTENCY ★ ★ ★

Increased earnings per share: 3 of the past 4 years
Increased sales: 4 consecutive years

AVANT! AT A GLANCE

Fiscal year ended: Dec. 31
Revenue and net income in $ millions

	1995	1996	1997	1998	1999	4-Year Growth Avg. Annual (%)	4-Year Growth Total (%)
Revenue ($)	68.9	124.0	181.1	248.3	303.6	45	341
Net income ($)	8.3	13.7	2.4	22.6	56.6	63	582
Earnings/share ($)	0.35	0.45	0.06	0.59	1.42	43	306
PE range	36–147	31–82	150–623	17–51	7–17		

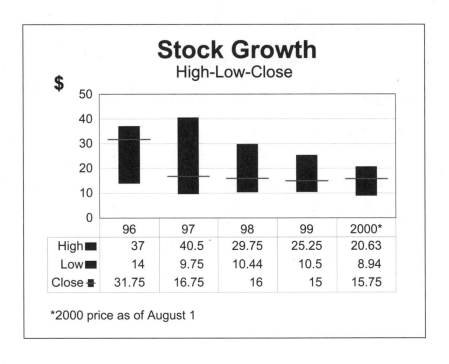

Stock Growth
High-Low-Close

	96	97	98	99	2000*
High■	37	40.5	29.75	25.25	20.63
Low■	14	9.75	10.44	10.5	8.94
Close ■	31.75	16.75	16	15	15.75

*2000 price as of August 1

Somera Communications

5383 Hollister Avenue
Santa Barbara, CA 93111
805-681-3322
Nasdaq: SMRA
www.somera.com

Chairman, President, and CEO:
Dan Firestone

Earnings Growth	★ ★ ★
Revenue Growth	★ ★ ★ ★
Stock Growth	★
Consistency	★ ★ ★
Total	**11 Points**

In the fast-growing area of telecommunications, Somera supplies a wide range of new and used equipment to many of the nation's leading telecommunications operations. Its customers include AT&T, GTE, the regional Bell companies, Alltel Communications, AirTouch, and nearly a thousand other businesses.

Somera's primary advantage is its ability to provide a wide range of equipment from more than 250 manufacturers. And because much of its equipment is used, Somera can often beat the competition dramatically on price.

The Santa Barbara, California operation often refurbishes the used equipment, cleaning, repairing, and reconfiguring it when necessary. It focuses on several key product categories, including:

- **Switching.** The company sells a wide range of switches and related equipment used by carriers to manage and direct call traffic.
- **Transmission.** Transmission equipment serves as the backbone of a telecommunications network, transmitting voice and data traffic across the network.
- **Access.** Used to provide local telephone service and Internet service, access equipment includes loop carriers, channel service units, multiplexors, and network interface units.
- **Wireless equipment.** The firm sells radio base stations, towers, shelters, combiners, transceivers, and related items used to transmit, amplify, and receive signals.
- **Microwave.** Somera sells antennas, dishes, coaxial cables, and connectors to transmit and receive voice, data, and video traffic.
- **Power.** The firm sells power bays, rectifiers, batteries, breaker panels, and converters used by carriers to provide power to the network infrastructure equipment.

Somera also offers technical services, materials management services, and asset recovery services in which the company agrees to purchase or trade equipment with carriers.

Most of the company's revenue is generated in the United States, but it is aggressively pushing into international markets.

Founded in 1995, Somera has about 140 employees and a market capitalization of about $700 million.

EARNINGS PER SHARE PROGRESSION ★ ★ ★

Past 2 years: 52 percent (23 percent per year)

REVENUE GROWTH ★ ★ ★ ★

Past 2 years: 261 percent (90 percent per year)

STOCK GROWTH ★

Past 6 months (since its IPO): 10 percent
Dollar growth: $10,000 over 6 months would have grown to $11,000.

CONSISTENCY ★ ★ ★

Increased earnings per share: 3 consecutive years
Increased sales: 3 consecutive years

SOMERA AT A GLANCE

Fiscal year ended: Dec. 31
Revenue and net income in $ millions

	1995	1996	1997	1998	1999	2-Year Growth Avg. Annual (%)	Total (%)
Revenue ($)	—	10.1*	34.6	72.2	125.1	90	261
Net income ($)	—	3.1*	9.8	11.5	14.8	23	51
Earnings/share ($)	—	0.08*	0.25	0.30	0.38	23	52
PE range	—	—	—	—	11–19		

*1996 figures represent just 6 months of revenue, net income, and earnings per share.

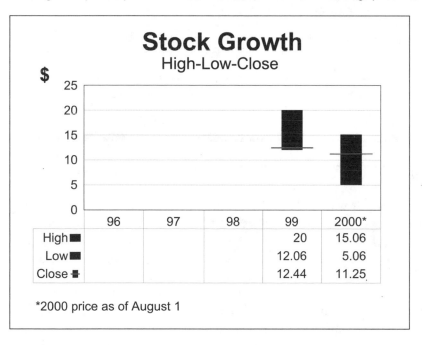

Stock Growth
High-Low-Close

$	96	97	98	99	2000*
High ■				20	15.06
Low ■				12.06	5.06
Close ▮				12.44	11.25

*2000 price as of August 1

48
NetScout Systems, Inc.

4 Technology Park Drive
Westford, MA 01886
978-614-4000
Nasdaq: NTCT
www.netscout.com

Chairman and CEO:
Anil K. Singhal
President:
Narendra Popat

Earnings Growth	★ ★ ★ ★
Revenue Growth	★ ★ ★ ★
Stock Growth	
Consistency	★ ★ ★
Total	**11 Points**

Businesses that want to keep their e-business applications up and running at optimum performance use NetScout System software to operate their networks. The Westford, Massachusetts operation makes software that helps companies direct, monitor, and analyze their computer traffic across both their corporate intranets and the Internet.

Its software is used by about half of the Fortune 500 companies, although by far its biggest customer is Cisco Systems, which integrates NetScout's software into its network management products.

The two companies have had a strategic alliance since 1994. Cisco works with NetScout to synchronize product development, then integrates the specially designed NetScout software into its networking systems. For instance, NetScout network management software is integrated into Cisco's Routed WAN management system, and the NetScout Application

Flow Management software is included in the CiscoWorks2000 network management console.

Sales through Cisco account for about 50 percent of NetScout's total annual revenue.

NetScout's Application Flow Management system tracks and analyzes traffic by software application, such as e-mail and order entry, across the network. Specific benefits include:

- Measuring response times for network-based software applications
- Monitoring and troubleshooting network usage to prevent malfunctions and to pinpoint problems
- Capacity planning to measure and identify trends in network usage
- Policy enforcement to ensure adherence to corporate guidelines
- Accounting and chargeback function, which breaks down usage by user, department, or application in order to charge for network use

Besides Cisco, the company's target market includes computer network service providers and businesses and organizations with large internal networks.

Formerly known as Frontier Software, the company was incorporated in 1984 and changed its name to NetScout in 1997. It went public with its initial stock offering in 1999. NetScout has about 250 employees and a market capitalization of about $900 million.

EARNINGS PER SHARE PROGRESSION ★ ★ ★ ★

Past 4 years: 520 percent (58 percent per year)

REVENUE GROWTH ★ ★ ★ ★

Past 4 years: 448 percent (53 percent per year)

STOCK GROWTH

The stock went public in 1999 and dropped about 60 percent in the first half of 2000.

CONSISTENCY ★ ★ ★

Increased earnings per share: 3 of the past 4 years
Increased sales: 4 consecutive years

NETSCOUT SYSTEMS AT A GLANCE

Fiscal year ended: March 31
Revenue and net income in $ millions

	1996	1997	1998	1999	2000	4-Year Growth Avg. Annual (%)	Total (%)
Revenue ($)	15.7	30.6	42.8	67.5	86.1	53	448
Net income ($)	2.0	5.9	5.4	10.3	15.2	67	660
Earnings/share ($)	0.09	0.26	0.23	0.43	0.56	58	520
PE range	—	—	—	25–95			

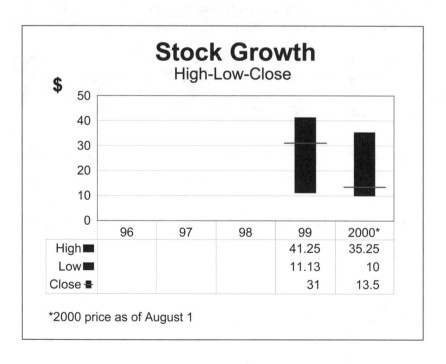

Stock Growth
High-Low-Close

	96	97	98	99	2000*
High				41.25	35.25
Low				11.13	10
Close				31	13.5

*2000 price as of August 1

Manatron, Inc.

510 East Milham Avenue
Portage, MI 49002
616-375-5300
Nasdaq: MANA
www.manatron.com

Chairman:
Randall L. Peat
President and CEO:
Paul R. Sylvester

Earnings Growth	★ ★ ★ ★
Revenue Growth	
Stock Growth	★ ★ ★ ★
Consistency	★ ★ ★
Total	**11 Points**

Sparing people a trip to the local courthouse to fish out records on their property or tax information is one of the charms of Manatron's Internet-based software.

Homeowners, attorneys, and real estate brokers using Manatron's MVP-Connect software can access data from their home or office.

Manatron's software allows local governments—counties, cities, and townships—to create what it calls a "virtual courthouse," where citizens get more convenient access to public records via the World Wide Web. Its software for court administration can monitor everything from the court docket to traffic fines, bail bonds to alimony. The program also allows users to search a court docket and schedule via the Internet.

The Portage, Michigan operation provides both Internet-based and client-server application software to more than 1,600 government entities in the United States and Canada.

Local governments are only too happy to streamline the normally labor-intensive task of collecting, analyzing, and warehousing data collected on each property. Manatron's Sabre Appraisal Division helps local governments create a digitized database of the land, building, and improvements of all the residential, commercial, industrial, public utility, farm, and tax-exempt properties in their jurisdictions.

Manatron's computer-assisted mass appraisal system ensures that governments have the most up-to-date information and that property evaluations are done fairly throughout the city, county, or township.

The company is confident it can tap a larger share of its target market, which currently is very fragmented among a number of suppliers of business-to-government software products. There are more than 3,000 counties, 19,000 cities, and 16,000 townships in the United States.

Manatron's software will also enhance the e-commerce capabilities of local governments by being able to process credit card payments over the Internet.

Founded in 1969, Manatron has about 380 employees and a market capitalization of about $25 million.

EARNINGS PER SHARE PROGRESSION   ★ ★ ★ ★

Past 3 years: 300 percent (100 percent per year)

REVENUE GROWTH

Past 4 years: 51 percent (11 percent per year)

STOCK GROWTH   ★ ★ ★ ★

Past 3 years: 267 percent (55 percent per year)
Dollar growth: $10,000 over 3 years would have grown to about $37,000.

CONSISTENCY   ★ ★ ★

Positive earnings progression: 4 consecutive years
Increased sales: 3 of the past 4 years

MANATRON AT A GLANCE

Fiscal year ended: April 30
Revenue and net income in $ millions

	1996	1997	1998	1999	2000	4-Year Growth Avg. Annual (%)	Total (%)
Revenue ($)	23.9	22.0	24.8	37.5	43.6	11	51
Net income ($)	−3.04	−0.41	0.32	1.3	1.6	125	400
Earnings/share ($)	−1.03	−0.14	0.11	0.41	0.44	100	300
PE range	12–24	—	—	13–68	7–19		

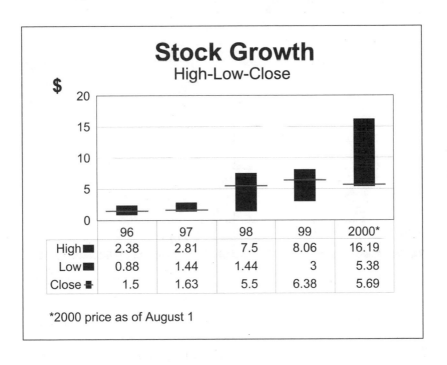

Stock Growth
High-Low-Close

$	96	97	98	99	2000*
High	2.38	2.81	7.5	8.06	16.19
Low	0.88	1.44	1.44	3	5.38
Close	1.5	1.63	5.5	6.38	5.69

*2000 price as of August 1

Extended Stay America

450 East Las Olas Boulevard
Fort Lauderdale, FL 33301
954-713-1600
NYSE: ESA
www.extendedstayamerica.com

Chairman:
H. Wayne Huizenga
CEO:
George D. Johnson Jr.
President:
Robert A. Brannon

Earnings Growth	★ ★ ★ ★
Revenue Growth	★ ★ ★ ★
Stock Growth	
Consistency	★ ★ ★
Total	**11 Points**

H. Wayne Huizenga appears to have another blockbuster on his hands—Extended Stay America.

Huizenga, the driving force behind several other successful enterprises including Blockbuster Entertainment, Waste Management, and AutoNation, is cofounder and chairman of Extended Stay America, a chain of value-priced extended stay hotels. Fortune magazine recently named it one of the fastest-growing companies in America. The extended stay market is the hottest niche in the lodging industry.

Extended Stay America consists of more than 380 properties in 38 states operating under three different brands. Extended Stay America Efficiency Suites is the largest of three with more than 250 properties nationwide. The company operates more than 90 StudioPLUS Deluxe Suites and about 40 Crossland Economy Studios.

The company's target audience consists of corporate employees on long-term training or consulting assignments. Other customers include people relocating, those attending family functions, or even people who are building a home and need a place to hang their hat for several weeks. Extended Stay America customers typically stay from three to eight weeks at one of the properties.

The 300-square-foot guest rooms at Extended Stay America include a queen-size bed, recliner, cable TV, free voice mail and local calls, and a data port. Rooms are equipped with a refrigerator, range, microwave, utensils, and tableware. Guests are provided with weekly housekeeping service and twice-weekly towel service. Weekly rates at one of the company's newest hotels in suburban Chicago begins at just over $350 a week.

The company's StudioPLUS Deluxe suites are the largest offering about 450 square feet of living space. The smallest units are the Crossland Economy Studios with about 225 square feet of living space.

The company was founded in 1995 and went public with its initial stock offering later that same year. It has about 5,600 employees and a market capitalization of about $1.25 billion.

EARNINGS PER SHARE PROGRESSION   ★ ★ ★ ★

Past 4 years: 900 percent (78 percent per year)

REVENUE GROWTH   ★ ★ ★ ★

Past 3 years: 2,385 percent (120 percent per year)

STOCK GROWTH

Past 3 years: −41 percent
Dollar growth: $10,000 over 3 years would have dropped to about $ 6,000.

CONSISTENCY   ★ ★ ★

Increased earnings per share: 3 of the past 4 years
Increased sales: 4 consecutive years

EXTENDED STAY AMERICA AT A GLANCE

Fiscal year ended: Dec. 31
Revenue and net income in $ millions

	1995	1996	1997	1998	1999	Avg. Annual (%)	Total (%)
						4-Year Growth	
Revenue ($)	16.8	38.8	130.8	283.1	417.7	120	2,385
Net income ($)	1.6	7.8	2.6	28.0	48.8	133	2,950
Earnings/share ($)	0.05	0.11	0.03	0.29	0.50	78	900
PE range	—	95–219	379–741	20–52	14–25		

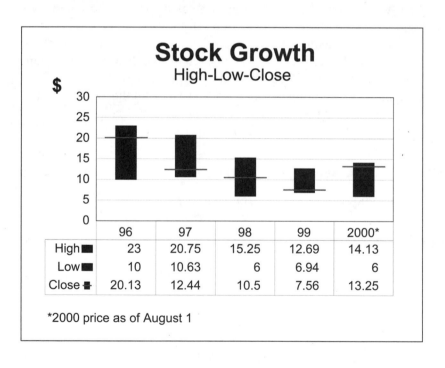

Stock Growth
High-Low-Close

$

	96	97	98	99	2000*
High■	23	20.75	15.25	12.69	14.13
Low■	10	10.63	6	6.94	6
Close ■	20.13	12.44	10.5	7.56	13.25

*2000 price as of August 1

AmSurg Corp.

AMSURG

20 Burton Hills Boulevard,
5th Floor
Nashville, TN 37215
615-665-1283
Nasdaq: AMSGA
www.amsurg.com

Chairman:
Thomas G. Cigarran
President and CEO:
Ken P. McDonald

Earnings Growth	★ ★ ★ ★
Revenue Growth	★ ★ ★ ★
Stock Growth	
Consistency	★ ★ ★
Total	**11 Points**

Freestanding outpatient surgery centers give doctors greater control, insurers lower costs, and patients higher satisfaction, according to health care analysts. That helps explain why AmSurg has been aggressively buying and developing the centers throughout the United States.

The Nashville operation owns a majority interest in about 65 of the centers and has 11 more under development. The centers are operated in partnership with physician groups.

About half of the six million surgical procedures done each year in the United States take place at freestanding or ambulatory surgical centers.

The ambulatory surgery industry is projected to grow by about 8 percent per year due to an aging population, and because more advanced technology allows surgery to take place outside of hospitals. Higher costs are associated with the traditional, hospital-based surgical centers, which provide more intensive services in a broader array of surgical specialties.

AmSurg's licensed centers are generally equipped and staffed for a single medical specialty and are typically located in or adjacent to a physician group practice.

AmSurg focuses on several specialties, including gastroenterology, ophthalmology, orthopedics, urology, and otolaryngology (surgery of the tonsils and larynx). By focusing on a single specialty at each center, the company can significantly lower operating costs. Satisfaction surveys indicate that patients feel more comfortable in the less-threatening environment of an outpatient surgical center.

AmSurg also develops and owns eight specialty physician networks, which help it obtain additional contracts with managed care payers and increase the profitability of its centers. The company envisions further growth through acquisition. Logical candidates would be some of the 1,000 U.S. surgical centers operating in AmSurg's specialties that are primarily physician owned.

AmSurg was founded in 1992 and went public in 1998. The company has about 285 employees and a market capitalization of about $85 million.

EARNINGS PER SHARE PROGRESSION   ★ ★ ★ ★

Past 4 years: 292 percent (42 percent per year)

REVENUE GROWTH   ★ ★ ★ ★

Past 4 years: 353 percent (46 percent per year)

STOCK GROWTH

Past 3 years: −43 percent
Dollar growth: $10,000 over 3 years would have declined to about $5,700.

CONSISTENCY   ★ ★ ★

Increased earnings per share: 3 of the past 4 years
Increased sales: 4 consecutive years

AMSURG AT A GLANCE

Fiscal year ended: Dec. 31
Revenue and net income in $ millions

	1995	1996	1997	1998	1999	4-Year Growth Avg. Annual (%)	4-Year Growth Total (%)
Revenue ($)	22.4	34.9	57.4	80.3	101.4	46	353
Net income ($)	1.05	1.48	0.08	0.76	7.05	62	571
Earnings/share ($)	0.12	0.16	−0.22	0.06	0.47	42	292
PE range	—	—	—	101–191	10–19		

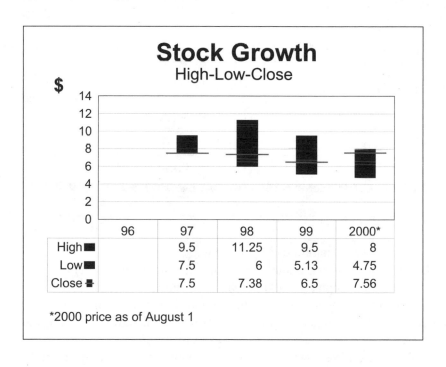

Stock Growth
High-Low-Close

$	96	97	98	99	2000*
High		9.5	11.25	9.5	8
Low		7.5	6	5.13	4.75
Close		7.5	7.38	6.5	7.56

*2000 price as of August 1

Dataram Corp.

P.O. Box 7528
Princeton, NJ 08543
609-799-0071
Nasdaq: DRAM
www.dataram.com

Chairman, President, and CEO:
R.V. Tarantino

Earnings Growth	★ ★ ★ ★
Revenue Growth	
Stock Growth	★ ★ ★ ★
Consistency	★ ★
Total	**10 Points**

Short of memory? Dataram can fill the gap.

Dataram is a leading manufacturer of gigabyte capacity memory circuit boards for computer workstations and network servers. The company's memory chips are used to power many of the leading computer brands, including Compaq/Digital, Dell, Hewlett-Packard, IBM, and Sun Microsystems.

The Princeton, New Jersey operation also manufactures a line of high-capacity Intel-certified memory boards for computer manufacturers.

Dataram, which has been making computer components for more than 30 years, introduces more than 70 new memory products each year.

Demand for the company's memory boards has been increasing in recent years with the growth of the Internet. Its products are used for a wide range of Internet applications, including e-commerce, Internet service provision, online transactions, and Internet infrastructure.

Its powerful memory boards also enable computers to create Hollywood special effects, track airline reservations, execute stock transactions, support communications activities and utility transmissions, and execute a wide range of other functions.

Dataram sells memory products for new machines as well as for installed computers—generally at prices that are below what the original computer manufacturer would charge. Dataram's customer base is made up primarily of distributors, value-added resellers, and large end-users. The company does business worldwide. About 25 percent of its revenue is generated outside the United States in Europe, Canada, and the Asia Pacific region.

The firm markets its low-cost, high-quality memory products through a direct sales force. Dataram is strong on service, working closely with customers to engineer upgraded products. Orders are generally shipped within hours of when they're received, and all of its products carry a lifetime guarantee.

The company spends about $1.3 million a year in research and development.

Dataram has about 150 employees and a market capitalization of about $180 million.

EARNINGS PER SHARE PROGRESSION ★ ★ ★ ★

Past 3 years: 531 percent (58 percent per year)

REVENUE GROWTH

Past 4 years: 1 percent

STOCK GROWTH ★ ★ ★ ★

Past 3 years: 733 percent (103 percent per year)
Dollar growth: $10,000 over 3 years would have grown to about $20,000.

CONSISTENCY ★ ★

Increased earnings per share: 4 consecutive years
Increased sales: 2 of the past 4 years

DATARAM AT A GLANCE

Fiscal year ended: April 30
Revenue and net income in $ millions

	1996	1997	1998	1999	2000	4-Year Growth Avg. Annual (%)	Total (%)
Revenue ($)	107.6	68.9	77.3	75.8	109.1	—	1
Net income ($)	1.4	3.8	3.7	5.6	7.8	53*	447*
Earnings/share ($)	0.13	0.37	0.40	0.60	0.82	58*	531*
PE range	10–23	7–11	7–18	5–29			

*Net income and earnings per share growth figures are based on 3-year performance.

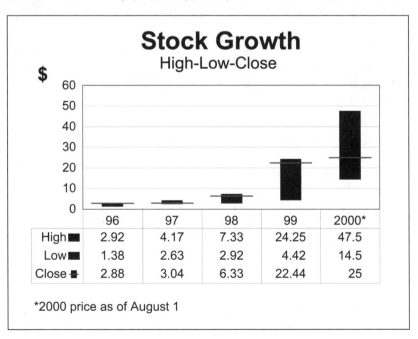

Stock Growth
High-Low-Close

$	96	97	98	99	2000*
High ■	2.92	4.17	7.33	24.25	47.5
Low ■	1.38	2.63	2.92	4.42	14.5
Close ■	2.88	3.04	6.33	22.44	25

*2000 price as of August 1

53

Taro Pharmaceutical Industries Ltd.

Five Skyline Drive
Hawthorne, NY 10532
914-345-9001
Nasdaq: TARO
www.taropharma.com

Chairman:
Barrie Levitt, MD
President:
Aaron Levitt

Earnings Growth	★ ★ ★
Revenue Growth	★
Stock Growth	★ ★ ★
Consistency	★ ★ ★
Total	**10 Points**

Taro Pharmaceutical is best known to the nation's doctors and pharmacists for its ointments and creams for such skin conditions as excema and dermatitis.

But the successful debut of its generic form of the anticlotting medication warfarin sodium speaks to the company's product breadth and research skills. Taro's warfarin tablets have been widely accepted by doctors, who typically prescribe them to patients over 60 for the prevention of strokes and heart attacks. The medication has proven to be one of Taro's most financially vibrant products and represents the company's best new product opportunity in a market estimated at $500 million annually.

The company has a knack for gaining government approval of generic drugs, perhaps because it spends a disproportionate amount of its revenues on research. While the pharmaceutical industry average is 9 percent, Taro devotes 14 percent of its revenues to research and development. The company has about 40 products in various stages of development.

Taro is better able to control its costs than most makers of generic drugs, because it makes its own supply of active ingredients that go into a drug at its Israeli chemical facilities. Taro is ensured a steady supply of active ingredients at a low price.

The company was founded in Israel. The name Taro is derived from the first two letters of two Hebrew words. One means "industry" and the other translates to "pharmaceutical."

The company's recent initiatives include the development of its Non-Spil drug delivery system, which makes it easier for children and the elderly to take liquid medications; the launch of an over-the-counter three-day vaginal cream to treat yeast infections; and the development of a nonsedating treatment for epilepsy.

The company was founded in 1950 and went public with its initial stock offering in 1961. It has about 500 employees and a market capitalization of about $110 million.

EARNINGS PER SHARE PROGRESSION   ★ ★ ★

Past 4 years: 168 percent (28 percent per year)

REVENUE GROWTH   ★

Past 4 years: 69 percent (14 percent per year)

STOCK GROWTH   ★ ★ ★

Past 3 years: 78 percent (21 percent per year)
Dollar growth: $10,000 over 3 years would have grown to about $18,000.

CONSISTENCY   ★ ★ ★

Increased earnings per share: 3 of the past 4 years
Increased sales: 4 consecutive years

TARO PHARMACEUTICAL AT A GLANCE

Fiscal year ended: Dec. 31
Revenue and net income in $ millions

	1995	1996	1997	1998	1999	4-Year Growth Avg. Annual (%)	Total (%)
Revenue ($)	49.6	56.5	60.9	66.7	83.8	14	69
Net income ($)	2.0	2.2	1.4	2.3	5.5	29	175
Earnings/share ($)	0.19	0.21	0.14	0.23	0.51	28	168
PE range	30–43	23–39	31–90	16–31	9–36		

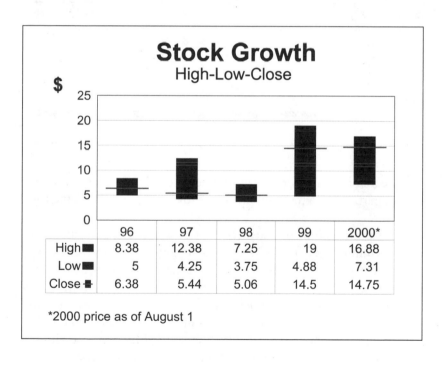

Stock Growth
High-Low-Close

	96	97	98	99	2000*
High	8.38	12.38	7.25	19	16.88
Low	5	4.25	3.75	4.88	7.31
Close	6.38	5.44	5.06	14.5	14.75

*2000 price as of August 1

54

BackWeb Technologies Ltd.

3 Abba Hillel Street
Ramat Gan, Israel
408-933-1713
Nasdaq: BWEB
www.backweb.com

Chairman and CEO:
Eli Barkat

Earnings Growth	★ ★
Revenue Growth	★ ★ ★ ★
Stock Growth	★ ★
Consistency	★ ★
Total	**10 Points**

BackWeb Technologies is a leader in Internet "push" technology, which is designed, in part, to push the right messages to the right people at the right time.

With the proliferation of "spam"—that barrage of junk e-mail promoting everything from porno Web sites to get-rich-quick schemes—businesses have found it necessary to find a new way to get important messages noticed. The spam epidemic has become such a big problem that corporate Web users sometimes miss important e-mail messages, because they get lost in all the spam-mail that lands in their e-boxes each day.

The Israeli-based operation makes a suite of software products designed to improve communications within an organization and between businesses. Its signature software suite, BackWeb Foundation, features several key components, including:

- **BackWeb Server.** This software is able to receive digital data from various sources, such as the Internet, intranet sites, and databases, and automatically sends the information to the proper computer users.
- **BackWeb Client.** This application allows computer users to receive data communications from BackWeb servers while they are using other applications. The system displays information through "flashes" and other displays and user interfaces, so that important messages are conveyed quickly to the designated recipient.
- **Add-on components.** BackWeb offers a variety of add-on components, such as Enhanced Security Module, which provides encrypted communications between BackWeb Server and BackWeb Client, and AutoFile Update Manager, which can automatically copy and organize files from any directory accessible to BackWeb Server and send them to any computer in the user's system.

BackWeb Technologies went public with its initial stock offering in 1999. It has about 150 employees and a market capitalization of about $1.5 billion.

EARNINGS PER SHARE PROGRESSION ★ ★

Losses have been declining recently.

REVENUE GROWTH ★ ★ ★ ★

Past 2 years: 316 percent (104 percent per year)

STOCK GROWTH ★ ★

Past year: 27 percent
Dollar growth: $10,000 over 1 year would have grown to about $12,700.

CONSISTENCY ★ ★

Positive earnings progression: 2 of the past 4 years
Increased sales: 4 consecutive years

BACKWEB TECHNOLOGIES AT A GLANCE

Fiscal year ended: Dec. 31
Revenue and net income in $ millions

	1995	1996	1997	1998	1999	2-Year Growth Avg. Annual (%)	Total (%)
Revenue ($)	0	0.071	5.6	9.54	23.3	104	316
Net income ($)	−0.238	−7.68	−14.9	−14.6	−11.5	NA	NA
Earnings/share ($)	−0.21	−6.95	−6.96	−6.07	−0.59	NA	NA
PE range	—	—	—	—	—		

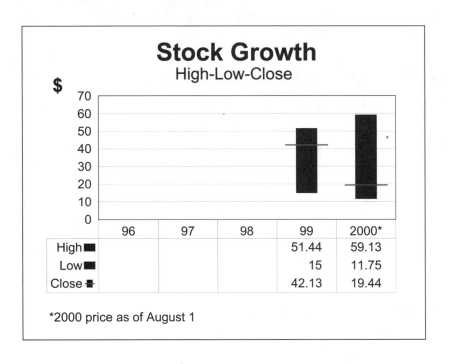

Stock Growth
High-Low-Close

$	96	97	98	99	2000*
High				51.44	59.13
Low				15	11.75
Close				42.13	19.44

*2000 price as of August 1

55

Monterey Pasta Company

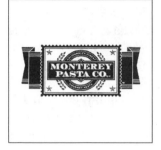

1528 Moffett Street
Salinas, CA 93905
831-753-6262
Nasdaq: PSTA
www.montereypasta.com

President and CEO:
R. Lance Hewitt

Earnings Growth	★ ★ ★
Revenue Growth	★
Stock Growth	★ ★ ★
Consistency	★ ★ ★
Total	**10 Points**

Monterey Pasta Company serves up a mouth-watering product line based on more than 100 recipes for gourmet pasta, sauces, fresh refrigerated soups, and little Italian-style potato dumplings known as gnocchi.

The company's products are sold in the United States and Canada through some 5,000 major grocery chains and warehouse and club stores. Retailers carrying Monterey Pasta products include Safeway, Jewel, Albertsons, Kroger, and Sam's Club. Initially, the company sold gourmet ravioli and sauces to restaurants and grocers on California's Monterey Peninsula.

The Salinas, California operation also peddles its pasta and other products through its online Pasta Store at <www.MontereyPasta.com>, where customers can buy products for overnight delivery. The site also offers cookbooks, cooking utensils, and other gourmet products. The company has also struck an agreement with online grocer Webvan, which will deliver Monterey Pasta products in many major cities.

America's growing appetite for freshly prepared, healthy foods bodes well for Monterey Pasta, whose flavorful products are made with no preservatives or artificial ingredients. Americans also have a growing taste for easily prepared home meals that are as good as meals ordered at a restaurant. Typical prep time for a refrigerated Monterey Pasta product is about four minutes.

Monterey Pasta prides itself on being the only premium pasta maker that distributes on a national basis that is not operated under the corporate umbrella of a large, diversified foodmaker. The company says that allows it to focus strictly on the quality of its food.

Its retail product list includes such items as Gorgonzola roasted-walnut ravioli, garlic basil fettuccine, Italian sausage sauce, Southwest-style tortilla soup, and Tuscan minestrone soup.

The company was founded in 1989 and went public with its initial stock offering in 1993. It has about 180 employees and a market capitalization of about $50 million.

EARNINGS PER SHARE PROGRESSION   ★ ★ ★

Has gone from –20 cents to a positive 54 cents the past 4 years.

REVENUE GROWTH   ★

Past 4 years: 97 percent (18 percent per year)

STOCK GROWTH   ★ ★ ★

Past 3 years: 98 percent (26 percent per year)
Dollar growth: $10,000 over 3 years would have grown to about $20,000.

CONSISTENCY   ★ ★ ★

Positive earnings progression: 4 consecutive years
Increased sales: 3 of the past 4 years

MONTEREY PASTA AT A GLANCE

Fiscal year ended: Dec. 31
Revenue and net income in $ millions

	1995	1996	1997	1998	1999	Avg. Annual (%)	Total (%)
						4-Year Growth	
Revenue ($)	18.7	24.5	23.4	26.2	36.9	18	97
Net income ($)	−1.3	−8.4	0.48	2.04	7.03	245*	245*
Earnings/share ($)	−0.20	−1.15	0.02	0.16	0.54	238*	238*
PE range	—	—	50–191	6–11	2–8		

*Net income and earnings per share growth figures are based on 1-year performance.

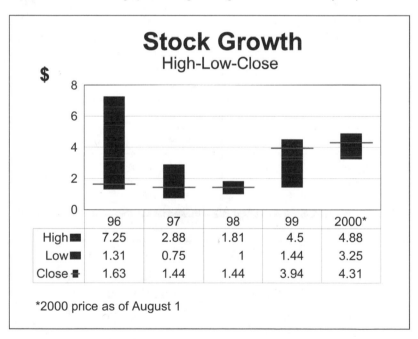

Stock Growth
High-Low-Close

	96	97	98	99	2000*
High	7.25	2.88	1.81	4.5	4.88
Low	1.31	0.75	1	1.44	3.25
Close	1.63	1.44	1.44	3.94	4.31

*2000 price as of August 1

◼ STV Group

---

205 West Welsh Drive
Douglassville, PA 19518
610-385-8200
Nasdaq: STVI
www.stvinc.com

Chairman:
Michael Haratunian
President and CEO:
Dominick M. Servedio

Earnings Growth	★ ★ ★ ★
Revenue Growth	
Stock Growth	★ ★
Consistency	★ ★ ★ ★
Total	**10 Points**

When New York City officials decided to extend the Long Island Railroad service into Grand Central Station, they hired STV Group to do the engineering. When Houston officials needed a program management firm for its light rail transit system, they hired STV.

STV handles engineering, architectural design, and project management for large and small construction projects throughout the country, including roads, bridges, prisons, hospitals, churches, office buildings, and a wide range of other projects.

The Douglassville, Pennsylvania operation does most of its work for state and local governments, which account for about 66 percent of its total revenue. Other leading clients include the U.S. government, 9 percent, and private contractors, 25 percent.

STV does business in several different segments, including:

- **Transportation engineering** (31 percent of revenue). The company designs track, terminals, stations, yards, and shops for the railway industry.
- **Architectural engineering** (24 percent). STV designs commercial, industrial, and government buildings; medical and educational facilities; laboratories; recreational, religious, and cultural centers; military installations; penal institutions; and public utility facilities.
- **Civil engineering** (24 percent). The company designs highways, bridges, airports, seaports, lighting, toll and service facilities, drainage and erosion control systems, aircraft hangars, and control towers.

The company also handles some defense systems engineering projects for the U.S. Department of Defense, although that division now accounts for just 1 percent of total revenue.

STV also provides industrial process engineering services and technical analyses, and it performs some other engineering and consulting work outside of its core areas, which accounts for about 8 percent of revenue. It also offers "design and build" services, handling both the architectural design for the project and construction management of the construction contractors.

STV Group has about 1,200 employees and a market capitalization of about $25 million.

EARNINGS PER SHARE PROGRESSION   ★ ★ ★ ★

Past 4 years: 1,027 percent (83 percent per year)

REVENUE GROWTH

Past 4 years: 56 percent (12 percent per year)

STOCK GROWTH   ★ ★

Past 3 years: 68 percent (19 percent per year)
Dollar growth: $10,000 over 3 years would have grown to about $17,000.

CONSISTENCY   ★ ★ ★ ★

Increased earnings per share: 4 consecutive years
Increased sales: 4 consecutive years

STV GROUP AT A GLANCE

Fiscal year ended: Sept. 30
Revenue and net income in $ millions

	1995	1996	1997	1998	1999	4-Year Growth Avg. Annual (%)	Total (%)
Revenue ($)	89.2	94.1	94.7	105.2	138.9	12	56
Net income ($)	0.39	0.595	0.86	2.19	5.18	91	1,215
Earnings/share ($)	0.11	0.16	0.23	0.55	1.24	83	1,027
PE range	21–28	18–25	16–19	6–23	5–7		

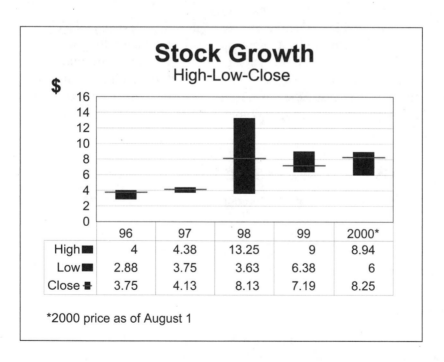

Stock Growth
High-Low-Close

$

	96	97	98	99	2000*
High■	4	4.38	13.25	9	8.94
Low■	2.88	3.75	3.63	6.38	6
Close ■	3.75	4.13	8.13	7.19	8.25

*2000 price as of August 1

Southwest Water Company

225 North Barranca Avenue,
Suite 200
West Covina, CA 91791
626-915-1551
Nasdaq: SWWC
www.southwestwater.com

Chairman, President, and CEO:
Anton C. Garnier

Earnings Growth	★ ★ ★ ★
Revenue Growth	
Stock Growth	★ ★
Consistency	★ ★ ★ ★
Total	**10 Points**

Water is a growth industry in the southwestern United States, where the Southwest Water Company has been soaking up rising profits by keeping the supply of H2O flowing.

The company supplies water and treats wastewater for communities in California, New Mexico, Texas, and Mississippi.

The West Covina, California company owns the water supply systems and wastewater treatment systems in several communities and operates other systems owned by cities, utility districts, and private companies. In all, the company serves more than 750,000 customers throughout its four-state area.

The company conducts business through three subsidiaries: Suburban Water Systems, New Mexico Utilities, and ECO Resources.

Suburban Water Systems is a regulated water utility that produces and supplies water for residents and businesses and for industrial and public authority use in Los Angeles and Orange County, California. The firm owns 15 wells and operates one other that pumps water from the Central Basin and the Main San Gabriel Basin in Southern California.

The suburban customer base is growing slowly, limited to extensions into new subdivisions along the periphery of the service area. There is little business or industrial growth in its service area.

The company acquired New Mexico Utilities in 1987 and has seen its customer base grow nearly tenfold since then. The firm offers both water and sewage collection services.

Its ECO Resources subsidiary focuses on operating water supply and wastewater systems owned by municipal utilities primarily in the Houston and Austin, Texas metropolitan areas. It takes over the maintenance operations of private and publicly owned municipal utility districts.

In 2000, Southwest Water acquired Master Tek International, which provides computerized utility submetering, billing, and collection services.

Founded in 1954, Southwest Water has about 560 employees and a market capitalization of about $88 million.

EARNINGS PER SHARE PROGRESSION ★ ★ ★ ★

Past 4 years: 278 percent (39 percent per year)

REVENUE GROWTH

Past 4 years: 42 percent (9 percent per year)

STOCK GROWTH ★ ★

Past 3 years: 68 percent (including 2 percent annual dividend; 19 percent per year)
Dollar growth: $10,000 over 3 years would have grown to about $17,000.

CONSISTENCY ★ ★ ★ ★

Increased earnings per share: 4 consecutive years
Increased sales: 4 consecutive years

SOUTHWEST WATER AT A GLANCE

Fiscal year ended: Dec. 31
Revenue and net income in $ millions

	1995	1996	1997	1998	1999	4-Year Growth Avg. Annual (%)	Total (%)
Revenue ($)	56.8	66.1	71.0	72.1	80.8	9	42
Net income ($)	1.44	1.92	2.60	3.35	5.82	42	304
Earnings/share ($)	0.23	0.31	0.41	0.51	0.87	39	278
PE range	12–18	12–24	12–24	13–22	8–21		

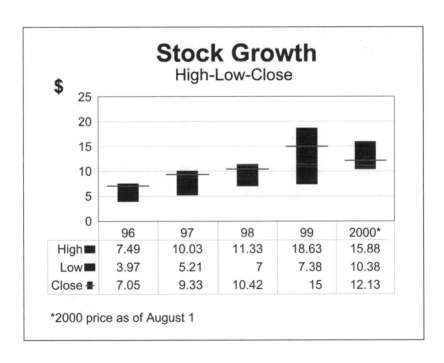

Stock Growth
High-Low-Close

	96	97	98	99	2000*
High ■	7.49	10.03	11.33	18.63	15.88
Low ■	3.97	5.21	7	7.38	10.38
Close ■	7.05	9.33	10.42	15	12.13

*2000 price as of August 1

58

Genesis Microchip, Inc.

165 Commerce Valley Drive West
Thornhill, Ontario, Canada
L3T 7V8
905-889-5400
Nasdaq: GNSS
www.genesis-video.com

Chairman:
Paul Russo
President and CEO:
A. Fisher

Earnings Growth	★ ★
Revenue Growth	★ ★ ★ ★
Stock Growth	
Consistency	★ ★ ★
Total	**9 Points**

As PC and TV head steadily toward convergence, Genesis Microchip is working on the technology that will make it all possible. The company specializes in designing integrated microchips that manipulate and process digital video and graphics images.

The company's semiconductors are used to project, sharpen, size, and control the images in digital displays, DVDs, home theater equipment, projection systems, video workstation gear, and a variety of related applications.

Still a small, young operation with revenues of well under $100 million a year, Genesis has amassed an impressive client list. Its chips are used in monitors of such market leaders as Dell, IBM, NEC, Philips, Apple, Fujitsu, Hitachi, and Sony. It also manufactures video components for Mitsubishi, Sharp, Texas Instruments, and more than 200 other companies.

Based in Canada, Genesis does most of its business in Asia—principally Japan, Korea, and Taiwan—home of most of the factories that make TVs, monitors, and related components. In all, about two-thirds of the company's revenue comes from Asia, a quarter comes from the United States, and the rest is generated in Europe and Canada.

The company has been focusing on image processing chips for flat panel computer monitors, flat panel TVs, and projection systems. In fact, Genesis already dominates the liquid crystal flat panel market, supplying the chips for at least half of the flat panel monitors manufactured worldwide.

Although flat monitors currently account for a small percentage of all monitors, they are expected to eventually replace all the traditional cathode ray monitors. The demand for flat screens is expected to double every year for several years to come, a trend that should bode well for Genesis.

Founded in 1987, Genesis went public in 1998. It has about 140 employees and a market capitalization of about $350 million.

EARNINGS PER SHARE PROGRESSION   ★ ★

Genesis has gone from losses to positive earnings the past 4 years.

REVENUE GROWTH   ★ ★ ★ ★

Past 4 years: 3,453 percent (142 percent per year)

STOCK GROWTH

Past year: −21 percent
Dollar growth: $10,000 over 1 year would have declined to about $8,000.

CONSISTENCY   ★ ★ ★

Positive earnings progression: 3 consecutive years
Increased sales: 4 consecutive years

GENESIS MICROCHIP AT A GLANCE

Fiscal year ended: March 31
Revenue and net income in $ millions

	1996	1997	1998	1999	2000	4-Year Growth Avg. Annual (%)	Total (%)
Revenue ($)	1.5	4.5	16.0	37.7	53.3	142	3,453
Net income ($)	−3.6	−4.6	−0.455	5.53	7.33	32	NA
Earnings/share ($)	−0.63	−0.70	−0.04	0.29	0.30	3	NA
PE range	—	—	—	52–125			

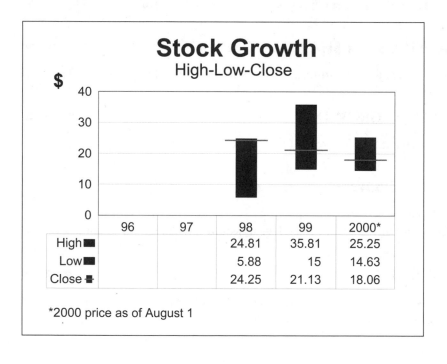

Stock Growth
High-Low-Close

	96	97	98	99	2000*
High			24.81	35.81	25.25
Low			5.88	15	14.63
Close			24.25	21.13	18.06

*2000 price as of August 1

59
Moldflow Corp.

91 Hartwell Avenue
Lexington, MA 02421
781-674-0085
Nasdaq: MFLO
www.moldflow.com

Chairman:
Charles D. Yie
President and CEO:
Marc J.L. Dulude

Earnings Growth	★ ★ ★ ★
Revenue Growth	★
Stock Growth	★
Consistency	★ ★ ★
Total	**9 Points**

Making molded plastic parts has always been a trial-and-error procedure. But Moldflow has taken the guesswork out of the process with a line of specialized software products that helps manufacturers of injection-molded plastic parts decrease manufacturing costs, reduce costly design and manufacturing errors, and speed their products to market.

Moldflow's software is used by more than 3,000 customers at manufacturing sites in more than 50 countries. Among its leading customers are DaimlerChrysler, DuPont, Fuji, Xerox, Hewlett-Packard, Lego, Lucent Technologies, and Motorola.

The Moldflow software helps plastics manufacturers in several stages of the design and production process:

- Assists part designers in the selection of plastic material based on their design criteria.

- Helps determine the strength and rigidity of a given part design.
- Evaluates the ease of manufacturing a given part design.
- Predicts the amount a part will shrink or warp during production.
- Determines the optimal locations in a mold to inject the plastic material.
- Selects the optimal machine temperatures, injection speeds, and cooling times for part production.
- Identifies and provides solutions for adverse variations during production.

Moldflow believes it is the world leader in plastic simulation software, a sector with strong growth potential. The company has identified about 750,000 injection molding machines that are currently operating without the benefit of integrated software.

The company markets its software through a direct sales staff with offices in nine countries and through a network of distributors and value-added resellers. The firm has also established a Web site, <www.plasticszone. com>, that assists engineers with technical aspects of the software.

The Massachusetts operation was originally founded in Australia in 1980 and moved its headquarters to the United States in 1997. The company went public with its initial stock offering in March 2000. Moldflow has about 170 employees and a market capitalization of about $145 million.

EARNINGS PER SHARE PROGRESSION ★ ★ ★ ★

Past 2 years: 2,300 percent (390 percent per year)

REVENUE GROWTH ★

Past 4 years: 96 percent (18 percent per year)

STOCK GROWTH ★

The stock went public in March 2000 and had a small gain after its IPO.

CONSISTENCY ★ ★ ★

Positive earnings progression: 3 consecutive years
Increased sales: 4 consecutive years

MOLDFLOW AT A GLANCE

Fiscal year ended: June 30
Revenue and net income in $ millions

	1996	1997	1998	1999	2000	4-Year Growth Avg. Annual (%)	4-Year Growth Total (%)
Revenue ($)	14.0	14.8	16.4	20.2	27.4	18	96
Net income ($)	−3.9	−3.9	0.35	0.66	3.5	215*	900*
Earnings/share ($)	−0.91	−0.96	0.02	0.08	0.48	390*	2,300*
PE range	—	—	—	—	—		

*Net income and earnings per share growth figures are based on 2-year performance.

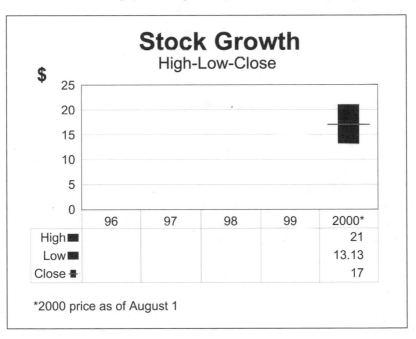

Stock Growth
High-Low-Close

$	96	97	98	99	2000*
High■					21
Low■					13.13
Close ■					17

*2000 price as of August 1

60

Spectrum Control, Inc.

8031 Avonia Road
Fairview, PA 16415
814-835-1650
Nasdaq: SPEC
www.spectrumcontrol.com

President and CEO:
Richard A. Southworth

Earnings Growth	★ ★
Revenue Growth	★
Stock Growth	★ ★ ★ ★
Consistency	★ ★
Total	**9 Points**

When you can't hear what a caller is telling you on your cell phone, it might be a case of electromagnetic interference.

Spectrum Control designs and markets filtering equipment that can reduce or eliminate the unwanted electromagnetic waves, so there's nothing lost in the conversation. Telecommunications is the company's largest customer segment, accounting for about 60 percent of its revenues.

The company's second-largest target audience is the military, whose aircraft and ships are loaded with extensive communication equipment, radar systems, and electronic countermeasure equipment to defend against enemy weapons. Without the proper electromagnetic filtering equipment, those military systems could be rendered useless. The military/aerospace segment accounts for about 20 percent of the company's business.

Other key industries targeted by Spectrum include health care, consumer electronics, computers, and industrial control. All are industries with an increasing dependency on various kinds of electronic equipment that can be inhibited by interference from electromagnetic signals. Demand for the company's products continues to be driven by growth in the communications equipment market for such applications as Internet servers, data communications switching equipment, fiber-optic networking equipment, global positioning systems, and wireless modems.

Spectrum has begun to broaden its focus and product lines beyond making electromagnetic filtering products by providing customers components and systems used to condition, regulate, transmit, receive, or govern electronic performance. The company believes a new line of products will better position it to sell into larger, high-growth markets.

The Pennsylvania-based operation has recently acquired several companies to fuel its new direction, including the purchase of AMP's Signal Conditioning Products Division.

Founded in 1968, the company has about 1,300 employees and a market capitalization of about $100 million.

EARNINGS PER SHARE PROGRESSION   ★ ★

Past 4 years: 75 percent (15 percent per year)

REVENUE GROWTH   ★

Past 4 years: 98 percent (18 percent per year)

STOCK GROWTH   ★ ★ ★ ★

Past 3 years: 220 percent (47 percent per year)
Dollar growth: $10,000 over 3 years would have grown to about $32,000.

CONSISTENCY   ★ ★

Increased earnings per share: 3 of the past 4 years
Increased sales: 3 of the past 4 years

SPECTRUM CONTROL AT A GLANCE

Fiscal year ended: Nov. 30
Revenue and net income in $ millions

	1995	1996	1997	1998	1999	4-Year Growth Avg. Annual (%)	Total (%)
Revenue ($)	49.3	57.3	56.5	59.9	97.7	18	98
Net income ($)	2.98	3.42	3.97	3.93	5.47	16	83
Earnings/share ($)	0.28	0.31	0.36	0.36	0.49	15	75
PE range	5–15	9–19	8–16	10–20	7–25		

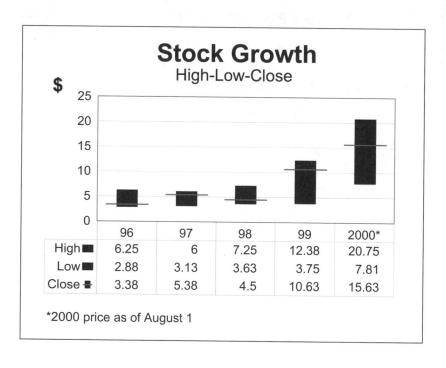

Stock Growth
High-Low-Close

$	96	97	98	99	2000*
High	6.25	6	7.25	12.38	20.75
Low	2.88	3.13	3.63	3.75	7.81
Close	3.38	5.38	4.5	10.63	15.63

*2000 price as of August 1

Drexler Technology Corp.

1077 Independence Avenue
Mountain View, CA 94043
650-969-7277
Nasdaq: DRXR
www.lasercard.com

Chairman and CEO:
Jerome Drexler
President:
Richard M. Haddock

Earnings Growth	★ ★ ★ ★
Revenue Growth	★ ★ ★
Stock Growth	
Consistency	★ ★
Total	**9 Points**

There's more to the green card than meets the eye. The Permanent Resident Card issued by the U.S. Immigration and Naturalization Service is rich with information laser-etched with a technology developed by Drexler Technology.

The so-called green card is actually a 4.1 megabyte optical memory card, or LaserCard, which is a patented, tamper-resistant card engineered by Drexler. The high-tech green card is designed to frustrate counterfeiters who've been known to sell illegally produced certificates of legitimacy for up to $15,000 each.

But counterfeiting the new cards will be a tall order. A wide magnetic strip on the green card now contains such information as a hologram of the Statue of Liberty, microimages of all the state flags, microimages of all the U.S. presidents, and the INS seal. The card, of course, also includes the holder's name, photo, fingerprints, and other data.

Drexler, which issues the credit-card-sized optical memory cards through its LaserCard Systems subsidiary, also develops optical data storage products used with personal computers for information recording, storage, and retrieval.

The U.S. government has been a big customer of Drexler. In 1999, the Feds placed a $7.5 million order for LaserCards for use in U.S. government programs, primarily at the U.S.–Mexico border. The cards, which can pack the equivalent of 128 printed pages onto the magnetic strip, have been snapped up for commercial purposes as well. For example, Honda owners in the Philippines store all of their automotive records on an optical memory card developed by Drexler.

The cards can store text, graphics, voice, pictures, and software—virtually any form of information that can be digitized.

Founded in 1968, the Mountain View, California operation has about 90 employees and a market capitalization of about $110 million.

EARNINGS PER SHARE PROGRESSION   ★ ★ ★ ★

Past 2 years: 184 percent (67 percent per year)

REVENUE GROWTH   ★ ★ ★

Past 4 years: 223 percent (34 percent per year)

STOCK GROWTH

Past 3 years: 25 percent (8 percent per year)
Dollar growth: $10,000 over 3 years would have grown to about $12,500.

CONSISTENCY   ★ ★

Increased earnings per share: 3 of the past 4 years
Increased sales: 3 of the past 4 years

DREXLER TECHNOLOGY AT A GLANCE

Fiscal year ended: March 31
Revenue and net income in $ millions

	1996	1997	1998	1999	2000	4-Year Growth Avg. Annual (%)	Total (%)
Revenue ($)	5.3	3.5	11.1	15.8	17.1	34	223
Net income ($)	−1.6	−2.3	1.8	4.1	5.4	75*	200*
Earnings/share ($)	−0.18	−0.26	0.19	0.41	0.54	67*	184*
PE range	—	—	—	38–103	15–33		

*Net income and earnings per share growth figures are based on 2-year performance.

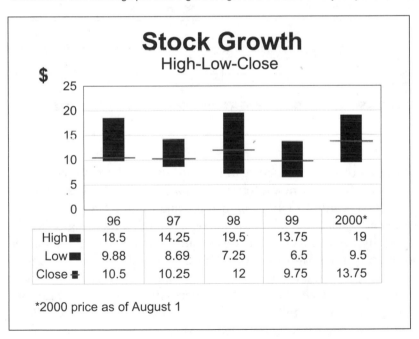

Stock Growth
High-Low-Close

	96	97	98	99	2000*
High	18.5	14.25	19.5	13.75	19
Low	9.88	8.69	7.25	6.5	9.5
Close	10.5	10.25	12	9.75	13.75

*2000 price as of August 1

62

Atrion Corp.

One Allentown Parkway
Allen, TX 75002
972-390-9800
Nasdaq: ATRI
www.atrioncorp.com

Chairman, President, and CEO:
Emile A. Battat

Earnings Growth	★ ★ ★
Revenue Growth	★ ★ ★ ★
Stock Growth	
Consistency	★ ★
Total	**9 Points**

Atrion keeps boaters afloat and heart patients alive with its diverse line of products. The Texas operation focuses primarily on medical devices and supplies for the cardiovascular, ophthalmic, and fluid delivery fields.

Atrion also makes a line of inflation devices for balloon angioplasties. The company has applied its expertise in inflation devices to the marine and aviation markets with its automatic inflator, a device that automatically inflates a life vest on impact with the water. The U.S. Coast Guard has approved the device, and it has been successfully marketed in Europe.

Through its three wholly owned subsidiaries—Atrion Medical Products, Halkey-Roberts, and Quest Medical—Atrion makes and markets a variety of medical products and components worldwide.

One of Atrion's leading products is the Myocardial Protection System (MPS), which delivers essential fluids to the heart during open-heart surgery. The system is particularly useful during what's called "off-pump" or "beating-heart" surgery. That procedure tends to be easier on the patient than conventional open-heart surgery, which temporarily stops the heart while a heart-lung machine pumps the blood.

Heart surgeons using the Atrion system enjoy an extra margin of safety during the off-pump procedure, because it enhances coronary blood flow and infuses additives directly to the heart as needed during the surgery. A growing number of surgeons are using the MPS for off-pump heart surgeries.

In 1999, Atrion introduced its new line of swabable valves, which eliminates the use of needles when injecting medication intravenously. Medical personnel are protected against possible infection from an accidental needle stick through use of a special valve that can be sterilized by swabbing before each use.

Atrion has about 440 employees and a market capitalization of about $25 million.

EARNINGS PER SHARE PROGRESSION ★ ★ ★

Past 4 years: 170 percent (28 percent per year)

REVENUE GROWTH ★ ★ ★ ★

Past 4 years: 326 percent (44 percent per year)

STOCK GROWTH

Past 3 years: −21 percent
Dollar growth: $10,000 over 3 years would have declined to about $8,000.

CONSISTENCY ★ ★

Increased earnings per share: 2 of the past 4 years
Increased sales: 4 consecutive years

ATRION AT A GLANCE

Fiscal year ended: Dec. 31
Revenue and net income in $ millions

	1995	1996	1997	1998	1999	4-Year Growth Avg. Annual (%)	Total (%)
Revenue ($)	11.7	22.1	30.2	43.4	49.9	44	326
Net income ($)	0.986	0.85	−2.00	1.50	2.10	21	113
Earnings/share ($)	0.30	0.26	−0.64	0.46	0.81	28	170
PE range	36–48	50–78	—	13–30	8–15		

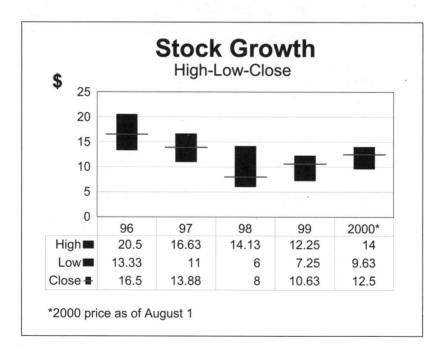

Stock Growth
High-Low-Close

$	96	97	98	99	2000*
High ■	20.5	16.63	14.13	12.25	14
Low ■	13.33	11	6	7.25	9.63
Close ▬	16.5	13.88	8	10.63	12.5

*2000 price as of August 1

63

Cheap Tickets, Inc.

1440 Kapiolani Boulevard
Honolulu, HI 96814
808-945-7439
Nasdaq: CTIX
www.cheaptickets.com

Chairman and CEO:
Michael J. Hartley
President:
Sam Galeotos

Earnings Growth	★ ★ ★ ★
Revenue Growth	★ ★ ★ ★
Stock Growth	
Consistency	★
Total	**9 Points**

Leisure travelers with flexible schedules can fly on the cheap thanks to the appropriately named Cheap Tickets, Inc.

Launched in 1986 as America's Travel Store, the company specializes in low-fare and discount tickets from about 35 air carriers, including all the major carriers like Continental, American, TWA, and Northwest. Tickets are for regularly scheduled flights out of major airports in the United States, Europe, Asia, and South America.

Cheap Tickets contracts for seats that the airlines aren't able to sell and resells the so-called nonpublished fares at a slight markup. Cheap Tickets pockets the difference, typically about 20 percent. The company does not carry an inventory of tickets, which keeps overhead costs low. It only sells a ticket upon a customer's request.

The company peddles tickets through its 4 call centers and 12 walk-in retail centers and increasingly through its Web site.

The site, launched in 1997, handled ?9 percent of the company's sales in 1999, but by the first quarter of 2000, it was already up to nearly 40 percent. And more traffic is anticipated through the site in years to come. The company boasts more than four million registered users of its Web site.

To keep its popular online site free of casual shoppers, Cheap Tickets requires standard profile information up front. The site stores a customer's seat and meal preferences. From the site, it's just four clicks to the purchase of a discounted airline ticket.

A small percentage—about 10 percent—of the company's revenues are generated through the sale of published airfares. It also has contracts with hotels, cruise lines, and car rental agencies for similar services.

The company was founded in 1986 and went public with its initial stock offering in 1999. It has about 950 employees and a market capitalization of about $270 million.

EARNINGS PER SHARE PROGRESSION   ★ ★ ★ ★

Past 3 years: 520 percent (58 percent per year)

REVENUE GROWTH   ★ ★ ★ ★

Past 4 years: 391 percent (49 percent per year)

STOCK GROWTH

Past 3 years: −64 percent
Dollar growth: $10,000 over 3 years would have dropped to about $4,600.

CONSISTENCY   ★

Increased earnings per share: 2 of the past 4 years
Increased sales: 3 of the past 4 years

CHEAP TICKETS AT A GLANCE

Fiscal year ended: Dec. 31
Revenue and net income in $ millions

	1995	1996	1997	1998	1999	4-Year Growth Avg. Annual (%)	4-Year Growth Total (%)
Revenue ($)	69.1	64.6	102.8	171.1	339.6	49	391
Net income ($)	0.017	0.675	−1.0	1.1	7.6	—	44,606
Earnings/share ($)	0.00	0.05	−0.08	0.03	0.31	58*	520*
PE range	—	—	—	—	38–213		

*Earnings per share growth figures are based on 3-year performance.

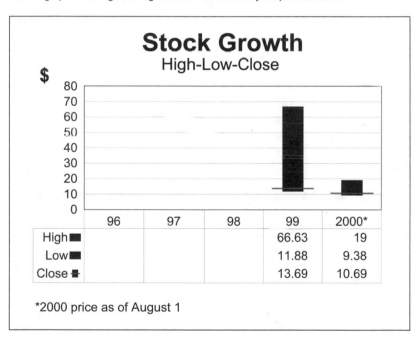

Stock Growth
High-Low-Close

$	96	97	98	99	2000*
High				66.63	19
Low				11.88	9.38
Close				13.69	10.69

*2000 price as of August 1

EarthLink, Inc.

1430 West Peachtree Street,
Suite 400
Atlanta, GA 30309
404-815-8805
Nasdaq: ELNK
www.earthlink.com

Chairman:
Charles Brewer
CEO:
C. Garry Betty
President:
Michael S. McQuary

Earnings Growth	
Revenue Growth	★ ★ ★ ★
Stock Growth	★ ★ ★ ★
Consistency	★
Total	**9 Points**

EarthLink has quietly established itself as one of the nation's leading Internet service providers (ISPs). It ranks number two behind America Online.

EarthLink has earned a reputation as one of the best ISPs because of its infrequent busy signals, speedy network performance, and an uncluttered portal that puts nothing extraneous between its subscribers and the Web. EarthLink has consistently placed at or near the top of ISP user satisfaction rankings.

But the company's young management team understands that being hip isn't enough. EarthLink's relentless growth strategy has given its dial-up network a presence in virtually every local market in North America.

The Atlanta operation currently claims more than 5,000 "points of presence" worldwide, although most of its business is in the United States.

Mergers and acquisitions have given the company nearly four million subscribers and a revenue stream approaching $1 billion a year. It has already surpassed such well-known names as Prodigy and Microsoft Network but remains far behind America Online's subscriber base of more than 25 million. But, EarthLink has a plan:

- **Establish the brand.** The company has launched a massive marketing campaign to burn the EarthLink brand into mass consumer consciousness.
- **Play Pepsi to AOL's Coca-Cola.** Position the company as the preferred alternative to millions of "sophomore" America Online customers who EarthLink's management team feel are becoming disaffected with AOL's service.
- **Focus on small business.** EarthLink offers small businesses end-to-end Internet solutions, including a full slate of Internet access, Web hosting, and e-commerce services. It is second only to Verio in hosting business Web sites.

With its recent acquisition of OneMain.com, EarthLink has also begun aggressively pushing its service in rural areas and smaller metropolitan areas of the United States—a stronghold of OneMain.com.

EarthLink made its initial public stock offering in 1997. It has about 1,400 employees and a market capitalization of about $1.4 billion.

EARNINGS PER SHARE PROGRESSION

No earnings and rising losses

REVENUE GROWTH ★ ★ ★ ★

Past 4 years: 22,025 percent (285 percent per year)

STOCK GROWTH ★ ★ ★ ★

Past 3 years: 400 percent (70 percent per year)
Dollar growth: $10,000 over 3 years would have grown to $50,000.

CONSISTENCY ★

Positive earnings progression: None
Increased sales: 4 consecutive years

EARTHLINK AT A GLANCE

Fiscal year ended: Dec. 31
Revenue and net income in $ millions

| | 1995 | 1996 | 1997 | 1998 | 1999 | 4-Year Growth | |
						Avg. Annual (%)	Total (%)
Revenue ($)	3.03	33.2	133.4	290.6	670.4	285	22,025
Net income ($)	–6.1	–31.1	–33.9	–53.2	–173.7	NA	NA
Earnings/share ($)	–0.80	–2.57	–0.44	–0.66	–1.65	NA	NA
PE range	—	—	—	—	—		

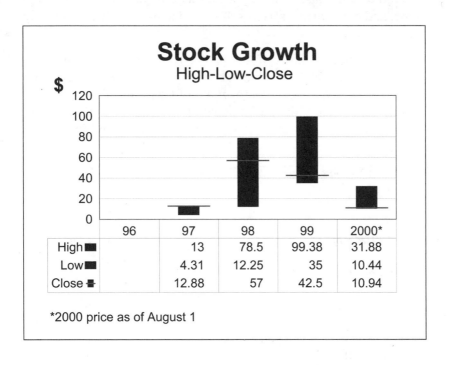

Stock Growth
High-Low-Close

	96	97	98	99	2000*
High ■		13	78.5	99.38	31.88
Low ■		4.31	12.25	35	10.44
Close ■		12.88	57	42.5	10.94

*2000 price as of August 1

65
Rubio's Restaurants, Inc.

1902 Wright Place, Suite 300
Carlsbad, CA 92008
760-929-8226
Nasdaq: RUBO
www.rubios.com

Chairman:
Rafael Rubio
President and CEO:
Ralph Rubio

Earnings Growth	★ ★
Revenue Growth	★ ★ ★ ★
Stock Growth	
Consistency	★ ★ ★
Total	**9 Points**

What do you get when you combine Mexican food with fish? You get the appetizing cuisine that's driving the rapid growth of Rubio's Baja Grill.

Operated by Rubio's Restaurants, Inc., the chain of casual-dining Mexican-style restaurants is now serving its zesty fare at more than 100 locations in five southwestern states. The menu includes its signature dish, the fish taco, as well as such plates as a lobster burrito or a shrimp quesadilla. The more standard Mexican fare of tacos and burritos is also available. The fresh, high-quality food is served promptly.

The restaurants are the brainchild of Chairman and CEO Ralph Rubio, who while on spring break in the Baja Peninsula of Mexico, was inspired to recreate the laid-back look and cuisine of Baja restaurants. He and his father, Rafael, opened their first restaurant in 1983 in the Mission Bay area of San Diego. It was called "Rubio's, Home of the Fish Taco." The largest percentage of its restaurants is in Southern California.

To give guests a taste of the Baja, the restaurants are decorated with natural woods, corrugated metals, and colorful tables. The ambiance also features beach photos, Mexican tiles, surfboards, saltwater aquariums, and thatched beach umbrellas. Rubio's locations average 2,200 square feet and feature 500-square-foot patios where diners are also seated.

Rubio's Restaurants have always been corporate owned and operated, but the chain is launching a franchise program to expedite its expansion into additional markets. The company believes that by partnering with reputable multiunit operators of other concept restaurants, it can expand on a national level without compromising the quality of its food and service.

Rubio's Restaurants went public with its initial stock offering in 1999. It has about 2,800 employees and a market capitalization of about $70 million.

EARNINGS PER SHARE PROGRESSION ★ ★

Past year: 43 percent

REVENUE GROWTH ★ ★ ★ ★

Past 4 years: 358 percent (48 percent per year)

STOCK GROWTH

Past year: −47 percent
Dollar growth: $10,000 over 3 years would have declined to about $5,300.

CONSISTENCY ★ ★ ★

Positive earnings progression: 3 of the past 4 years
Increased sales: 4 consecutive years

RUBIO'S RESTAURANTS AT A GLANCE

Fiscal year ended: Dec. 31
Revenue and net income in $ millions

	1995	1996	1997	1998	1999	4-Year Growth Avg. Annual (%)	4-Year Growth Total (%)
Revenue ($)	14.8	19.5	29.7	44.7	67.8	48	358
Net income ($)	0.016	0.072	–1.0	0.915	1.65	79	931
Earnings/share ($)	–0.04	0.00	–1.08	0.14	0.20	43	NA
PE range	—	—	—	—	29–80		

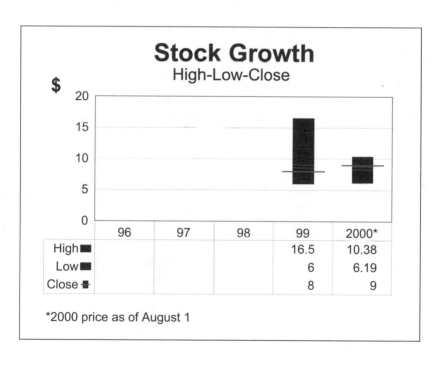

Stock Growth
High-Low-Close

$

	96	97	98	99	2000*
High				16.5	10.38
Low				6	6.19
Close				8	9

*2000 price as of August 1

66

Del Global Technologies Corp.

One Commerce Park
Valhalla, NY 10595
914-686-3600
Nasdaq: DGTC

Chairman, President, and CEO:
Leonard A. Trugman

Earnings Growth	★ ★ ★
Revenue Growth	★ ★
Stock Growth	
Consistency	★ ★ ★ ★
Total	**9 Points**

Del Global gives physicians a real view of the inner you. The company makes a line of cost-effective medical imaging systems, including mammography machines, neonatal imaging systems, and high-frequency X-ray machines.

The company, which sells its equipment worldwide to doctors, hospitals, and other medical and governmental facilities, competes in the low-cost end of the imaging market. Its units range in price from about $9,000 to $150,000.

The Valhalla, New York manufacturer operates through five divisions, including:

- **Gendex-Del.** This subsidiary manufactures mammography systems, stationary imaging systems, high-frequency X-ray generators, X-ray examination tables, and a full line of associated imaging accessories.
- **DynaRad.** DynaRad makes mobile medical imaging systems, portable dental X-ray units, and advanced neonatal imaging systems used by

hospitals, clinics, private practices, sports complexes, and defense forces.

- **Power conversion division.** This division sells high-voltage power supplies to medical, industrial, and defense customers. Applications include medical scanning, laser surgery, nuclear medicine, blood analysis, and cancer therapy, as well as airport security systems, ion implantation, electron beam welding, energy exploration, and radar systems.
- **Bertan High Voltage.** Bertan manufactures high-voltage power supplies and high-voltage instrumentation for a variety of medical applications, including bone densitometry imaging equipment, scanning electron microscopes, X-ray instrumentation, and electron beam systems.
- **RFI.** This division makes electronic noise suppression filters, high-voltage capacitors, pulse transformers, pulse forming networks, and specialty magnetics. Applications include cellular and hard-wired telecommunications systems, data communication equipment, and computer systems.

Del Global markets its medical imaging systems through a network of about 350 dealers in the United States. Its critical electronic subsystems are marketed separately through in-house and independent agents in the United States and throughout Europe, Asia, the Middle East, Australia, and India.

Del Global Technologies was founded in 1954. It has about 450 employees and a market capitalization of about $70 million.

EARNINGS PER SHARE PROGRESSION ★ ★ ★

Past 4 years: 134 percent (24 percent per year)

REVENUE GROWTH ★ ★

Past 4 years: 109 percent (20 percent per year)

STOCK GROWTH

Past 3 years: −15 percent
Dollar growth: $10,000 over 3 years would have declined to about $8,500.

CONSISTENCY ★ ★ ★ ★

Increased earnings per share: 4 consecutive years
Increased sales: 4 consecutive years

DEL GLOBAL TECHNOLOGIES AT A GLANCE

Fiscal year ended: July 31
Revenue and net income in $ millions

	1995	1996	1997	1998	1999	4-Year Growth Avg. Annual (%)	Total (%)
Revenue ($)	32.6	43.7	54.7	62.3	68.0	20	109
Net income ($)	1.9	2.9	4.9	5.8	6.7	37	253
Earnings/share ($)	0.35	0.48	0.61	0.71	0.82	24	134
PE range	12–18	13–39	11–20	8–18	9–14		

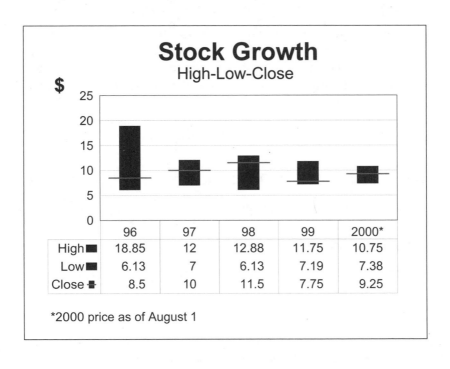

Stock Growth
High-Low-Close

$	96	97	98	99	2000*
High	18.85	12	12.88	11.75	10.75
Low	6.13	7	6.13	7.19	7.38
Close	8.5	10	11.5	7.75	9.25

*2000 price as of August 1

Catellus Development Corp.

201 Mission Street
San Francisco, CA 94105
415-974-4500
NYSE: CDX
www.catellus.com

Chairman:
William M. Kahane
President and CEO:
Nelson C. Rising

Earnings Growth	★ ★ ★ ★
Revenue Growth	★
Stock Growth	
Consistency	★ ★ ★ ★
Total	**9 Points**

Although it has been building offices, factories, and retail buildings for more than 15 years, Catellus Development Corp. is still years away from developing all the land in its portfolio. The company has the land to build more than 41 million square feet of new commercial development and an estimated 16,000 residential units in the western United States.

The San Francisco–based operation was originally formed in 1984 to conduct the non-railroad real estate activities of the Santa Fe Pacific Corp. It was spun off to shareholders in 1990. Its railroad background led to the acquisition of a diverse base of real estate properties located near transportation corridors of major urban areas.

The firm has successfully developed many of those areas as industrial parks, retail centers, offices, and residential areas, but other large tracts of the company's land remain undeveloped. One of the company's key strate gies is to develop the remaining lands as profitable properties.

Most of the property is located in California, although Catellus also has properties in Texas, Colorado, Illinois, Arizona, Oklahoma, Oregon, and Kansas. In all, the company has about 200 industrial properties, 225 rental properties, 25 office sites, 20 retail centers, several land developments, and 60 land leases. It also owns 782,000 acres of desert land in the western United States.

The company is currently building a massive "Pacific Commons" development in the Silicon Valley area that will include nearly 10 million square feet of office buildings and other businesses.

Catellus pursues an aggressive program of acquiring promising new properties. It has recently acquired a large residential tract in Southern California, a 300-acre site adjacent to Stapleton Airport in Denver, and other commercial and industrial properties in both Northern and Southern California.

Catellus has about 455 employees and a market capitalization of about $1.75 billion.

EARNINGS PER SHARE PROGRESSION ★ ★ ★ ★

Past 3 years: 4,350 percent (165 percent per year)

REVENUE GROWTH ★

Past 4 years: 68 percent (14 percent per year)

STOCK GROWTH

Past 3 years: −17 percent
Dollar growth: $10,000 over 3 years would have declined to about $8,300.

CONSISTENCY ★ ★ ★ ★

Increased earnings per share: 4 consecutive years
Increased sales: 4 consecutive years

CATELLUS DEVELOPMENT AT A GLANCE

Fiscal year ended: Dec. 31
Revenue and net income in $ millions

	1995	1996	1997	1998	1999	4-Year Growth Avg. Annual (%)	4-Year Growth Total (%)
Revenue ($)	102.8	115.9	128.9	149.3	172.3	14	68
Net income ($)	–33.0	25.4	25.2	59.9	70.2	29*	176*
Earnings/share ($)	–0.79	0.02	0.24	0.32	0.89	165*	4,350*
PE range	—	235–460	46–92	18–37	16–25		

*Net income and earnings per share growth figures are based on 3-year performance.

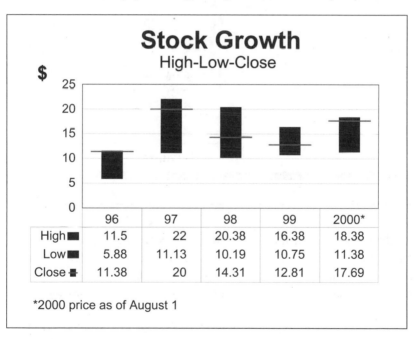

Stock Growth
High-Low-Close

	96	97	98	99	2000*
High■	11.5	22	20.38	16.38	18.38
Low■	5.88	11.13	10.19	10.75	11.38
Close ■	11.38	20	14.31	12.81	17.69

*2000 price as of August 1

Bell Microproducts, Inc.

1941 Ringwood Avenue
San Jose, CA 95131
408-451-9400
Nasdaq: BELM
www.bellmicro.com

Chairman, President, and CEO:
W. Donald Bell

Earnings Growth	★
Revenue Growth	★ ★ ★
Stock Growth	★ ★ ★
Consistency	★ ★
Total	**9 Points**

One of the challenges of the information age is finding a place to put all the digital content. Bell Microproducts makes the challenge less daunting for information-inundated corporations through the distribution of high-end storage devices made by the likes of IBM, Seagate Technology, and Fujitsu.

The nation's largest distributor of hard disk drives, Bell Microproducts has been riding the Internet wave, which is driving the need for mass storage in the commercial marketplace. Bell sells more than 100 brand-name product lines to original equipment manufacturers like IBM, as well as to resellers and systems integrators throughout Europe and the Americas.

Although its forte is storage devices, Bell also distributes semiconductors, computer peripherals, and computer platforms. The company adds value to the products it distributes through such services as testing, software loading, and integrating mass storage systems with a company's technology infrastructure.

Bell Microproducts was recently recognized by *Electronic Buyers News,* a leading industry journal, as the winner of the Best Managed Distributor Award. The magazine cited Bell for its top ranking among electronics distributors because of its key financial indicators and for its ability to closely partner with suppliers and meet the needs of its customers.

The San Jose operation adroitly manages its customer and supplier relationships through an e-commerce program that coordinates its supply chain. It also established an e-business program to drive business-to-business solutions to Internet reseller companies and other mass merchandisers.

Bell Microproducts has made several recent acquisitions to bolster its position as one of the world's top distributors of storage products. It also recently signed an agreement with IBM to become their Technology Group Solution Partner serving North and South America.

The company was founded in 1987 and went public with its initial stock offering in 1993. It has about 650 employees and a market capitalization of about $141 million.

EARNINGS PER SHARE PROGRESSION ★

Past 4 years: 60 percent (13 percent per year)

REVENUE GROWTH ★ ★ ★

Past 4 years: 206 percent (33 percent per year)

STOCK GROWTH ★ ★ ★

Past 3 years: 73 percent (20 percent per year)
Dollar growth: $10,000 over 3 years would have grown to about $17,000.

CONSISTENCY ★ ★

Increased earnings per share: 3 of the past 4 years
Increased sales: 3 of the past 4 years

BELL MICROPRODUCTS AT A GLANCE

Fiscal year ended: Dec. 31
Revenue and net income in $ millions

	1995	1996	1997	1998	1999	4-Year Growth Avg. Annual (%)	Total (%)
Revenue ($)	346	483	460	575	1,058	33	206
Net income ($)	4.0	7.9	6.3	8.5	8.9	22	123
Earnings/share ($)	0.48	0.92	0.53	0.68	0.77	13	60
PE range	14–29	6–10	9–19	5–11	5–11		

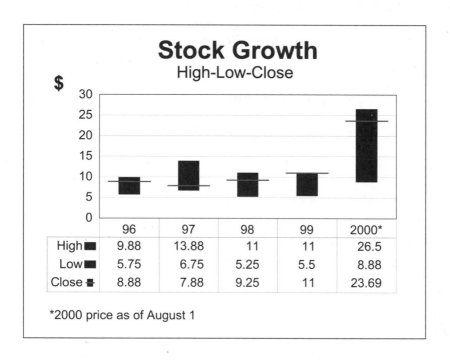

Stock Growth
High-Low-Close

$	96	97	98	99	2000*
High	9.88	13.88	11	11	26.5
Low	5.75	6.75	5.25	5.5	8.88
Close	8.88	7.88	9.25	11	23.69

*2000 price as of August 1

Hello Direct, Inc.

5839 Rue Ferrari
San Jose, CA 95138
408-972-1990
Nasdaq: HELO
www.hellodirect.com

Chairman:
John B. Mumford
President and CEO:
E. Alexander Glover

Earnings Growth	★
Revenue Growth	★ ★
Stock Growth	★ ★ ★
Consistency	★ ★ ★
Total	**9 Points**

Less than 10 percent of American office workers currently use a telephone headset, a fact Hello Direct would like to change. Hello Direct is a leading maker of headsets and related telecommunications equipment for small and midsized businesses. In addition to its own equipment, the company also sells business telephone equipment from other manufacturers.

The San Jose, California operation also specializes in integration of telephony products for business phone systems.

Unless properly configured, office telephone systems often do not function properly if equipment from several manufacturers is combined in a single system. Hello Direct has developed a technology that solves that problem. The company's LearnIt control device automatically configures the interface for virtually all phone handset protocols. It can also be used to provide access through the telephone handset jack to other analog communications products such as teleconferencing units, facsimiles, and modems.

Hello Direct markets its products aggressively through several channels, including a 60-page catalog that goes out to about 30 million prospects a year. It also sells through its Web site and telemarketing staff. Its customers include business offices, call centers, stockbrokers, consultants, real estate agents, and other salespeople.

About 50 percent of the company's revenue comes from sales of its line of headset products. Hello Direct has introduced a long line of innovative headsets, including lightweight and wireless models. Its brands include Ultralight, Solo, Executive, Cordless XLT, and Office Rover.

Other key areas for the company include audio/video-conferencing equipment, call/voice-processing equipment, computer/telephone integration services and equipment, and cellular/PCS equipment.

Hello Direct spends about $2 million a year in product development. Nearly all of its sales are in the United States. Founded in 1987, the company went public with its initial stock offering in 1995. It has about 250 employees and a market capitalization of about $65 million.

EARNINGS PER SHARE PROGRESSION   ★

Past 4 years: 70 percent (14 percent per year)

REVENUE GROWTH   ★ ★

Past 4 years: 120 percent (22 percent per year)

STOCK GROWTH   ★ ★ ★

Past 3 years: 71 percent (20 percent per year)
Dollar growth: $10,000 over 3 years would have grown to about $17,000.

CONSISTENCY   ★ ★ ★

Increased earnings per share: 3 of the past 4 years
Increased sales: 4 consecutive years

HELLO DIRECT AT A GLANCE

Fiscal year ended: Dec. 31
Revenue and net income in $ millions

	1995	1996	1997	1998	1999	4-Year Growth Avg. Annual (%)	Total (%)
Revenue ($)	36.8	51.6	63.8	68.7	81.0	22	120
Net income ($)	2.09	0.741	1.78	2.67	3.88	17	86
Earnings/share ($)	0.43	0.15	0.35	0.51	0.73	14	70
PE range	10–40	24–57	13–23	7–25	9–28		

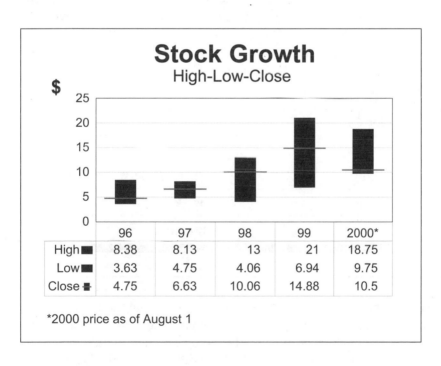

Stock Growth
High-Low-Close

	96	97	98	99	2000*
High	8.38	8.13	13	21	18.75
Low	3.63	4.75	4.06	6.94	9.75
Close	4.75	6.63	10.06	14.88	10.5

*2000 price as of August 1

California Micro Devices Corp.

215 Topaz Street
Milpitas, CA 95035
408-263-3214
Nasdaq: CAMD
www.californiamicrodevices.com

Chairman:
Wade F. Meyercord
President and CEO:
Jeffrey C. Kalb

Earnings Growth	★ ★
Revenue Growth	
Stock Growth	★ ★ ★ ★
Consistency	★ ★
Total	**8 Points**

As computers, cellular phones, heart pacemakers, and the growing array of portable electronic devices become smaller and more powerful, they need smaller, more powerful components to keep them running.

California Micro Devices fits the bill with its "thin film" technology. The micro components maker is able to combine multiple resistors, capacitors, diodes, and other components into a single, tiny, high-density device called "P/Active," which is used in a wide range of electronic devices.

The Milpitas, California operation also makes analog semiconductors for power management functions and low-voltage, micro-power operational amplifiers used in a variety of electronic devices. The company focuses on providing high-volume, cost-effective standard and custom components for computers, peripherals, networking systems, mobile phones, and telecommunications infrastructure equipment.

Its leading products, which generally range in price from about 20 cents to $1 per unit (and up to $10 for specialized products), include:

- Filters used in computers, mobile phones, personal digital assistants, and set-top boxes
- Termination devices, used in computers, base stations, and networks
- Resistor networks used in computers, automobiles, medical devices, audio equipment, test equipment, power supplies, and networks
- Protection devices used in mobile phones, personal digital assistants, computers, and set-top boxes
- Power management devices used for network interface cards and modems
- Amplifiers used in audio equipment, instrumentation, and mobile phones
- Microprocessors and peripherals used for telephone switching

The company's components are used in products made by Intel, Cisco Systems, Guidant, Nortel Networks, Samsung, 3Com, and other large computer and communications manufacturers. The company markets its products worldwide.

First incorporated in 1980, California Micro Devices went public with its initial stock offering in 1995. The company has about 285 employees and a market capitalization of about $260 million.

EARNINGS PER SHARE PROGRESSION

Past 4 years: −90 percent (But earnings are up from losses in 1998 and 1999.)

REVENUE GROWTH

Past 4 years: 10 percent (2 percent per year)

STOCK GROWTH

Past 3 years: 200 percent (45 percent per year)
Dollar growth: $10,000 over 3 years would have grown to $30,000.

CONSISTENCY   ★ ★

Positive earnings progression: 2 consecutive years
Increased sales: 3 consecutive years

CALIFORNIA MICRO DEVICES AT A GLANCE

Fiscal year ended: March 31
Revenue and net income in $ millions

| | | | | | | 4-Year Growth | |
| | | | | | | Avg. Annual (%) | Total (%) |
	1996	1997	1998	1999	2000		
Revenue ($)	39.9	32.9	33.0	33.6	43.8	2	10
Net income ($)	5.1	0.704	−3.0	−2.8	0.632	NA	−99
Earnings/share ($)	0.48	0.07	−0.30	−0.28	0.05	NA	−90
PE range	10–25	75–141	—	—			

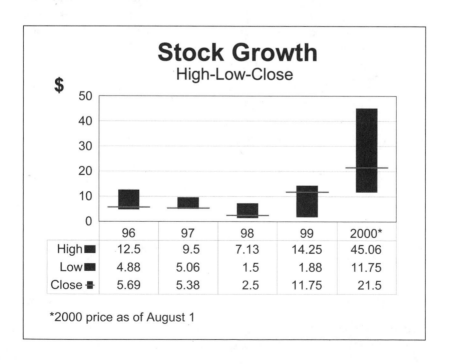

Stock Growth
High-Low-Close

$	96	97	98	99	2000*
High ■	12.5	9.5	7.13	14.25	45.06
Low ■	4.88	5.06	1.5	1.88	11.75
Close ■	5.69	5.38	2.5	11.75	21.5

*2000 price as of August 1

Camtek, Ltd.

P.O. Box 631
Migdal Haemek, Israel 10556
732-542-7711 (U.S.)
Nasdaq: CAMT
www.camtek.co.il

Chairman and CEO:
Rafi Amit

Earnings Growth	★
Revenue Growth	★ ★ ★ ★
Stock Growth	★
Consistency	★ ★
Total	**8 Points**

In this age of microcomponents—when you can fit a hundred transistors, resistors, and other electronic components on the head of pin—visual quality control inspections are no longer humanly possible. Camtek has developed an Automated Optical Inspection (AOI) system capable of seeing what we can't. The system is able to automatically detect defects in printed circuit boards during the manufacturing process.

The Israeli operation has installed its optical inspection systems at more than 450 manufacturing plants worldwide.

Camtek's AOI system helps manufacturers increase production by expediting the inspection process. In fact, operators can inspect and verify both sides of a circuit board panel in the same pass by using the system's "Flip" mode.

In addition to the standard circuit board inspections, Camtek's line of products also provides a number of other functions, including:

- **High-volume, high-resolution laser drilling inspections.** Its Orion AOI systems have been specifically designed to not only detect defects, but also to provide online verification, 3D-imaged display, multilanguage user interface, and other functions.

- **Camtek Verification and Repair station.** This cutting-edge tool provides offline verification, releasing the AOI system to focus strictly on inspections.
- **Camtek Process Control.** This system offers printed circuit board makers a real-time tool for inspection data collection, reporting, analysis, and alerting of process-related problems and repeat defects.
- **Camtek AOI Interface.** This interface product converts CAM data into AOI setup and reference data, allowing printed circuit board manufacturers to integrate Camtek equipment into their production lines.

The company markets its products to manufacturers around the world.

Camtek went public with its initial stock offering in July 2000. The company has about 200 employees and a market capitalization of about $150 million.

EARNINGS PER SHARE PROGRESSION ★

The company's earnings have declined since becoming profitable but were up considerably in the first half of 2000.

REVENUE GROWTH ★ ★ ★ ★

Past 4 years: 409 percent (50 percent per year)

STOCK GROWTH ★

The stock had solid growth after going public in July 2000.

CONSISTENCY ★ ★

Positive earnings progression: 1 of the past 4 years
Increased sales: 4 consecutive years

CAMTEK AT A GLANCE

Fiscal year ended: Dec. 31
Revenue and net income in $ millions

	1995	1996	1997	1998	1999	4-Year Growth Avg. Annual (%)	Total (%)
Revenue ($)	4.7	7.7	15.7	20.3	23.9	50	409
Net income ($)	−0.11	−0.34	2.0	1.32	0.63	NA	NA
Earnings/share ($)	−0.01	−0.02	0.13	0.09	0.04	NA	NA
PE range	—	—	—	—	—		

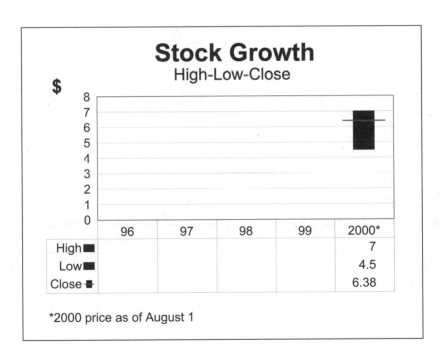

Stock Growth
High-Low-Close

$	96	97	98	99	2000*
High ■					7
Low ■					4.5
Close ■					6.38

*2000 price as of August 1

ANSYS Inc.

ANSYS

275 Technology Drive
Canonsburg, PA 15317
724-746-3304
Nasdaq: ANSS
www.ansys.com

Chairman:
Peter J. Smith
President and CEO:
James E. Cashman III

Earnings Growth	★ ★ ★ ★
Revenue Growth	
Stock Growth	★
Consistency	★ ★ ★
Total	**8 Points**

For the past 30 years, ANSYS has been putting the T-square out of business. The company makes computer-aided engineering (CAE) software that helps engineers operate more efficiently.

Design engineers use ANSYS software to accelerate product time-to-market, reduce production costs, and improve engineering processes.

ANSYS software allows engineers to construct computer models of structures, compounds, components, or systems to simulate performance conditions and physical responses to varying levels of stress, pressure, temperature, and velocity. The computer models allow engineers to make early, intelligent decisions about their design, materials, and other factors,

214

significantly accelerating product time-to-market. It also cuts down the expenses of prototyping and testing.

The Canonsburg, Pennsylvania operation offers CAE software and computer-aided design (CAD) software for a variety of industries. Leading customers come from the automotive, aerospace, and electronics industries. For instance, ANSYS software will be used to design the new Rolls Royce models through at least 2005. Its software is also used by universities around the world.

ANSYS markets its products through a global network of 29 independent regional ANSYS distributors, who operate 56 offices in 22 countries. The company also markets its products through alliances with a variety of leading computer makers, utilizes strategic corporate alliances in the development of its software, and has technical and marketing relationships with a number of other leading CAD creators.

The firm's design and analysis software programs, all of which are included in its ANSYS/Multiphysics program, are available as subsets or as stand-alone products. Its multiphysics products account for all of the company's annual revenue. ANSYS spends about $13 million a year for product research and development.

ANSYS was founded in 1970 as Swanson Analysis Systems. It went public with its initial stock offering in 1996. The firm has about 280 employees and a market capitalization of about $170 million.

EARNINGS PER SHARE PROGRESSION   ★ ★ ★ ★

Past 3 years: 878 percent (116 percent per year)

REVENUE GROWTH

Past 4 years: 59 percent (12 percent per year)

STOCK GROWTH   ★

Past 3 years: 38 percent (11 percent per year)
Dollar growth: $10,000 over 3 years would have grown to about $14,000.

CONSISTENCY   ★ ★ ★

Increased earnings per share: 3 of the past 4 years
Increased sales: 4 consecutive years

ANSYS AT A GLANCE

Fiscal year ended: Dec. 31
Revenue and net income in $ millions

	1995	1996	1997	1998	1999	4-Year Growth Avg. Annual (%)	Total (%)
Revenue ($)	39.6	47.1	50.5	56.5	63.1	12	59
Net income ($)	−1.58	1.65	7.40	11.30	14.70	108	791*
Earnings/share ($)	−0.18	0.09	0.05	0.68	0.88	116	878*
PE range	—	107–163	12–29	8–18	7–13		

*Net income and earnings per share growth figures are based on 3-year performance.

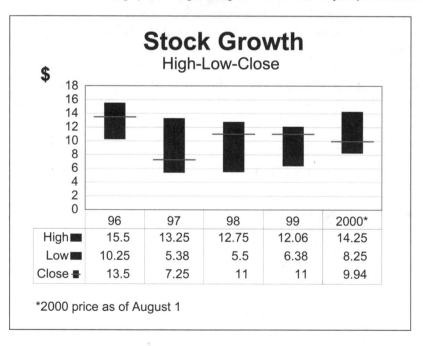

Stock Growth
High-Low-Close

$

	96	97	98	99	2000*
High ▪	15.5	13.25	12.75	12.06	14.25
Low ▪	10.25	5.38	5.5	6.38	8.25
Close ▪	13.5	7.25	11	11	9.94

*2000 price as of August 1

Digital Video Systems, Inc.

280 Hope Street
Mountain View, CA 94041
650-564-9699
Nasdaq: DVID
www.dvsystems.com

Co-Chairman:
Dr. Edmund Y. Sun
Co-Chairman and CEO:
Mali Kuo
President:
Edward M. Miller

Earnings Growth	★ ★
Revenue Growth	★ ★ ★ ★
Stock Growth	
Consistency	★ ★
Total	**8 Points**

The digital age has ushered in a broad range of new opportunities for technically savvy operations. Digital Video Systems specializes in the development of digital video technologies that facilitate the convergence of data, digital audio, digital photography, and high-end graphics.

The company develops and markets DVD-ROM drives, DVD players, DVD subassemblies and components, and video engines for the consumer, commercial, and computer peripherals markets.

Digital Video Systems controls worldwide rights to more than 100 patents and patent applications relating to DVD applications, as well as intellectual properties including video-on-demand and ad-insertion technologies.

The company has acquired its technology through its own original research as well as through acquisitions of other companies. Its major turning point came in 1998 when it acquired the DVD-ROM operations of Korea-based Hyundai Electronics.

Most of the firm's products are manufactured in Korea and China, although some products are made in the United States. The firm's DVD loader, which is the core subassembly of a DVD player, has captured more than 50 percent of the market in China, where a growing number of DVD players are assembled.

The Mountain View, California operation also has offices or subsidiaries in Taiwan, Hong Kong, and Bermuda.

Company Co-Chairman Edmund Y. Sun has been instrumental in the development of DVD technology. He was given the Lifetime Achievement Award at the 1999 DVD Summit Conference in Ireland for his contribution to the development of MPEG technologies.

In addition to its line of DVD-related products, the company also designs and produces a number of other computer peripherals, such as rewritable compact disc drives and thin-film-transistor liquid crystal display monitors. Rewritable CD drives allow computer users to record data, audio, images, or video on a compact disc.

Founded in 1992, the company went public with its initial stock offering in 1997. It has about 100 employees and a market capitalization of about $40 million.

EARNINGS PER SHARE PROGRESSION   ★ ★

The company has gone from losses to a gain in fiscal 2000.

REVENUE GROWTH   ★ ★ ★ ★

Past 4 years: 4,207 percent (154 percent per year)

STOCK GROWTH

Past 3 years: −58 percent
Dollar growth: $10,000 over 3 years would have dropped to about $4,200.

CONSISTENCY   ★ ★

Positive earnings progression: 2 consecutive years
Increased sales: 3 of the past 4 years

DIGITAL VIDEO SYSTEMS AT A GLANCE

Fiscal year ended: March 31
Revenue and net income in $ millions

	1996	1997	1998	1999	2000	4-Year Growth Avg. Annual (%)	Total (%)
Revenue ($)	1.4	14.1	17.6	17.1	60.3	154	4,207
Net income ($)	−1.4	−11.6	−25.7	−20.8	0.9	NA	NA
Earnings/share ($)	−2.3	−9.8	−14.6	−8.9	0.16	NA	NA
PE range	—	—	—	—	—		

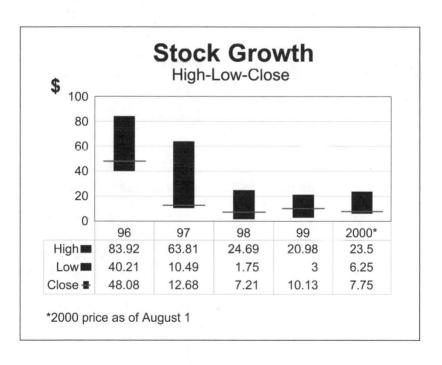

Stock Growth
High-Low-Close

	96	97	98	99	2000*
High ■	83.92	63.81	24.69	20.98	23.5
Low ■	40.21	10.49	1.75	3	6.25
Close ■	48.08	12.68	7.21	10.13	7.75

*2000 price as of August 1

Sound Advice, Inc.

SoundAdvice

1901 Tigertail Boulevard
Dania Beach, FL 33004
954-922-4434
Nasdaq: SUND
www.wegivesoundadvice.com

Chairman, President, and CEO:
Peter Beshouri

Earnings Growth	★ ★ ★
Revenue Growth	
Stock Growth	★ ★ ★ ★
Consistency	★
Total	**8 Points**

In the age of electronics superstores, Sound Advice has built its business by keeping its focus narrow. The Florida retailer concentrates on the upscale end of the home entertainment market.

The company operates about 24 Sound Advice stores located throughout Florida. Each store sells home and car audio systems, large screen televisions, video products, personal electronics, car security systems, home entertainment furniture, and related products. The product mix includes plasma, digital, and high-definition TVs and digital satellite systems.

Most of the products the stores carry are not available in mass market stores and electronics superstores, such as Best Buy and Circuit City.

In addition to its flagship Sound Advice stores, the company also operates five smaller Bang & Olufsen stores that feature high-end Bang & Olufsen audio products.

In addition to its electronics products, Sound Advice also offers customized services designing, installing, and servicing integrated multiroom systems.

Each Sound Advice store is equipped with state-of-the-art demonstration areas, where customers are enveloped in the sight and sound of its video and audio systems.

The company opens about two to three new stores each year. It opened its first Electronic Environments store in the summer of 2000. The 5,700-square-foot facility is entirely demonstration-oriented, built to simulate a residential environment in order to showcase its integrated sound and video systems as customers would experience them in their homes.

Because superior service is a key component of the company's success, its sales and service associates receive extensive technical product training.

Sound Advice stores are typically located in freestanding buildings of about 15,000 to 17,000 square feet. Its Bang & Olufsen stores are much smaller—about 1,500 square feet—and are located in shopping malls.

Founded in 1974, Sound Advice has a market capitalization of about $35 million.

EARNINGS PER SHARE PROGRESSION   ★ ★ ★

The company has had losses changing to positive earnings the past 4 years.

REVENUE GROWTH

Past 4 years: 6 percent (1.3 percent per year)

STOCK GROWTH   ★ ★ ★ ★

Past 3 years: 352 percent (65 percent per year)
Dollar growth: $10,000 over 3 years would have grown to about $45,000.

CONSISTENCY   ★

Positive earnings progression: 3 of the past 4 years
Increased sales: 2 consecutive years

SOUND ADVICE AT A GLANCE

Fiscal year ended: Jan. 31
Revenue and net income in $ millions

	1996	1997	1998	1999	2000	4-Year Growth Avg. Annual (%)	Total (%)
Revenue ($)	168.9	155.6	96.8	154.6	179.2	1.3	6
Net income ($)	−4.23	.871	−.955	.707	6.53	NA	NA
Earnings/share ($)	−1.13	−0.23	−0.26	0.18	1.53	NA	NA
PE range	—	—	—	12–70			

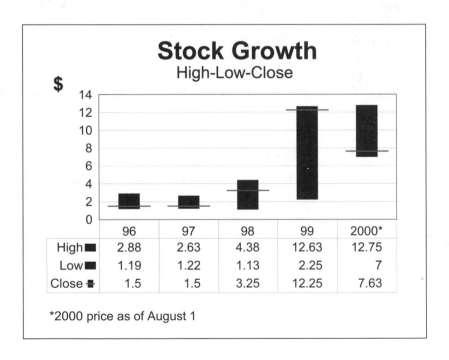

Stock Growth
High-Low-Close

$

	96	97	98	99	2000*
High	2.88	2.63	4.38	12.63	12.75
Low	1.19	1.22	1.13	2.25	7
Close	1.5	1.5	3.25	12.25	7.63

*2000 price as of August 1

75
Mail-Well, Inc.

23 Inverness Way East, Suite 160
Englewood, CO 80112
303-790-8023
NYSE: MWL
www.mail-well.com

Chairman and CEO:
Gerald F. Mahoney
President:
Paul V. Reilly

Earnings Growth	★ ★ ★
Revenue Growth	★ ★
Stock Growth	
Consistency	★ ★ ★
Total	**8 Points**

The name Mail-Well reflects this company's role as the nation's leading envelope manufacturer. But its name could just as easily be Acquire-Well. After a rapid-fire series of corporate buyouts—including ten acquisitions in 1999 alone—Mail-Well now operates more than 100 envelope and commercial printing facilities throughout North America.

The Englewood, Colorado operation has a strong presence in the consumer direct segment of the envelope market in which envelopes are designed, printed, and manufactured to customer specifications. The company makes a wide range of specialty envelopes with color graphics or action devices.

In addition to its envelope and high impact color printing services, the company has a strong business in label printing for foods, beverages, and spirits.

Commercial printing makes up about 42 percent of the company's total revenue, envelope production accounts for about 40 percent of revenue, printing for distributors accounts for 8 percent, and label printing makes up 10 percent.

Mail-Well, in its present form, began operations in 1994 with the acquisition of the envelope business of Georgia-Pacific and Pavey Envelope & Tag Corp. Mail-Well continued to buy up companies at an increasing pace through 2000, adding printing and envelope plants throughout the United States and Canada.

The printing and envelope industry is highly fragmented, with about 200 independent envelope companies and 500 high-impact color commercial printing companies in the United States. Mail-Well's long-term strategy is to continue to swallow up the independent operations and take advantage of the operating efficiencies of consolidation to increase profits.

Mail-Well may face one major threat in the coming years—e-mail. An increasing amount of correspondence is done over the Internet, which could lead to a declining demand for envelopes.

Mail-Well went public with its initial stock offering in 1995. The company has about 13,350 employees and a market capitalization of about $500 million.

EARNINGS PER SHARE PROGRESSION   ★ ★ ★

Past 4 years: 169 percent (28 percent per year)

REVENUE GROWTH   ★ ★

Past 4 years: 144 percent (25 percent per year)

STOCK GROWTH

Past 3 years: –40 percent
Dollar growth: $10,000 over 3 years would have dropped to about $6,000.

CONSISTENCY   ★ ★ ★

Increased earnings per share: 3 of the past 4 years
Increased sales: 4 consecutive years

MAIL-WELL AT A GLANCE

Fiscal year ended: Dec. 31
Revenue and net income in $ millions

	1995	1996	1997	1998	1999	4-Year Growth Avg. Annual (%)	4-Year Growth Total (%)
Revenue ($)	758	945	1,074	1,505	1,848	25	144
Net income ($)	13.0	21.2	28.9	28.9	64.5	50	396
Earnings/share ($)	0.49	0.53	0.71	0.47	1.32	28	169
PE range	8–10	4–10	6–24	10–46	9–15		

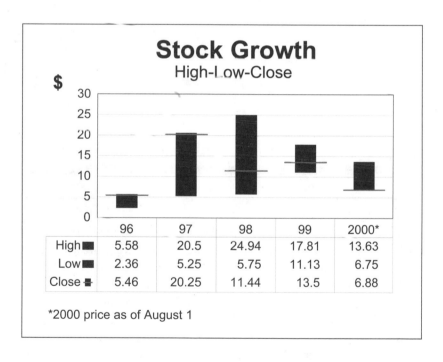

Stock Growth
High-Low-Close

$

	96	97	98	99	2000*
High	5.58	20.5	24.94	17.81	13.63
Low	2.36	5.25	5.75	11.13	6.75
Close	5.46	20.25	11.44	13.5	6.88

*2000 price as of August 1

76

International Home Foods, Inc.

100 North Field Street
Greenwich, CT 06830
203-622-6010
NYSE: IHF
www.intlhomefoods.com

Chairman and CEO:
C. Dean Metropoulos
President:
Lawrence K. Hathaway

Earnings Growth	★ ★ ★	
Revenue Growth	★ ★ ★	
Stock Growth		
Consistency	★ ★	
Total	**8 Points**	

Although it's hardly a household name, International Home Foods (IHF) has stuffed its corporate cupboard with some of America's most familiar brands—Chef Boyardee, Bumblebee tuna, Gulden's mustard, Libby's, and PAM cooking spray.

IHF has bought nine food companies with leading brands since it was established 1996. The leading brands aren't just gathering dust on IHF's shelves. Many of the brands are enjoying double-digit sales growth, thanks to the company's aggressive advertising and promotional campaigns.

To drive sales of its Chef Boyardee products, the company used television ads targeting its core audiences—moms and teens. The TV spots used the theme: "Say Yes to the Chef" to remind moms that Chef Boyardee products, such as its ravioli or beefaroni, are not only a hit with the kids but nutritious as well.

Spots targeting teens featured stars from the rough-and-tumble World Wrestling Federation. The ad campaign was complemented with in-store displays and other trade and consumer promotions.

To further leverage its roster of brand-name products, IHF has redesigned the packaging of the majority of its products to make them more visually appealing on store shelves. To bolster the bottom line, the company has introduced a variety of productivity improvements in every area of the company, resulting in savings of $20 million a year.

Other initiatives include expanding into the institutional food service markets, such as restaurants and institutions, and expanding its line of private label offerings. Through acquisitions and the leveraging of its popular brands, IHF has launched or expanded its presence in such international markets as Mexico, Canada, the United Kingdom, and Australia.

The Greenwich, Connecticut operation was founded in 1996 and went public with its initial stock offering in 1997. It has about 7,200 employees and a market capitalization of about $1.5 billion.

EARNINGS PER SHARE PROGRESSION　　★ ★ ★

Past 4 years: 116 percent (21 percent per year).

REVENUE GROWTH　　★ ★ ★

Past 4 years: 162 percent (27 percent per year)

STOCK GROWTH

Past 3 years: −13 percent
Dollar growth: $10,000 over 3 years would have declined to about $8,700.

CONSISTENCY　　★ ★

Increased earnings per share: 2 of the past 4 years
Increased sales: 4 consecutive years

INTERNATIONAL HOME FOODS AT A GLANCE

Fiscal year ended: Dec. 31
Revenue and net income in $ millions

	1995	1996	1997	1998	1999	4-Year Growth Avg. Annual (%)	Total (%)
Revenue ($)	819	943	1,222	1,700	2,144	27	162
Net income ($)	39.2	83.0	23.9	16.5	103.4	28	164
Earnings/share ($)	0.63	1.34	0.30	0.21	1.36	21	116
PE range	—	—	58–78	49–169	10–15		

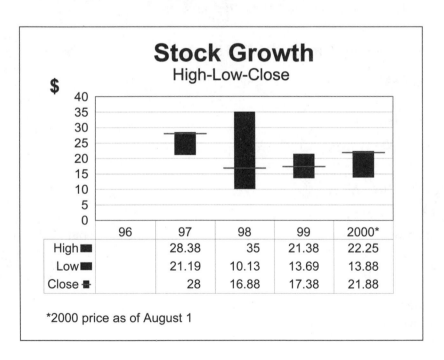

Stock Growth
High-Low-Close

$	96	97	98	99	2000*
High		28.38	35	21.38	22.25
Low		21.19	10.13	13.69	13.88
Close		28	16.88	17.38	21.88

*2000 price as of August 1

Chinadotcom Corp.

chinadotcom corporation

20 Floor, Citicorp Centre
18 Whitfeld Road
Causeway Bay, Hong Kong
800-997-8970 (or 852-2961-2719)
Nasdaq: CHINA
www.china.com

Chairman:
Raymond K. F. Ch'ien
CEO:
Peter Yip

Earnings Growth	
Revenue Growth	★ ★ ★ ★
Stock Growth	★ ★ ★
Consistency	★
Total	**8 Points**

It may be years before most Chinese citizens have personal computers, but when they do, Chinadotcom will be there to serve them. No question, the Internet portal's biggest prospects for growth are well into the future, but Chinadotcom is already busy attempting to establish itself as the America Online of Asia. In fact, America Online is one of the leading investors in Chinadotcom.

Chinadotcom offers news, sports, market information, horoscopes, message boards, online shopping options, e-mail, Web search, and other options similar to AOL. It recently acquired the nation's largest online travel service, Chinaholiday.com.

The company has Web sites in both English and Chinese. Its other portals include <www.hongkong.com>, <www.taiwan.com>, and <www.cww.com>. All three are Chinese language sites. On the other hand, <www.china.com> is an English language site that focuses on Chinese and Asian issues.

Chinadotcom also offers Internet advertising services and corporate Internet strategy and development services. Its advertising division, which includes the sale, economic delivery, and tracking of advertisements on a network of Web sites, has been developed in connection with U.S.-based 24/7 Media. Its advertising market base includes not just China and Taiwan, but Japan, South Korea, Singapore, India, Australia, Vietnam, Thailand, the Philippines, Malaysia, Laos, and Cambodia.

Although the company has already signed up about half a million users, its growth may be slower than one might expect in a country this big, because computers remain a relatively scarce commodity in China. According to industry estimates, by 2004 there will be about 33 million Chinese on the Internet—and a billion still waiting for service.

Chinadotcom was incorporated in the Cayman Islands in 1997 and went public with its initial stock offering in 1999. It has a market capitalization of about $1.8 billion and claims nearly 2,000 employees in 28 offices in its ten leading markets.

EARNINGS PER SHARE PROGRESSION

Losses have increased the past 2 years.

REVENUE GROWTH   ★ ★ ★ ★

Past 2 years: 3,868 percent

STOCK GROWTH   ★ ★ ★

Past year: 150 percent (but highly volatile)
Dollar growth: $10,000 over 1 year would have grown to about $25,000.

CONSISTENCY   ★

Positive earnings progression: None
Increased sales: 2 consecutive years

CHINADOTCOM AT A GLANCE

Fiscal year ended: Dec. 31
Revenue and net income in $ millions

	1995	1996	1997	1998	1999	2-Year Growth Avg. Annual (%)	Total (%)
Revenue ($)	—	—	0.509	3.45	20.2	NA	3,868
Net income ($)	—	—	−4.15	−8.82	−18.7	NA	NA
Earnings/share ($)	—	—	−0.09	−0.18	−0.26	NA	NA
PE range	—	—	—	—	—		

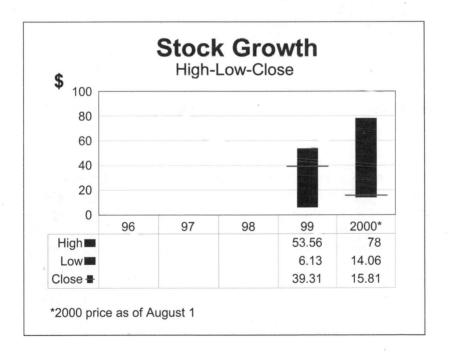

Stock Growth
High-Low-Close

$	96	97	98	99	2000*
High■				53.56	78
Low■				6.13	14.06
Close ■				39.31	15.81

*2000 price as of August 1

78
PFF Bancorp, Inc.

350 South Garey Avenue
Pomona, CA 91766
909-623-2323
Nasdaq: PFFB
www.pffbank.com

President and CEO:
Larry M. Rinehart

Earnings Growth	★ ★ ★ ★
Revenue Growth	
Stock Growth	
Consistency	★ ★ ★ ★
Total	**8 Points**

PFF Bancorp has enjoyed boom times recently, serving the fast-paced economy of Southern California. The Pomona, California regional bank continues to post strong earnings and revenue gains, while catering primarily to retail banking customers in the Los Angeles area.

Formerly known as the Pomona First Federal Savings and Loan Association, PFF remains a fairly small bank by industry standards. It has 23 full-service branches, two trust offices, and two regional loan centers in the Pomona area. It serves the eastern Los Angeles area, San Bernardino, Riverside, and northern and central Orange County.

PFF also operates its own Web site and a state-of-the-art loan and telebanking center, which it launched in 1997.

PFF focuses primarily on customers interested in savings and checking accounts and home mortgages. Home mortgages (for one- to four-family residences) account for about 60 percent of PFF's total gross loans. Multifamily mortgages account for about 3 percent; commercial real estate loans make up about 7 percent; construction and land loans account for about 20 percent; consumer loans, 5 percent; and commercial business loans, 5 percent.

The bank has begun to put more emphasis recently on attracting business deposit accounts and originating commercial business and real estate loans.

PFF was founded in 1892 as The Mutual Building and Loan. It changed its name to Pomona First Federal in 1938. The bank made the switch from savings and loan to bank—technically known as changing from a mutual form of ownership to a stock form—in 1996. It raised about $200 million in its initial public stock offering in 1996. Since the changeover, PFF has seen its earnings grow steadily from 11 cents a share in fiscal 1996 to $2.01 in fiscal 2000.

The company has about 450 employees and a market capitalization of about $240 million.

EARNINGS PER SHARE PROGRESSION ★ ★ ★ ★

Past 4 years: 1,736 percent (104 percent per year)

REVENUE GROWTH

Past 4 years: 58 percent (12 percent per year)

STOCK GROWTH

Past 3 years: Even, but it pays a 1.4 percent annual dividend (5 percent over 3 years).
Dollar growth: $10,000 over 3 years (including dividend) would have grown to about $10,500.

CONSISTENCY ★ ★ ★ ★

Increased earnings per share: 4 consecutive years
Increased sales: 4 consecutive years

PFF BANCORP AT A GLANCE

Fiscal year ended: March 31
Revenue and net income in $ millions

	1996	1997	1998	1999	2000	4-Year Growth Avg. Annual (%)	4-Year Growth Total (%)
Revenue ($)	136.2	168.5	191.4	206.9	215.3	12	58
Net income ($)	2.06	2.73	15.9	19.0	26.6	90	1,191
Earnings/share ($)	0.11	0.15	0.95	1.29	2.02	104	1,736
PE range	—	89–130	90–145	11–22	11–18		

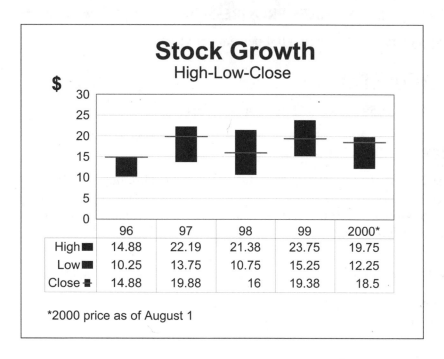

Stock Growth
High-Low-Close

	96	97	98	99	2000*
High■	14.88	22.19	21.38	23.75	19.75
Low■	10.25	13.75	10.75	15.25	12.25
Close■	14.88	19.88	16	19.38	18.5

*2000 price as of August 1

White Electronic Designs Corp.

3601 East University Drive
Phoenix, AR 85034
602-437-1520
Nasdaq: WEDC
www.whiteedc.com

President and CEO:
Hamid Shokrgozar

Earnings Growth	★
Revenue Growth	★ ★ ★ ★
Stock Growth	
Consistency	★ ★
Total	**8 Points**

White Electronics makes microchips for some of the fastest-growing sectors of the electronics market. The company designs and manufactures high-density, microelectronic memory and microprocessor products for commercial, industrial, and military applications.

White sells its products to more than 400 manufacturers around the world, including Cisco Systems, Lucent, 3Com, Allied Signal, Lockheed, Qualcomm, Samsung, and Rockwell. International sales account for nearly 20 percent of its total revenue.

The company works closely with the engineering departments of its customers to design and manufacture electronics components customized to the customer's specifications.

White was formed in 1998 through the merger of Bowmar Instrument Corp. and Electronic Designs. Bowmar was founded in 1951.

The company makes semiconductor products for wired and wireless telecommunications applications, such as network systems, switches, base stations, and other hardware platforms. It also makes products for a wide range of other industries, including medical electronics, consumer electronics, avionics, transportation, and network systems.

White specializes in high-density memory products and multichip modules for data communications and telecommunications providers, ruggedized high-legibility flat panel displays for commercial and military aircraft, and interface storage and retrieval devices and electromechanical assemblies for manufacturers in commercial and military markets.

Among its offerings are commercial and high-reliability manufacturing fabrication, test engineering, surface mount assembly, display, interface and mechanical manufacturing, electrical and electronic design, software design, and semiconductor assembly and test services.

Key applications for its products include backbone servers, routers, optical switches, wireless base stations, network hubs, bridges, LAN/WAN backbone switches, and Internet server hardware. "Overall, our products make the Internet run faster and wider and deeper," explains CEO Hamid Shokrgozar.

The Phoenix-based operation has manufacturing plants in Arizona, Massachusetts, and Indiana. The firm has about 260 employees and a market capitalization of about $200 million.

EARNINGS PER SHARE PROGRESSION ★

White's losses have declined over the past 4 years.

REVENUE GROWTH ★ ★ ★ ★

Past 4 years: 3,436 percent (142 percent per year)

STOCK GROWTH

Past 3 years: −48 percent
Dollar growth: $10,000 over 3 years would have declined to about $5,200.

CONSISTENCY ★ ★

Positive earnings progression: 3 of the past 4 years
Increased sales: 3 of the past 4 years

WHITE ELECTRONIC DESIGNS AT A GLANCE

Fiscal year ended: Sept. 30
Revenue and net income in $ millions

	1995	1996	1997	1998	1999	4-Year Growth Avg. Annual (%)	Total (%)
Revenue ($)	1.64	25.3	42.1	32.8	58.0	142	3,436
Net income ($)	−4.2	1.3	5.1	−3.3	−.558	NA	NA
Earnings/share ($)	−1.29	0.14	0.50	−0.47	−0.08	NA	NA
PE range	—	21–49	3–8	—	—		

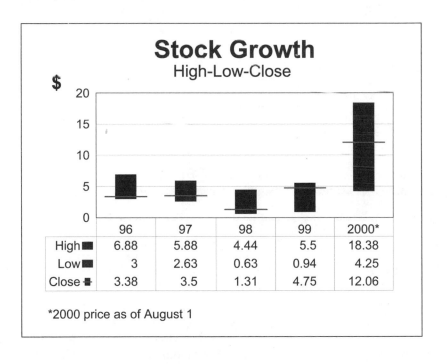

Stock Growth
High-Low-Close

	96	97	98	99	2000*
High	6.88	5.88	4.44	5.5	18.38
Low	3	2.63	0.63	0.94	4.25
Close	3.38	3.5	1.31	4.75	12.06

*2000 price as of August 1

80
Alpha Technologies Group, Inc.

306 Pasadena Avenue South
Pasadena, CA 91030
626-799-9171
Nasdaq: ATGI
www.alphatgi.com/sitemap.html

Chairman and CEO:
Lawrence Butler
President:
Robert C. Streiter

Earnings Growth	★ ★
Revenue Growth	
Stock Growth	★ ★ ★ ★
Consistency	★
Total	**7 Points**

Alpha Technologies Group knows how to take the heat. The company makes thermal management products engineered to dissipate unwanted heat generated by electronic components.

As electronic components become smaller yet mightier, they generate an increasing level of heat that threatens the reliability and functionality of electronic systems. Alpha's thermal management products, which are made primarily from fabricated aluminum extrusions, are used to reduce heat in a variety of high-tech applications, including microprocessors, computers, telecommunications, industrial controls, power supplies, factory automation, consumer electronics, aerospace and defense, and transportation. The company has more than 3,000 customers.

About two-thirds of Alpha's revenue comes from its thermal management products. Its other two leading product lines are electrical connectors and electronic subsystems.

Alpha's electrical connectors are electro-mechanical devices that permit electronic components, such as printed circuit boards, power supplies, and input-output cable assemblies, to be coupled and separated. Its connector products include sub-miniature, micro-miniature, and ultra-miniature connectors and wire harness connector assemblies.

Alpha's electronic subsystems are used in major networks for data transmission, retrieval, and transfer functions.

The company's thermal management products include:

- **Penguin coolers.** Used in personal computers and servers, these heat-sink products address thermal problems for the latest high-speed microprocessors.
- **Extruded heat sinks.** These products are designed for high-power industrial applications, such as transportation equipment, stereo amplifiers, and industrial equipment.
- **Active cooling components.** These products use air or liquid to dissipate heat for telecommunications, military, and aerospace systems.
- **Accessory products.** Alpha makes high-performance thermal compounds, adhesives, interface materials, precision compression mounting clamp systems, and other accessories.

The Pasadena, California operation was founded in 1969 as Synercom Technology. It changed to its present name in 1995. The company has about 600 employees and a market capitalization of about $100 million.

EARNINGS PER SHARE PROGRESSION ★ ★

Past 4 years: 5 percent (1 percent per year)
The company has gone from losses to strong gains the past 3 years.

REVENUE GROWTH

Past 4 years: 6 percent (1 percent per year)

STOCK GROWTH ★ ★ ★ ★

Past 3 years: 255 percent (53 percent per year)
Dollar growth: $10,000 over 3 years would have grown to about $35,000.

CONSISTENCY   ★

Positive earnings progression: 2 years
Increased sales: 3 of the past 4 years

ALPHA TECHNOLOGIES GROUP AT A GLANCE

Fiscal year ended: Oct. 31
Revenue and net income in $ millions

	1995	1996	1997	1998	1999	4-Year Growth Avg. Annual (%)	Total (%)
Revenue ($)	61.4	67.1	75.7	77.0	65.2	1	6
Net income ($)	4.04	−0.62	−4.02	−2.78	4.10	NA	1
Earnings/share ($)	0.57	−0.05	−0.50	−0.41	0.60	1	5
PE range	8–24	—	—	—	2–12		

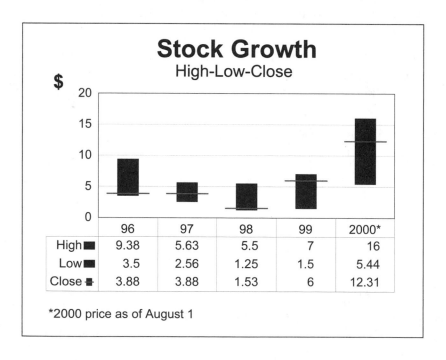

Stock Growth
High-Low-Close

$	96	97	98	99	2000*
High ■	9.38	5.63	5.5	7	16
Low ■	3.5	2.56	1.25	1.5	5.44
Close ■	3.88	3.88	1.53	6	12.31

*2000 price as of August 1

81
Interliant, Inc.

Two Manhattanville Road
Purchase, NY 10577
914-640-9000
Nasdaq: INIT
www.interliant.com

Co-Chairman:
Leonard Fassler
Co-Chairman:
Bradley Feld
CEO:
Herb Hribar

Earnings Growth	★ ★
Revenue Growth	
Stock Growth	★ ★ ★ ★
Consistency	★
Total	**7 Points**

Interliant can put you on the Net. The company is a leading Application Service Provider (ASP), offering a wide range of services designed to get companies up and running on the World Wide Web.

The Purchase, New York operation is a Web site host for more than 40,000 businesses. Interliant makes it easy and inexpensive for companies to establish and operate a Web site without going to the trouble of building and maintaining an internal network infrastructure.

According to Gartner Group, a Web research company, the ASP market is experiencing explosive growth and is expected to generate $23 billion in revenue by 2003 (compared to just $1 billion in 1998).

Interliant has three state-of-the-art Web hosting data centers in Atlanta, Houston, and Washington, D.C., with high-speed network connectivity and uninterruptible power supplies to keep its clients' sites up and running 24 hours a day.

Interliant offers several hosting options, including:

- **Virtual hosting.** The firm provides low-cost site hosting for multiple customers on a server Interliant owns and operates.
- **Dedicated hosting.** Interliant can assign a server specifically to a single customer who needs to host high-traffic or complex Web sites and applications but wants to avoid incurring significant infrastructure and overhead costs.
- **Co-located hosting.** Interliant can manage and house servers owned by its customers.
- **Application hosting.** The firm can manage online software applications for customers through the Lotus Notes/Domino platform.
- **Groupware hosting.** The company's Groupware software applications can enable people from remote locations to work together on the same applications. Options include e-mail and other messaging methods, project team collaboration and document sharing, business process automation and workflow, and document libraries.

Interliant has formed strategic alliances with leading technology companies, including Dell, IBM, Lotus, Microsoft, BMC, and Network Solutions. The company went public with its initial stock offering in 1999. It has about 750 employees and a market capitalization of about $1 billion.

EARNINGS PER SHARE PROGRESSION

None

REVENUE GROWTH   ★ ★ ★ ★

Past 1 year: 317 percent

STOCK GROWTH   ★ ★

Past 1 year: 19 percent
Dollar growth: $10,000 over 1 year would have grown to about $12,000.

CONSISTENCY ★

Increased earnings per share: None
Increased sales: 1 year

INTERLIANT AT A GLANCE

Fiscal year ended: Dec. 31
Revenue and net income in $ millions

	1995	1996	1997	1998	1999	1-Year Growth Avg. Annual (%)	1-Year Growth Total (%)
Revenue ($)	—	—	—	4.91	20.5	317	317
Net income ($)	—	—	—	–10.7	–53.9	NA	NA
Earnings/share ($)	—	—	—	–1.22	–1.50	NA	NA
PE range	—	—	—	—	—		

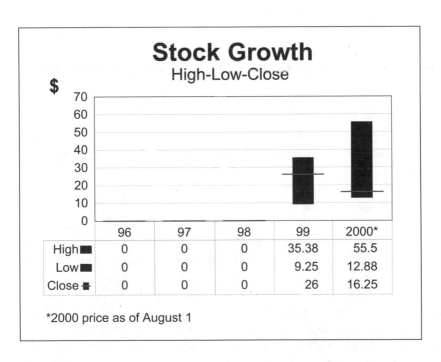

Stock Growth
High-Low-Close

$	96	97	98	99	2000*
High ■	0	0	0	35.38	55.5
Low ■	0	0	0	9.25	12.88
Close ▪	0	0	0	26	16.25

*2000 price as of August 1

82
inSilicon Corp.

411 East Plumeria Drive
San Jose, CA 95134
408-894-1900
Nasdaq: INSN
www.insilicon.com

Chairman:
Albert E. Sisto
President and CEO:
Wayne C. Cantwell

Earnings Growth	
Revenue Growth	★ ★ ★ ★
Stock Growth	★
Consistency	★ ★
Total	**7 Points**

With ever-increasing pressure to get their digital or Internet-related products to market in a hurry, electronics and semiconductor companies turn to inSilicon to help them design their complex systems.

inSilicon licenses its communication and connectivity software to more than 450 companies that design systems on a chip for digital devices. Some of the more than 600 applications include loudspeakers, microprocessors, set-top boxes, personal digital assistants, digital cameras, cable modems, routers, and switches. inSilicon's technology has also been used in telecommunications, networking, and industrial products.

The company's customers range from start-ups to Fortune 500 companies such as Intel, Cisco, Lucent, Motorola, AMD, Hewlett-Packard, and Raytheon. Companies turn to inSilicon to help speed the products time-to-market, reduce the engineering risk, and lessen research and development costs when developing complex communications-based silicon chips. Thanks to rapidly improving design and silicon technologies, entire systems can now be created on a single chip.

inSilicon's growth strategy calls for its continued targeting of companies that produce digital devices to meet the demands of customers who want to stay ahead of the curve in a wired world. Companies that are first to market with an innovatively designed product are often the ones that grab the early lead in market share.

One of inSilicon's newest technologies is its JVX accelerator, which speeds up performance tenfold on wireless Web systems. The technology should serve as a key catalyst for inSilicon's stock price and revenues. Other growth initiatives include creating new lines of communications technology software, expanding its U.S. and international distribution channels, building brand awareness among the electronics manufacturing and semiconductor communities, and developing e-commerce channels.

The San Jose operation was founded in 1999 and went public with its initial stock offering in 2000. It has about 70 employees and a market capitalization of about $240 million.

EARNINGS PER SHARE PROGRESSION

Increasing losses the past 2 years

REVENUE GROWTH ★ ★ ★ ★

Past 2 years: 270 percent (92 percent per year)

STOCK GROWTH ★

The stock just went public in 2000. It dropped and rebounded after its IPO.

CONSISTENCY

Positive earnings progression: None
Increased sales: 2 consecutive years

INSILICON AT A GLANCE

Fiscal year ended: Sept. 30
Revenue and net income in $ millions

	1995	1996	1997	1998	1999	2-Year Growth Avg. Annual (%)	Total (%)
Revenue ($)	—	—	5.11	8.79	18.9	92	270
Net income ($)	—	—	-1.99	-7.10	-12.1	NA	NA
Earnings/share ($)	—	—	-0.19	-0.68	-1.16	NA	NA
PE range	—	—	—	—	—		

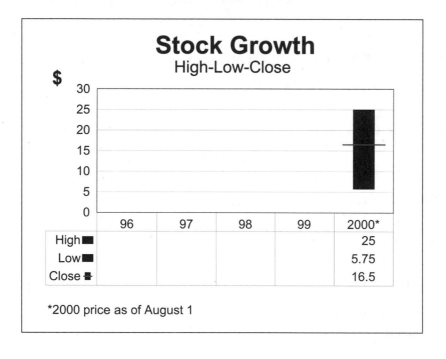

Stock Growth
High-Low-Close

$	96	97	98	99	2000*
High					25
Low					5.75
Close					16.5

*2000 price as of August 1

Computer Network Technology

6000 Nathan Lane North
Plymouth, MN 55442
763-268-6000
Nasdaq: CMNT
www.cnt.com

Chairman, President, and CEO:
Thomas Hudson

Earnings Growth	
Revenue Growth	★
Stock Growth	★ ★ ★ ★
Consistency	★ ★
Total	**7 Points**

Information is power. But when it is scattered hither and yon, it is of little value to an organization.

Computer Network Technology (CNT) helps corporations and government agencies bridge the disparate islands of information and meet the growing demand for instant access to data through a storage area network, or SAN. CNT can connect old systems with new, the local with the distant across systems as varied as the mainframe, the Internet, or open systems.

Storage systems like tape libraries and disks are attached to a SAN, creating a shared resource that is accessible and manageable for members of an organization. The bottom line: An organization is more productive through greater connectivity to information.

CNT makes what it calls its UltraNet family of networking products, including the UltraNet Storage Director, which allows users to move and share data between diverse servers, be they open system or mainframe, and storage systems. Other products are the UltraNet Open Systems Director and the UltraNet Storage Gateway.

The Minneapolis operation has customers in such industries as financial services, e-commerce, health care, aerospace, and telecommunications. More than half of the nation's 100 largest companies, including Boeing and GTE, use CNT products.

In addition to its hardware and software, CNT offers an array of professional services to help information technology managers grapple with an increasingly complex mix of servers, protocols, storage devices, channels, and networks. An early leader in the high-growth SAN market, CNT and its team of consultants have expertise in design, planning and management, protecting information, and preventing network downtime.

The company was founded in 1983 and went public with its initial stock offering in 1985. It has more than 600 employees and a market capitalization of about $327 million.

EARNINGS PER SHARE PROGRESSION

Past 4 years: 6 percent (1.5 percent per year)

REVENUE GROWTH   ★

Past 4 years: 93 percent (18 percent per year)

STOCK GROWTH   ★ ★ ★ ★

Past 3 years: 287 percent (57 percent per year)
Dollar growth: $10,000 over 3 years would have grown to about $39,000.

CONSISTENCY   ★ ★

Increased earnings per share: 1 of the past 4 years
Increased sales: 4 consecutive years

COMPUTER NETWORK TECHNOLOGY AT A GLANCE

Fiscal year ended: Dec. 31
Revenue and net income in $ millions

	1995	1996	1997	1998	1999	4-Year Growth Avg. Annual (%)	Total (%)
Revenue ($)	78.8	97.1	97.8	133.5	151.7	18	93
Net income ($)	4.02	1.36	−2.31	4.73	7.05	15	75
Earnings/share ($)	0.17	0.06	−0.10	0.21	0.18	1.5	6
PE range	23–74	69–181	—	16–67	41–170		

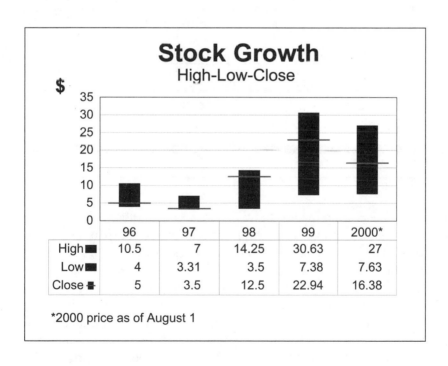

Stock Growth
High-Low-Close

	96	97	98	99	2000*
High	10.5	7	14.25	30.63	27
Low	4	3.31	3.5	7.38	7.63
Close	5	3.5	12.5	22.94	16.38

*2000 price as of August 1

84

Kewaunee Scientific Corp.

2700 West Front Street
Statesville, NC 28677
704-873-7202
Nasdaq: KEQU
www.kewaunee.com

Chairman and CEO:
Eli Manchester, Jr.
President:
William A. Shumaker

Earnings Growth	★ ★ ★ ★
Revenue Growth	
Stock Growth	
Consistency	★ ★ ★
Total	**7 Points**

Kewaunee Scientific provides the work surfaces and other accessories to support everything from a simple high school chemistry experiment to sophisticated medical and industrial laboratory research.

In addition to work surfaces, Kewaunee makes scientific laboratory and technical workstations, wood and steel laboratory furniture, hoods to remove laboratory fumes, sinks, and workbenches. The company sells its products to industrial, commercial, educational, government, and health care markets through a network of laboratory products dealers and distributors. To smooth the distribution process, Kewaunee has introduced a new electronic order management system.

The majority of customers for Kewaunee's wood furniture products are in the educational area—high schools, colleges, and universities. It has been a vibrant market as schools grow and enhance their lab facilities.

Kewaunee's largest-volume product is its metal furniture, made of heavy gauge steel and favored by the industrial research marketplace. A key company goal is to increase its sales of laboratory and technical products to international markets. The company has established relationships in Singapore, England, and the Middle East. Its joint venture project in Singapore, Kewaunee Labway Asia, has been awarded several lucrative contracts.

Another corporate objective is to expand the product offering for its line of technical products targeted to fast-growing computer and Internet-related industries. The company's manufacturing facilities are in Statesville, North Carolina, and Lockhart, Texas.

Kewaunee adds value to its product and engenders loyalty by having its sales representatives, who are knowledgeable about laboratory products and procedures, work with customers from preplanning through final installation. The services include laboratory design and layout, product selection, ordering, and scheduling.

The North Carolina–based operation has about 650 employees and a market capitalization of about $30 million.

EARNINGS PER SHARE PROGRESSION   ★ ★ ★ ★

Past 4 years: 820 percent (101 percent per year)

REVENUE GROWTH

Past 4 years: 24 percent (6 percent per year)

STOCK GROWTH

Past 3 years: –43 percent
Dollar growth: $10,000 over 3 years would have declined to about $5,700.

CONSISTENCY   ★ ★ ★

Positive earnings progression: 4 consecutive years
Increased sales: 3 of the past 4 years

KEWAUNEE SCIENTIFIC AT A GLANCE

Fiscal year ended: April 30
Revenue and net income in $ millions

	1996	1997	1998	1999	2000	4-Year Growth Avg. Annual (%)	Total (%)
Revenue ($)	62.5	57.5	62.0	73.0	77.5	6	24
Net income ($)	−1.09	0.361	2.26	2.56	3.4	102*	842*
Earnings/share ($)	−0.46	0.15	0.95	1.06	1.38	101*	820*
PE range	18–43	5–14	8–14	6–8			

*Net income and earnings per share growth are based on 3-year performance.

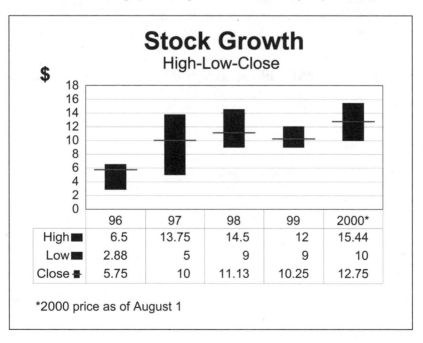

Stock Growth
High-Low-Close

$	96	97	98	99	2000*
High■	6.5	13.75	14.5	12	15.44
Low■	2.88	5	9	9	10
Close■	5.75	10	11.13	10.25	12.75

*2000 price as of August 1

85
Mitek Systems, Inc.

10070 Carroll Canyon Road
San Diego, CA 92131
619-635-5900
Nasdaq: MITK
www.miteksys.com

Chairman, President, and CEO:
John M. Thornton

Earnings Growth	
Revenue Growth	
Stock Growth	★ ★ ★ ★
Consistency	★ ★
Total	**6 Points**

There's nothing too cryptic for Mitek Systems, a maker of advanced character recognition products that allow companies to automatically process documents.

Mitek can help organizations such as banks, manufacturers, and government agencies decipher and process hand-printed, machine-printed, or even scribbled documents with what it calls its Intelligent Character Recognition and Automatic Document Recognition technologies. There are plenty of opportunities for Mitek, because U.S. businesses produce more than 900 million documents per day.

Mitek got its start as a supplier of computer products to government agencies and defense contractors dealing in sensitive and classified information. When the Cold War ended, the company switched to the emerging commercial market of document imaging.

Mitek's QuickStrokes program is designed to process and store some of the most difficult documents—application forms filled out with smeared felt pen; faxed orders in blurry, broken type; and mail-order forms that arrive torn or dirty. The QuickStrokes technology, for example, allows banks to automatically read both handwritten and encoded information on a check with a single pass through a document scanner.

The company's new DOCTUS document understanding system automatically distinguishes among thousands of document types and formats them for classification, indexing, or data entry. The system can handle both structured and unstructured documents. The latter often lack ID numbers, registration marks, or entry fields that are often in the same place.

Mitek is introducing a Web browser in 2000 that will locate, capture, and save to a database or file information from the Internet. The WEBrowz technology is designed to make it easier for anyone who routinely gathers and analyzes information from the Internet. For example, a stockbroker could use it to capture and save information about a particular stock he or she is following.

Founded in 1982, Mitek has about 40 employees and a market capitalization of about $75 million.

EARNINGS PER SHARE PROGRESSION

Past 3 years: 27 percent (8 percent per year)

REVENUE GROWTH

Past 4 years: 47 percent (10 percent per year)

STOCK GROWTH   ★ ★ ★ ★

Past 3 years: 269 percent (55 percent per year)
Dollar growth: $10,000 over 3 years would have grown to about $37,000.

CONSISTENCY

Positive earnings progression: 3 of the past 4 years
Increased sales: 3 of the past 4 years

MITEK SYSTEMS AT A GLANCE

Fiscal year ended: Sept. 30
Revenue and net income in $ millions

	1995	1996	1997	1998	1999	4-Year Growth Avg. Annual (%)	Total (%)
Revenue ($)	6.63	8.15	4.84	6.50	9.74	10	47
Net income ($)	–0.07	1.23	–2.57	–1.5	2.03	18*	65*
Earnings/share ($)	–0.01	0.15	–0.25	–0.13	0.19	8*	27*
PE range	—	9–40	—	—	5–28		

*Net income and earnings per share growth figures are based on 3-year performance.

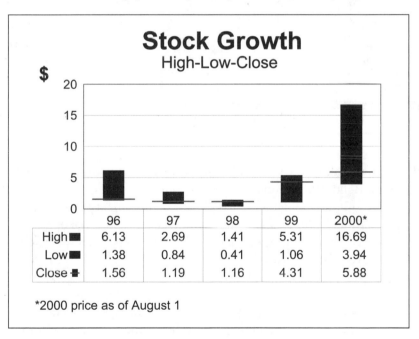

Stock Growth
High-Low-Close

$	96	97	98	99	2000*
High ■	6.13	2.69	1.41	5.31	16.69
Low ■	1.38	0.84	0.41	1.06	3.94
Close ■	1.56	1.19	1.16	4.31	5.88

*2000 price as of August 1

86

Gehl Company

143 Walter Street
West Bend, WI 53095-0179
262-334-9461
Nasdaq: GEHL
www.gehl.com

Chairman, President, and CEO:
William D. Gehl

Earnings Growth	★ ★
Revenue Growth	★
Stock Growth	
Consistency	★ ★ ★
Total	**6 Points**

Gehl has been making agricultural implements for more than 140 years. But the West Bend, Wisconsin operation now makes more money on light construction equipment than it does on its farm equipment.

In this high-tech era, Gehl may be considered an old-school operation, but both of its manufacturing segments—farm equipment and light construction—have been growing like high-tech start-ups. The strong economy has helped pump up the construction industry, which tends to be cyclical.

Gehl's agriculture division makes a wide range of equipment used primarily in the dairy and livestock industries, including haymaking, forage harvesting, materials handling, manure handling, and feedmaking equipment. Its construction division makes skid steer loaders, rough-terrain telescopic forklifts, and asphalt pavers.

Construction equipment accounts for about 60 percent of Gehl's annual revenue, while farm equipment makes up the other 40 percent. Gehl construction equipment is manufactured at plants in Minnesota and South

Dakota, while its agricultural equipment is manufactured in Wisconsin, South Dakota, and Pennsylvania.

Gehl offers a full line of related products along with its main staples. For instance, its haymaking line includes disc mowers, pull-type disc mower conditioners, hay rakes, and variable chamber round balers. Its forage harvesting line includes harvesters, wagons, and blowers. Its feed-making line includes grinder mixers, mixer feeders, and feeder wagons for mixing and delivery to livestock feeders.

Gehl sells its equipment worldwide; in fact, it has been selling outside of North America since about 1950. The company sells both farm and construction equipment in Europe, the Middle East, Australia, the Pacific Rim, and Latin America through a network of independent distributors. In the United States, it uses about 300 independent dealers.

Gehl was founded in 1859. It has about 1,100 employees and a market capitalization of about $102 million.

EARNINGS PER SHARE PROGRESSION   ★ ★

Past 4 years: 120 percent (20 percent per year)

REVENUE GROWTH   ★

Past 4 years: 86 percent (17 percent per year)

STOCK GROWTH

Past 3 years: −13 percent
Dollar growth: $10,000 over 3 years would have declined to about $8,700.

CONSISTENCY   ★ ★ ★

Increased earnings per share: 4 consecutive years (but dropping in 2000)
Increased sales: 4 consecutive years

GEHL AT A GLANCE

Fiscal year ended: Dec. 31
Revenue and net income in $ millions

	1995	1996	1997	1998	1999	4-Year Growth Avg. Annual (%)	4-Year Growth Total (%)
Revenue ($)	153.4	159.7	197.1	262.2	285.8	17	86
Net income ($)	9.0	9.6	12.8	15.3	20.2	22	124
Earnings/share ($)	1.44	1.54	1.95	2.29	3.17	20	120
PE range	4–6	4–8	5–13	5–10	4–7		

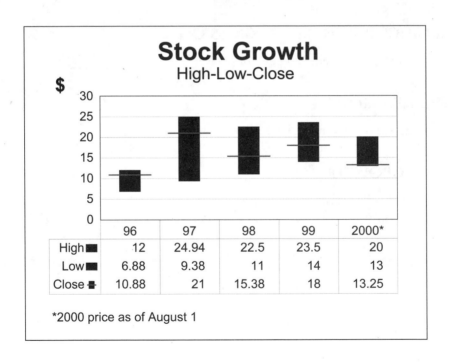

Stock Growth
High-Low-Close

$	96	97	98	99	2000*
High	12	24.94	22.5	23.5	20
Low	6.88	9.38	11	14	13
Close	10.88	21	15.38	18	13.25

*2000 price as of August 1

87

Amtech Systems, Inc.

131 South Clark Drive
Tempe, AZ 85281
480-967-5146
Nasdaq: ASYS
www.amtechsystems.com

Chairman, President, and CEO:
Jong S. Whang

Earnings Growth	★ ★
Revenue Growth	★
Stock Growth	
Consistency	★ ★ ★
Total	**6 Points**

Amtech is helping the high-tech industry meet the growing demand for semiconductors through its growing line of equipment used in the manufacture of semiconductor wafers.

Semiconductor chips, which are fabricated on a silicon wafer substrate, make up part of the circuitry of a vast range of electrical components. Amtech's products are used in the fabrication and processing of silicon wafers.

Its line of products includes:

- **Diffusion furnaces.** Through its Tempress Systems subsidiary, the firm makes diffusion furnace systems, which are used in the manufacturing of large-size chips and multimodel manufacturing.
- **Processing and robotic equipment.** Amtech's "Atmoscan" is a wafer processing system for use with the diffusion furnaces. The Atmoscan provides increased control of the environment of the wafers during the gaseous and heating process.

- **Automation systems.** The company's automation system includes quartz trays that hold silicon wafers while they are being processed in diffusion furnaces. They also come with hardware and software that automatically places the quartz trays into Atmoscan tubes before they are inserted into the diffusion furnaces—and automatically removes them after the process has been completed.

The company also makes loading stations and polishing machines and a variety of related equipment used in the fabrication of semiconductor wafers. It also makes "carriers," which hold the wafers during the lapping and polishing process.

Amtech markets its products worldwide through its corporate sales staff. The company sells almost exclusively to semiconductor manufacturing operations. Among its leading customers are Intel, Lucent Technologies, Motorola, Texas Instruments, Philips, Samsung, and Hyundai.

Founded in 1981, the company went public with its initial stock offering in 1983. Amtech Systems has about 100 employees and a market capitalization of about $15 million.

EARNINGS PER SHARE PROGRESSION   ★ ★

Past 4 years: 89 percent (17 percent per year)

REVENUE GROWTH   ★ ★

Past 4 years: 116 percent (21 percent per year)

STOCK GROWTH

Past 3 years: −30 percent
Dollar growth: $10,000 over 3 years would have declined to about $7,000.

CONSISTENCY   ★

Increased earnings per share: 2 of the past 4 years
Increased sales: 3 of the past 4 years

AMTECH SYSTEMS AT A GLANCE

Fiscal year ended: Sept. 30
Revenue and net income in $ millions

	1995	1996	1997	1998	1999	4-Year Growth Avg. Annual (%)	Total (%)
Revenue ($)	6.86	8.41	11.1	16.2	14.8	21	116
Net income ($)	0.170	0.199	0.236	–0.590	0.363	21	114
Earnings/share ($)	0.09	0.08	0.10	–0.28	0.17	17	89
PE range	44–108	80–150	39–79	—	5–34		

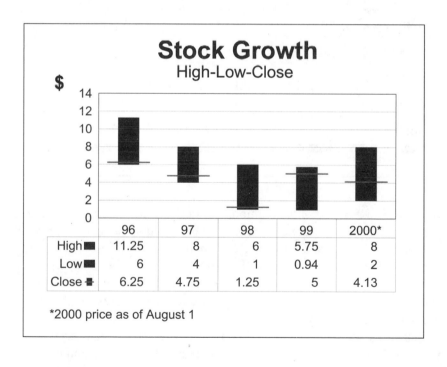

Stock Growth
High-Low-Close

	96	97	98	99	2000*
High	11.25	8	6	5.75	8
Low	6	4	1	0.94	2
Close	6.25	4.75	1.25	5	4.13

*2000 price as of August 1

88

Channell Commercial Corp.

26040 Ynez Road
Temecula, CA 92591
909-719-2600
Nasdaq: CHNL

Chairman and CEO:
William Channell, Sr.
President:
William Channell, Jr.

Earnings Growth	
Revenue Growth	★ ★ ★
Stock Growth	
Consistency	★ ★
Total	**5 Points**

In the fast-growth world of telecommunications, the big hitters are starting to turn to Channell Commercial for a broad range of equipment and supplies.

Based in Temecula, California, Channell makes a line of advanced copper termination and connection devices, fiber-optic cable management systems, coaxial-based passive radio frequency electronics and heat-shrink products, and thermoplastic and metal fabricated enclosures for the telecommunications industry.

Channell's special enclosures house, protect, and provide access to advanced telecommunications hardware—such as fiber optics and copper wire—and are deployed in the "last mile" or "local loop" that connects the network provider's signal origination office with residences and businesses.

The last-mile hardware is one of the hottest areas of communications, as consumers look for faster service for their Internet and communications hookups.

Channell sells its equipment to telephone, cable television, and power utility networks worldwide. Its leading markets outside the United States are Australia, Canada, and the United Kingdom.

In addition to its specialized enclosures, Channell's product line includes:

- Radio frequency electronics used for outdoor and indoor taps, signal splitters, and cable TV and broadband telecommunications networks
- Copper connectivity products that provide advanced telephone termination systems for copper wires, the predominant medium used in the last mile for telecommunications services
- Fiber-optic products designed for use in telephone, broadband, and power utility telecommunications networks

Channell has helped build its business through several key acquisitions. The company acquired RMS Electronics and Standby Electronics in 1997 and A.C. Egerton, PLC, in 1998.

Channell Commercial went public with its initial stock offering in 1996. It has about 850 employees and a market capitalization of about $125 million.

EARNINGS PER SHARE PROGRESSION

Past 4 years: 21 percent (5 percent per year)

REVENUE GROWTH ★ ★ ★

Past 4 years: 195 percent (32 percent per year)

STOCK GROWTH

Past 3 years: −20 percent
Dollar growth: $10,000 over 3 years would have declined to about $8,000.

CONSISTENCY ★ ★

Increased earnings per share: 2 of the past 4 years
Increased sales: 4 consecutive years

CHANNELL COMMERCIAL AT A GLANCE

Fiscal year ended: Dec. 31
Revenue and net income in $ millions

	1995	1996	1997	1998	1999	Avg. Annual (%)	Total (%)
						4-Year Growth	
Revenue ($)	40.9	47.3	59.9	92.7	120.7	32	195
Net income ($)	6.4	8.2	8.5	8.1	9.3	10	45
Earnings/share ($)	0.84	0.97	0.92	0.88	1.02	5	21
PE range	—	8–14	10–18	6–15	6–13		

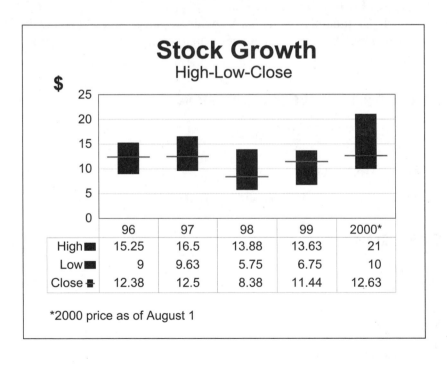

Stock Growth
High-Low-Close

	96	97	98	99	2000*
High	15.25	16.5	13.88	13.63	21
Low	9	9.63	5.75	6.75	10
Close	12.38	12.5	8.38	11.44	12.63

*2000 price as of August 1

BTU International Inc.

23 Esquire Road
North Billerica, MA 01862
978-667-4111
Nasdaq: BTUI
www.btu.com

Chairman, President, and CEO:
Paul J. van der Wansem

Earnings Growth	
Revenue Growth	
Stock Growth	★ ★ ★ ★
Consistency	★
Total	**5 Points**

When the electronics industry gets hot, BTU International is more than happy to turn up the heat.

The company makes sophisticated furnaces and thermal processing systems for electronics manufacturers and chip makers to "cure" their hot-off-the-press semiconductors, circuit boards, and other electronic circuitry—key components for cell phones, palm-top computers, and networking devices.

Industrial customers have been buying more of the kilns to meet the growing demand for electronic components in an era of fast-paced communications. In the first quarter of 2000, BTU's sales to PC circuit board makers increased 125 percent over the same quarter the year before, accounting for 50 percent of the company's total sales for that quarter.

BTU's furnaces aren't cheap. Depending on the features, a BTU furnace can cost from $700,000 to $900,000. The company's biggest customers are specialty contract manufacturers that produce components and products for electronics, computer, and telecommunications companies attempting to reduce production, inventory, and other overhead costs. Contract manufacturing is expanding at a rate of more than 20 percent a year, a trend that bodes well for BTU.

The company is introducing several new products that are expected to fan the flames for its revenues, profits, and share price. One new product is a furnace that has more precise temperature controls than those manufactured by BTU's competitors, which are primarily based in Japan. The company sells U.S. manufacturers on the advantage of doing business with a supplier that's much closer to home.

BTU is also introducing a new line of thermal processing machines for printed circuit boards that are easier to operate than older machines.

The company has about 300 employees and a market capitalization of about $60 million.

EARNINGS PER SHARE PROGRESSION

Past 4 years: −40 percent

REVENUE GROWTH

Past 4 years: 21 percent (3 percent per year)

STOCK GROWTH ★ ★ ★ ★

Past 3 years: 167 percent (39 percent per year)
Dollar growth: $10,000 over 3 years would have grown to about $27,000.

CONSISTENCY ★

Increased earnings per share: 2 of the past 4 years
Increased sales: 3 of the past 4 years

BTU INTERNATIONAL AT A GLANCE

Fiscal year ended: Dec. 31
Revenue and net income in $ millions

	1995	1996	1997	1998	1999	4-Year Growth Avg. Annual (%)	4-Year Growth Total (%)
Revenue ($)	58.3	45.8	52.1	56.5	70.5	3	21
Net income ($)	5.07	3.56	1.25	1.53	2.84	NA	−65
Earnings/share ($)	0.68	0.48	0.17	0.21	0.41	NA	−40
PE range	5–20	5–15	14–43	9–26	6–15		

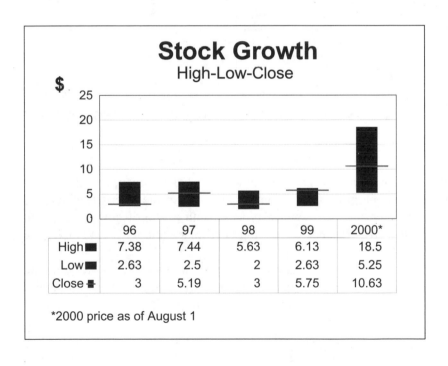

Stock Growth
High-Low-Close

	96	97	98	99	2000*
High	7.38	7.44	5.63	6.13	18.5
Low	2.63	2.5	2	2.63	5.25
Close	3	5.19	3	5.75	10.63

*2000 price as of August 1

AltiGen Communications

47427 Fremont Boulevard
Fremont, CA 94538
510-252-9712
Nasdaq: ATGN
www.altigen.com

President and CEO:
Gilbert Hu

Earnings Growth	
Revenue Growth	
Stock Growth	★ ★ ★ ★
Consistency	★
Total	**5 Points**

Convergence is only a matter of time, with voice, video, and data communications merging into a common medium on the Internet. AltiGen is helping hasten the convergence process with a line of computer circuit boards that gives businesses the ability to place telephone calls over the Internet.

AltiGen's circuit boards and communications software systems are installed in the business's main computer, where they serve as a central communications system, answering and routing calls, coordinating e-mail and voice mail, and tracking call activity.

AltiGen's systems are marketed to small and midsized businesses that can realize some cost savings by placing certain types of calls over a data network, such as the Internet or their corporate intranet. AltiGen's systems give users the choice between calling over the traditional telephone network or the Internet.

The California-based operation has several product options, including:

- **AltiWare IP software.** This software enables users to place and receive phone calls over data networks.
- **AltiView software.** AltiView gives computer users the ability to receive and place calls, listen to voice mail messages, and identify the phone number of the caller.
- **AltiWare OE.** This is a graphical user interface program that provides phone service for computer users.
- **Triton IP.** This is a circuit board that allows calls to be carried over public and private data networks that support Internet Protocol.
- **Triton T1.** This circuit board allows calls to be carried over digital telecommunications lines.

The company markets its products through a network of distributors and more than 400 dealers, who sell its systems to end users. The company provides 24/7 customer support, assisting customers with questions on installing and using AltiGen's products.

AltiGen has about 85 employees and a market capitalization of about $85 million.

EARNINGS PER SHARE PROGRESSION

Losses have become larger in recent years.

REVENUE GROWTH   ★ ★ ★ ★

Past 3 years: 2,782 percent (207 percent per year)

STOCK GROWTH

Past 1 year: −50 percent
Dollar growth: $10,000 over 1 year would have declined to about $5,000.

CONSISTENCY   ★

Positive earnings progression: None
Increased sales: 4 consecutive years

ALTIGEN COMMUNICATIONS AT A GLANCE

Fiscal year ended: Dec. 31
Revenue and net income in $ millions

	1995	1996	1997	1998	1999	3-Year Growth Avg. Annual (%)	Total (%)
Revenue ($)	0	0.23	1.38	3.89	6.60	207	2,782
Net income ($)	−1.07	−1.63	−3.12	−3.92	−6.89	NA	NA
Earnings/share ($)	−1.77	−2.14	−3.91	−4.75	−5.76	NA	NA
PE range	—	—	—	—	—		

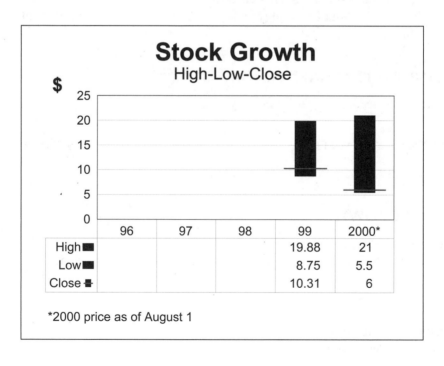

	96	97	98	99	2000*
High				19.88	21
Low				8.75	5.5
Close				10.31	6

*2000 price as of August 1

All American Semiconductor, Inc.

16115 Northwest 52nd Avenue
Miami, FL 33014
305-621-8282
Nasdaq: SEMI
www.allamerican.com

Chairman:
Paul Goldberg
President and CEO:
Bruce M. Goldberg

Earnings Growth	
Revenue Growth	★
Stock Growth	★ ★ ★
Consistency	★
Total	**5 Points**

The electronics revolution has spurred an insatiable demand for transistors, capacitors, inductors, and the whole realm of microcomponents. All American has cashed in on that boom as one of the nation's leading distributors of semiconductors and related electronics components.

The Miami distributor sells to manufacturers of a wide variety of high-tech products, including computers and computer-related products; networking, satellite, wireless, and other communications products; Internet infrastructure and appliances; consumer goods; robotics and industrial equipment; defense and aerospace equipment; and medical instrumentation. In all, the company has about 12,000 accounts.

All American carries more than 60,000 different products representing about 75 component manufacturers. Its leading product categories include:

- **Semiconductors.** Considered "active" components because they respond to or activate upon receipt of an electronic current, semiconductors include transistors, diodes, memory devices, and other integrated circuits.
- **Passive components.** Certain components are referred to as "passive," because they do not respond to electronic current but rather facilitate the completion of electronic functions. These products include capacitors, resistors, inductors, and electromechanical products, such as cable, switches, connectors, filters, and sockets.
- **Flat panel display components.** Used for computer monitors and high-definition TV, flat panel displays represent a rapidly growing market. All American distributes flat panel display back-light inverters, driver boards, and related components. It also provides technical support and product integration.
- **Memory modules.** The company designs and manufactures memory modules under the Aved Memory Products (AMP) label. Memory products represent the largest product sector of semiconductor revenues. Memory modules facilitate the incorporation of expanded memory in limited space. In addition to AMP, the company distributes memory modules from other manufacturers.

Foreign sales account for about 7 percent of the company's annual revenue.

Founded in 1964, All American has about 650 employees and a market capitalization of about $60 million.

EARNINGS PER SHARE PROGRESSION

Past 4 years: −24 percent

REVENUE GROWTH   ★

Past 4 years: 82 percent (16 percent per year)

STOCK GROWTH   ★ ★ ★

Past 3 years: 96 percent (25 percent per year)
Dollar growth: $10,000 over 3 years would have grown to about $20,000.

CONSISTENCY

Increased earnings per share: 2 of the past 4 years
Increased sales: 3 of the past 4 years

ALL AMERICAN SEMICONDUCTOR AT A GLANCE

Fiscal year ended: Dec. 31
Revenue and net income in $ millions

	1995	1996	1997	1998	1999	4-Year Growth Avg. Annual (%)	4-Year Growth Total (%)
Revenue ($)	180.8	237.8	265.6	250	329.5	16	82
Net income ($)	1.9	−8.2	3.25	0.83	1.8	NA	−5.5
Earnings/share ($)	0.60	−2.51	0.80	0.20	0.46	NA	−24
PE range	12–32	—	5–15	18–59	5–11		

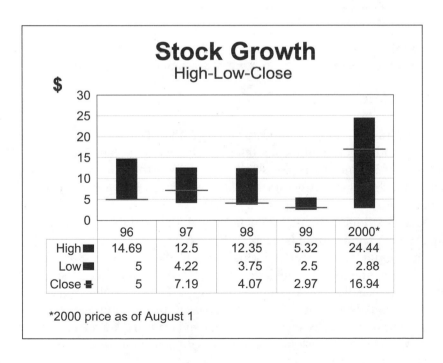

Stock Growth
High-Low-Close

	96	97	98	99	2000*
High	14.69	12.5	12.35	5.32	24.44
Low	5	4.22	3.75	2.5	2.88
Close	5	7.19	4.07	2.97	16.94

*2000 price as of August 1

Network Access Solutions

100 Carpenter Drive
Sterling, VA 20164
703-742-7700
Nasdaq: NASC
www.nas-corp.com

Chairman and CEO:
Jonathan P. Aust
President:
Nicholas Williams

Earnings Growth	
Revenue Growth	★ ★ ★ ★
Stock Growth	
Consistency	★
Total	**5 Points**

The standard 56K computer modem simply isn't fast enough to deliver the growing variety of multimedia Internet content at acceptable speeds. That's why Internet users are steadily switching to high-speed access, such as the digital subscriber lines (DSLs) offered by Network Access Solutions (NAS).

NAS is stringing high-speed data lines throughout the Northeast and Mid-Atlantic regions from Norfolk to Boston.

The Virginia-based operation's hallmark CopperNet service can make normal copper phone lines run like lightning. NAS handles the "last mile" between its backbone and customers with DSL circuits that run up to seven megabits per second—substantially faster than dial-up modems.

In addition to greatly increasing speed and efficiency, CopperNet can save NAS's corporate customers as much as 70 percent in voice/data communications expenses.

NAS offers its customers a full line of telecommunications products and services, including setup, network consulting, integration, management, and security services.

The company is well positioned for growth. Broadband needs worldwide have been soaring recently and are expected to double every two years. NAS's revenue has been doubling about every year, but the company is still posting losses as it pours money into efforts to land as many subscribers as possible. Subscriber recruitment is very important in this business, because the monthly income stream from subscribers can continue for many years.

NAS, which is focusing its efforts on the business sector of the broadband market, has been busy the past three years setting up a DSL high-speed network that should be accessible to nearly 100 percent of the businesses in the Bell Atlantic region.

Founded in 1995, Network Access Solutions went public with its initial stock offering in 1999. The company has about 400 employees and a market capitalization of about $500 million.

EARNINGS PER SHARE PROGRESSION

The company has posted only losses.

REVENUE GROWTH   ★ ★ ★ ★

Past 4 years: 801 percent (73 percent per year)

STOCK GROWTH

Past year: −31 percent
Dollar growth: $10,000 over 1 year would have declined to about $7,000.

CONSISTENCY   ★

Positive earnings progression: None
Increased sales: 3 of the past 4 years

NETWORK ACCESS SOLUTIONS AT A GLANCE

Fiscal year ended: Dec. 31
Revenue and net income in $ millions

	1995	1996	1997	1998	1999	Avg. Annual (%)	Total (%)
						4-Year Growth	
Revenue ($)	1.93	14.5	8.9	11.6	17.4	73	801
Net income ($)	—	0.09	0.04	−2.07	−40.3	NA	NA
Earnings/share ($)	—	—	—	−0.09	−0.99	NA	NA
PE range	—	—	—	—	—		

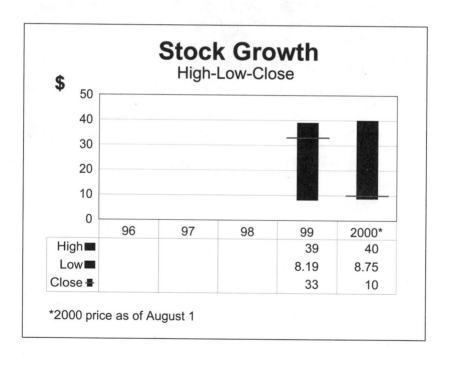

Stock Growth
High-Low-Close

$	96	97	98	99	2000*
High				39	40
Low				8.19	8.75
Close				33	10

*2000 price as of August 1

Sage, Inc.

2460 North First Street, #100
San Jose, CA 95131
408-383-5300
Nasdaq: SAGI
www.sageinc.com

President and CEO:
Chandrashekar M. Reddy

Earnings Growth	
Revenue Growth	★ ★ ★ ★
Stock Growth	
Consistency	
Total	**4 Points**

Sales of PCs and TVs are going flat. But that's good news for Sage, which makes digital display processors for the flat panels that are becoming increasingly popular with their crisper images on PC monitors and TVs.

Electronics manufacturers such as Sony, Fujitsu, Sanyo, and NEC use the company's display processors to digest the signals entering the display devices. Display signals that will produce an image's resolution and color must be recognized and processed to produce a high-quality image on a PC or TV screen.

Sage processors are also used in projection devices, Internet appliances, touchscreens, and digital cathode ray tubes. As their production costs continue to fall, flat panel displays are expected to become commonplace in offices, homes, and industrial settings in the form of PC desk monitors, flat-panel TVs, and various Internet appliances. Sage's chip design can handle analog, digital, and video signals, ensuring compatibility with the various manufacturers' systems.

It's no wonder flat panel screens have become so popular with consumers. Unlike the traditional cathode ray tube monitors, the flat screens offer high-quality, flicker-free images, lower heat emissions, and no radiation; require less electricity; and take up only a fraction of the space of old-style monitors.

Sage controls about 25 percent of the digital display processor market, a market that analysts predict will top $2 billion by 2004. Digital TV broadcasting, which is expected to replace traditional analog TV transmission in the next few years, holds enormous promise for Sage, as the number of digital TVs is expected to reach 10 million units in 2004, up from a half million units in 1998.

In 2000, Sage acquired as a subsidiary Faroudja Inc., a leading maker of video processing products, which gives Sage an expanded presence over the entire display market.

The company was founded in 1994 and went public with its initial stock offering in 1999. It has about 90 employees and a market capitalization of about $170 million.

EARNINGS PER SHARE PROGRESSION

Losses the past 4 years

REVENUE GROWTH   ★ ★ ★ ★

Past 4 years: 7,031 percent (427 percent per year)

STOCK GROWTH

Past 1 year: −45 percent since company went public in 1999
Dollar growth: $10,000 over 1 year would have dropped to about $5,500.

CONSISTENCY

Positive earnings progression: 1 of the past 4 years
Increased sales: 3 of the past 4 years

SAGE AT A GLANCE

Fiscal year ended: March 31
Revenue and net income in $ millions

	1995	1996	1997	1998	1999	4-Year Growth Avg. Annual (%)	Total (%)
Revenue ($)	0.251	1.76	1.49	7.13	17.9	427	7,031
Net income ($)	–0.384	–0.708	–2.78	–4.7	–4.6	NA	NA
Earnings/share ($)	–0.19	–0.31	–1.08	–1.99	–1.04	NA	NA
PE range	—	—	—	—	—		

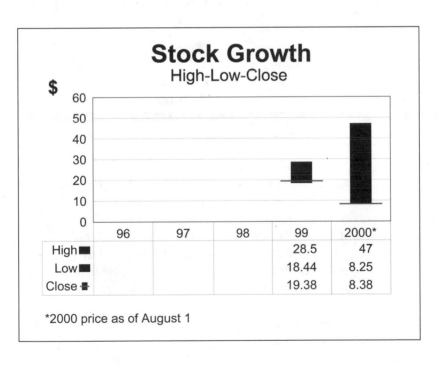

Stock Growth
High-Low-Close

	96	97	98	99	2000*
High ■				28.5	47
Low ■				18.44	8.25
Close ■				19.38	8.38

*2000 price as of August 1

94
Semitool, Inc.

655 West Reserve Drive
Kalispell, MT 59901
406-752-2107
Nasdaq: SMTL
www.semitool.com

Chairman, President, and CEO:
Raymon F. Thompson

Earnings Growth	★
Revenue Growth	
Stock Growth	★ ★ ★
Consistency	
Total	**4 Points**

The exploding demand for semiconductors has spurred strong growth in a range of industries tied to the semiconductor industry. Semitool has become a key player in the industry by designing and manufacturing specialized equipment that cleans and coats semiconductor wafers.

Its equipment, which prepares and cleans the surface of semiconductor wafers during the manufacturing process, utilizes a centrifugal spray technology, spraying wafers with a chemical solution in an enclosed chamber.

The spray helps enhance the chemical reactions on the wafer surface, which increases process reliability and shortens process cycle times. It also increases uniformity and reduces contamination of the microchips.

Semitool equipment is also used to manufacture materials and devices fabricated with similar processes, such as thin film heads used for disk drives, flat panel displays, multichip modules, ink jet print heads, compact disc masters, smart cards, and systems on a chip.

The company also operates a software control systems division that makes software to monitor and control the semiconductor fabrication process.

The Montana operation offers a range of products, including:

- **Batch processing tools.** These systems process multiple wafers in groups of 25 to 50.
- **Spectrum and Magnum.** These automated batch multimodule surface processing products cluster the solvent, acid, and spin rinser capabilities into a single automated unit.
- **Single substrate processing tools.** This equipment employs chemical spray and allows multiple chemicals to be used within a self-cleaning, enclosed process chamber.
- **Wafer carrier cleaning systems.** Semitool systems clean and dry the wafer carriers in a unique rinsing and drying process.

Semitool sells its equipment to manufacturers worldwide. International sales account for about 53 percent of the company's total revenue.

Founded in 1979, Semitool has about 1,000 employees and a market capitalization of about $400 million.

EARNINGS PER SHARE PROGRESSION   ★

No growth through 1999, but strong earnings in 2000.

REVENUE GROWTH

Past 4 years: −5 percent

STOCK GROWTH   ★ ★ ★

Past 3 years: 96 percent (25 percent per year)
Dollar growth: $10,000 over 5 years would have grown to about $20,000.

CONSISTENCY

Positive earnings progression: None of the past 4 years
Increased sales: 2 of the past 4 years

SEMITOOL AT A GLANCE

Fiscal year ended: Sept. 30
Revenue and net income in $ millions

	1995	1996	1997	1998	1999	4-Year Growth Avg. Annual (%)	Total (%)
Revenue ($)	128.3	174.2	193.9	180.5	122.5	NA	−5
Net income ($)	14.9	15.1	12.5	4.8	−6.7	NA	NA
Earnings/share ($)	0.57	0.55	0.45	0.17	−0.24	NA	NA
PE range	9–32	6–16	10–31	12–42	—		

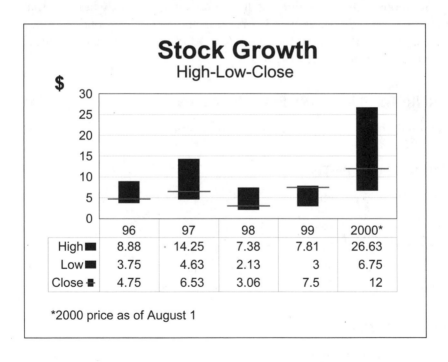

Stock Growth
High-Low-Close

$

	96	97	98	99	2000*
High	8.88	14.25	7.38	7.81	26.63
Low	3.75	4.63	2.13	3	6.75
Close	4.75	6.53	3.06	7.5	12

*2000 price as of August 1

95

ESS Technology, Inc.

48401 Fremont Boulevard
Fremont, CA 94538
510-492-1088
Nasdaq: ESST
www.esstech.com

Chairman:
Fred S. L. Chan
President and CEO:
Robert L. Blair

Earnings Growth	
Revenue Growth	★ ★ ★
Stock Growth	
Consistency	★
Total	**4 Points**

ESS Technology has positioned itself at the intersection of multimedia and the Internet. And these days, that's a busy intersection.

ESS established its reputation as a maker of digital audio chips for the consumer electronics and personal computer markets. But it's no longer content to be the world's largest supplier of digital audio and digital video chips. ESS is developing new systems, services, content, and concepts to revolutionize the Internet, which is rapidly moving from the desktop to the palmtop to the set-top TV box or even to smart kitchen appliances.

To capitalize on the explosive growth of the Internet, ESS created in 1999 a new subsidiary, ViAlta.com, which will introduce multimedia appliances, applications, and content for the Internet, including browsers, set-top boxes, and multifunction devices.

The company's other Internet-related initiatives include the introduction of its SuperLink broadband and analog high-speed modems. They are designed to increase the speed and capabilities of the next generation of Internet appliances.

For homes and businesses, ESS is introducing a new line of DSL (digital subscriber line) modems that will allow connections to the Internet 50 times faster than analog modems. ESS is also introducing a new computing and Internet platform for the Chinese market.

ESS's proprietary set-top box technology will allow the booming number of cable TV users in China to view around-the-clock news and information, stock quotes, video-on-demand entertainment, online MP3 music, and other content via an interactive, Internet-like browser. The system features an easy-to-use set-top box that connects to existing TV networks. ESS is also creating and marketing devices to allow it to become a player in the burgeoning global e-commerce field.

The company was founded in 1984 and went public with its initial stock offering in 1995. It has about 470 employees and a market capitalization of about $500 million.

EARNINGS PER SHARE PROGRESSION

Past 4 years: 11 percent (2 percent per year)

REVENUE GROWTH   ★ ★ ★

Past 4 years: 194 percent (32 percent per year)

STOCK GROWTH

Past 3 years: 8 percent (2 percent per year)
Dollar growth: $10,000 over 3 years would have grown to about $11,000.

CONSISTENCY   ★

Positive earnings progression: 2 of the past 4 years
Increased sales: 3 of the past 4 years

ESS TECHNOLOGY AT A GLANCE

Fiscal year ended: Dec. 31
Revenue and net income in $ millions

	1995	1996	1997	1998	1999	4-Year Growth Avg. Annual (%)	Total (%)
Revenue ($)	105.7	226.4	249.5	218.2	310.6	32	194
Net income ($)	29.9	21.6	−10.9	−28.0	40.1	8	34
Earnings/share ($)	0.79	0.52	−0.27	−0.68	0.88	2	11
PE range	16–50	17–58	—	—	5–27		

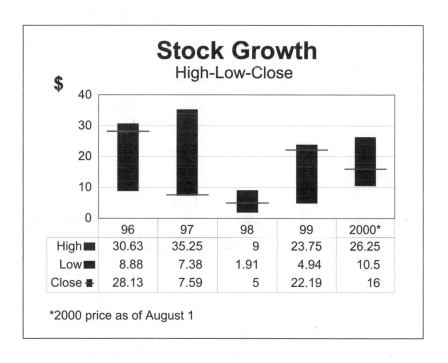

Stock Growth
High-Low-Close

	96	97	98	99	2000*
High■	30.63	35.25	9	23.75	26.25
Low■	8.88	7.38	1.91	4.94	10.5
Close■	28.13	7.59	5	22.19	16

*2000 price as of August 1

Ace*Comm Corp.

704 Quince Orchard Road
Gaithersburg, MD 20878
301-721-3000
Nasdaq: ACEC
www.acec.com

Chairman and CEO:
George T. Jimenez
President:
Gino O. Picasso

Earnings Growth	★
Revenue Growth	★
Stock Growth	
Consistency	★ ★
Total	**4 Points**

You make the call—then you pay the bill. Ace*Comm makes telecommunications billing systems that help telephone companies monitor phone usage in order to compute long-distance charges and analyze traffic patterns.

The Maryland-based operation makes hardware and software systems for both local and long-distance carriers, as well as wireless carriers and larger enterprises operating internal networks.

Ace*Comm makes a full line of related products, including:

- **Distributed Call Measurement System.** This hardware and software-based microprocessor-controlled system collects call record data from telephone switches and other network elements and electronically transmits the data to a central location. The data is processed for such purposes as billing, business analysis, traffic analysis, and fraud management.

- **N*Usage.** This software data collection system enables service providers who operate data networks and Internet Protocol (IP) networks to collect billing data and charge their customers on a usage-sensitive basis.
- **N*Vision.** N*Vision monitors network data in real time and provides information for subscriber and wholesale billing, carrier settlements, fraud detection, subscriber management, and network management.
- **AMAT Network Management System.** This surveillance, alarm, and traffic monitoring software collects and reports on alarms sent by data collection systems to ensure that no billing data is lost or duplicated.
- **NetPlus Voice and Data Network Management System.** This product line automates network operations and management functions for circuit-switched and IP-based networks.

Ace*Comm sells its products worldwide. It markets and installs some of its products through strategic alliances with other companies. For instance, it has been working with General Dynamics to set up phone systems at military sites worldwide. Ace has also been working with Samsung to create a billing data collection system for Korea Telecom.

Founded in 1983, Ace*Comm has about 180 employees and a market capitalization of about $60 million.

EARNINGS PER SHARE PROGRESSION ★

Past 4 years: 6 percent (but strong growth past 2 years)

REVENUE GROWTH ★

Past 4 years: 70 percent (14 percent per year)

STOCK GROWTH

Past 3 years: −73 percent
Dollar growth: $10,000 over 3 years would have dropped to about $3,000.

CONSISTENCY ★ ★

Increased earnings per share: 3 of the past 4 years
Increased sales: 3 of the past 4 years

ACE*COMM AT A GLANCE

Fiscal year ended: June 30
Revenue and net income in $ millions

	1996	1997	1998	1999	2000	4-Year Growth Avg. Annual (%)	Total (%)
Revenue ($)	19.9	33.7	22.5	29.6	33.8	14	70
Net income ($)	1.1	2.6	−9.2	0.62	2.2	19	100
Earnings/share ($)	0.18	0.32	−1.06	0.07	0.24	1	6
PE range	38–88	23–76	—	26–173	—		

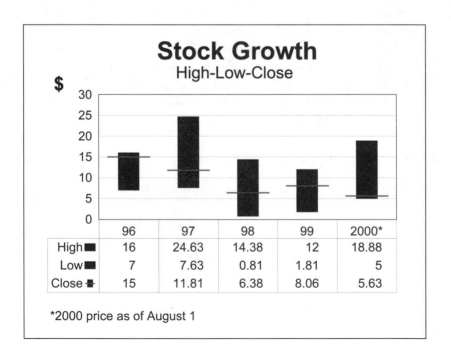

Stock Growth
High-Low-Close

	96	97	98	99	2000*
High ■	16	24.63	14.38	12	18.88
Low ■	7	7.63	0.81	1.81	5
Close ■	15	11.81	6.38	8.06	5.63

*2000 price as of August 1

CollaGenex Pharmaceuticals, Inc.

41 University Drive
Newtown, PA 18940
215-579-7388
Nasdaq: CGPI
www.collagenex.com

Chairman, President, and CEO:
Brian M. Gallagher, Ph.D.

Earnings Growth	
Revenue Growth	★ ★ ★ ★
Stock Growth	
Consistency	
Total	**4 Points**

CollaGenex Pharmaceuticals's flagship medication gets to the root of severe gum disease. The specialty pharmaceutical company recently launched its latest blockbuster, Periostat, a drug to treat adult periodontitis.

Gum disease is a widespread problem, according to the American Dental Association. Some 54 million Americans have adult periodontitis, and about 18 million periodontal procedures are performed in the United States.

CollaGenex's 135-member sales force has been educating the nation's periodontists and dentists who have a significant portion of their work in soft-tissue treatment on the benefits of Periostat. It works by suppressing certain enzymes that attack and degrade periodontal tissues that anchor teeth to gums. Periodontists and dentists have been writing a growing number of prescriptions for the drug.

In addition to selling Periostat, the CollaGenex sales force sells Vioxx, a painkiller developed by Merck & Company, and Denavir, a prescription drug for treating cold sores, manufactured by SmithKline Beecham, PLC. The marketing arrangement with the two drug giants, which recognizes CollaGenex's tight bond with its target audience, has provided Colla-Genex with additional revenue.

The unique arrangement with the larger companies also validates the much-smaller specialty pharmaceutical company's reputation as a leading marketer of dental medications. Typically, it's the smaller drug companies that produce the breakthrough drugs and then team up with larger companies to market their products.

Although primarily focused on building its dental pharmaceutical franchise, CollaGenex is exploring additional avenues for growth. It is collaborating with the National Cancer Institute in the development of a medication called Metastat for the possible treatment of Kaposi's sarcoma, a condition that often afflicts people with AIDS.

The company was founded in 1992 and went public with its initial stock offering in 1996. It has about 140 employees and a market capitalization of about $88 million.

EARNINGS PER SHARE PROGRESSION

Past 4 years: No earnings

REVENUE GROWTH   ★ ★ ★ ★

Past 3 years: 3,902 percent

STOCK GROWTH

Past 3 years: −22 percent
Dollar growth: $10,000 over 3 years would have declined to about $8,000.

CONSISTENCY

Positive earnings progression: 1 of the past 4 years
Increased sales: 3 of the past 4 years

COLLAGENEX PHARMACEUTICALS AT A GLANCE

Fiscal year ended: Dec. 31
Revenue and net income in $ millions

	1995	1996	1997	1998	1999	4-Year Growth Avg. Annual (%)	Total (%)
Revenue ($)	0.0	0.400	0.334	3.46	16.1	NA	3,902
Net income ($)	−5.3	−5.9	−8.6	−11.6	−14.6	NA	NA
Earnings/share ($)	−1.10	−0.90	−1.04	−1.35	−1.82	NA	NA
PE range	—	—	—	—	—		

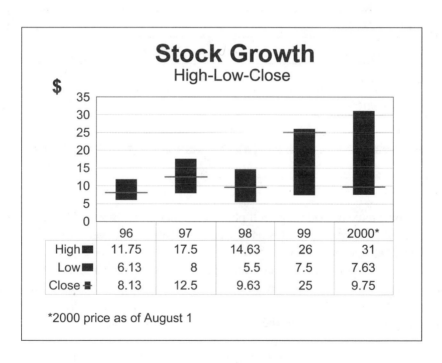

Stock Growth
High-Low-Close

	96	97	98	99	2000*
High	11.75	17.5	14.63	26	31
Low	6.13	8	5.5	7.5	7.63
Close	8.13	12.5	9.63	25	9.75

*2000 price as of August 1

98
Xicor, Inc.

1511 Buckeye Drive
Milpitas, CA 95035
408-432-8888
Nasdaq: XICO
www.xicor.com

Chairman and CEO:
Raphael Klein
President:
Bruce Gray

Earnings Growth	★
Revenue Growth	
Stock Growth	★ ★
Consistency	
Total	**3 Points**

Xicor's chips have helped make cell phones smaller and laptop PC batteries more reliable. They have also been key components in the ever-expanding fiber-optic/Internet backbone.

Xicor's chips or integrated circuits can also be found in cars, industrial controls, and consumer electronics. Designers of leading-edge electronics products are fond of Xicor's chips, because they can be reprogrammed without being removed from the electronic system in which they are being used.

Another advantage is that they operate at low power levels and come in ultra-small packages. Xicor's chips can also retain information even when a system is turned off or when the power is inadvertently lost. Because Xicor's chips are reprogrammable and can retain information if and when the power goes out, customers such as consumer electronics or telecommunication products manufacturers can simplify their production processes and get their wares to market much more quickly.

To allow the company to save on overhead costs and to focus on chip design, Xicor closed its silicon wafer fabrication plant in Northern California and outsourced its manufacturing to chip manufacturers in Germany and Japan. Xicor markets its products from its California headquarters and from its U.S. regional and foreign sales offices.

The California operation's international sales have been steadily increasing. In 1999, international sales constituted 56 percent of the company's revenues, compared with 46 percent in 1998 and 44 percent in 1997. To fuel growth in the domestic and international markets, the company will target high-growth markets like fiber optics and manufacturers that embed microcontrollers into their electronic products. Xicor's chips allow microcontroller devices to mark times and dates.

Xicor has about 500 employees and a market capitalization of about $140 million.

EARNINGS PER SHARE PROGRESSION   ★

Mixed returns the past 4 years, with strong growth in the first half of 2000.

REVENUE GROWTH

Past 4 years: 1 percent

STOCK GROWTH

Past 3 years: 50 percent (15 percent per year)
Dollar growth: $10,000 over 3 years would have grown to $15,000.

CONSISTENCY

Positive earnings progression: 2 of the past 4 years
Increased sales: 2 of the past 4 years

XICOR AT A GLANCE

Fiscal year ended: Dec. 31
Revenue and net income in $ millions

	1995	1996	1997	1998	1999	4-Year Growth Avg. Annual (%)	Total (%)
Revenue ($)	113.5	123.5	122.4	106.1	114.9	NA	1
Net income ($)	10.0	13.8	−2.3	−29.5	−26.9	NA	NA
Earnings/share ($)	0.53	0.70	−0.13	−1.53	−1.32	NA	NA
PE range	3–17	7–20	—	—	—		

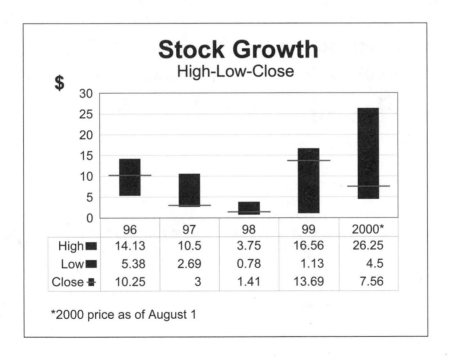

Stock Growth
High-Low-Close

	96	97	98	99	2000*
High	14.13	10.5	3.75	16.56	26.25
Low	5.38	2.69	0.78	1.13	4.5
Close	10.25	3	1.41	13.69	7.56

*2000 price as of August 1

99

Wabash National Corp.

1000 Sagamore Parkway South
Lafayette, IN 47905
765-771-5300
NYSE: WNC
www.wabashnational.com

Chairman, President, and CEO:
Jerry Ehrlich

Earnings Growth	
Revenue Growth	★
Stock Growth	
Consistency	★ ★
Total	**3 Points**

Wabash National helps the world to keep on truckin'. Although the company name suggests it's a bank or an insurance company, Wabash National is the world's largest manufacturer of truck trailers.

Motorists see Wabash's truck trailers everywhere on the road, operating under the names of some of its leading customers—Schneider, FedEx, Heartland Express, and Safeway. The company's biggest seller is its Dura-Plate trailer, whose sidewalls consist of high-strength steel and a vinyl core. The company produces more than 70,000 customized and standard truck trailers and railcars a year.

The company also makes refrigerated truck trailers and what it calls its RoadRailer, a trailer that doubles as a railroad car. The RoadRailer bi-modal system of transportation allows shippers to operate more efficiently than using alternate systems, such as piggyback or stack railcars that require railroad terminal operators to transfer truck trailers to railcars. Road-Railer is a global system with operations on four continents. The newest one is in South America between São Paulo, Brazil, and Buenos Aires, Argentina.

Wabash National also offers replacement parts and accessories and provides maintenance service for both its own and competitors' trailers and related equipment. It produces and sells aftermarket products through its parts division and its wholly owned subsidiary Fruehauf Trailer Services, which also distributes new and used trailers.

The company has a unique industrial culture that emphasizes design and new product development teams. The team-based approach has allowed the company to substantially boost productivity. Productivity is further enhanced through extensive employee training. Every employee who's been on the job at least a year is given salary incentives to take courses in business economics, statistical process control, and just-in-time manufacturing.

The company was founded in 1985 and went public with its initial stock offering in 1991. It has about 5,600 employees and a market capitalization of about $280 million.

EARNINGS PER SHARE PROGRESSION

Past 4 years: 19 percent (3 percent per year)

REVENUE GROWTH ★

Past 4 years: 97 percent (18 percent per year)

STOCK GROWTH

Past 3 years: −54 percent
Dollar growth: $10,000 over 3 years would have declined to about $5,000.

CONSISTENCY ★ ★

Increased earnings per share: 3 of the past 4 years
Increased sales: 3 of the past 4 years

WABASH NATIONAL AT A GLANCE

Fiscal year ended: Dec. 31
Revenue and net income in $ millions

	1995	1996	1997	1998	1999	4-Year Growth Avg. Annual (%)	4-Year Growth Total (%)
Revenue ($)	0.734	0.631	0.846	1.29	1.45	18	97
Net income ($)	0.025	3.64	15.2	23.3	38.8	NA	155,100
Earnings/share ($)	1.34	0.19	0.74	0.99	1.59	3	19
PE range	14–30	73–129	21–48	10–32	6–14		

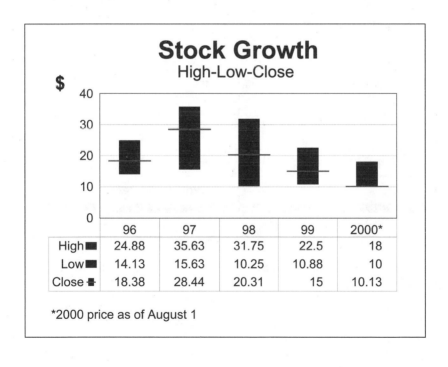

Stock Growth
High-Low-Close

	96	97	98	99	2000*
High ■	24.88	35.63	31.75	22.5	18
Low ■	14.13	15.63	10.25	10.88	10
Close ■	18.38	28.44	20.31	15	10.13

*2000 price as of August 1

Sevenson Environmental Services, Inc.

S Sevenson

2749 Lockport Road
Niagara Falls, NY 14035
716-284-0431
Nasdaq: SEVN
www.sevenson.com

President and CEO:
Michael A. Elia

Earnings Growth	★
Revenue Growth	
Stock Growth	
Consistency	★
Total	**2 Points**

Sevenson Environmental Services put itself on the map with the cleanup of the notorious Love Canal.

The uncompleted canal became a nationally known chemical waste disposal site that contaminated an entire neighborhood in Niagara Falls, New York, in the late 1970s. In addition to Love Canal, Sevenson has tackled cleanup or what's known as remediation at more than 800 other contaminated sites, including 79 Environmental Protection Agency Superfund sites, the worst of the worst. The combined value of all the projects handled by Sevenson comes to about $1 billion.

It's a dirty job, but Sevenson knows how to handle it. The company was founded in 1917 as a general construction contractor but transitioned into remediation work when it became the principal contractor at Love Canal. Remediation entails the containment, excavation, and removal of contaminated sites. The company uses a variety of specialized treatment techniques.

Sevenson performs its remediation work for major industrial companies and for state and federal governments. About 55 percent of its work is done for the private sector, and about 45 percent is done in the public sector. Although many governmental budgets for environmental programs have been reduced, an increasing percentage of those budgets have been dedicated to cleanup work, which remains a priority for the public and for policymakers.

About a quarter of the company's revenues are generated by performing large-scale cleanups of contaminated sediments in rivers, basins, and lagoons. It's a growing business, and the trend favors companies such as Sevenson, which have the technical expertise for the projects.

Other services provided by the company include the decontamination, demolition, and closing of industrial sites and the removal of contaminated materials.

Founded in 1969, Sevenson has about 230 employees and a market capitalization of about $104 million.

EARNINGS PER SHARE PROGRESSION ★

Past 4 years: 1 percent (but strong growth past 2 years)

REVENUE GROWTH

Past 4 years: 24 percent (6 percent per year)

STOCK GROWTH

Past 3 years: −9 percent
Dollar growth: $10,000 over 3 years would have declined to about $9,000.

CONSISTENCY ★

Increased earnings per share: 2 consecutive years
Increased sales: 2 consecutive years

SEVENSON ENVIRONMENTAL SERVICES AT A GLANCE

Fiscal year ended: Dec. 31
Revenue and net income in $ millions

	1995	1996	1997	1998	1999	4-Year Growth Avg. Annual (%)	4-Year Growth Total (%)
Revenue ($)	102.5	85.7	81.9	84.7	127.2	6	24
Net income ($)	10.1	6.3	4.7	6.5	9.7	NA	−4
Earnings/share ($)	1.00	0.62	0.47	0.66	1.02	1	1
PE range	9–13	15–20	20–43	11–19	7–11		

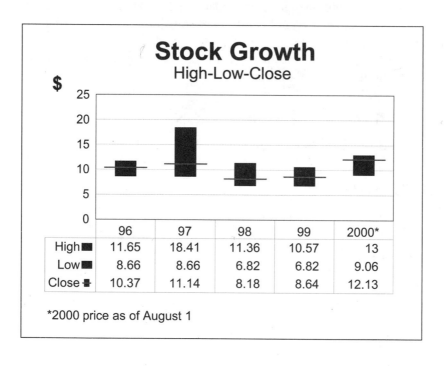

Stock Growth
High-Low-Close

	96	97	98	99	2000*
High■	11.65	18.41	11.36	10.57	13
Low■	8.66	8.66	6.82	6.82	9.06
Close■	10.37	11.14	8.18	8.64	12.13

*2000 price as of August 1

The 100 Best Stocks Under $25
by State/Country

State	Ranking
ARIZONA	
Amtech Systems, Inc.	87
International FiberCom	35
Radyne ComStream, Inc.	30
ARKANSAS	
White Electronic Designs Corp.	79
CALIFORNIA	
Abaxis, Inc.	23
AltiGen Communications	90
Alpha Technologies Group, Inc.	80
Avant! Corp.	46
Bell Microproducts, Inc.	68
California Micro Devices Corp.	70
Catellus Development Corp.	67
Channell Commercial Corp.	88
Digital Video Systems, Inc.	73
Drexler Technology Corp.	61
ESS Technology, Inc.	95
Galileo Technology Ltd.	31
Hello Direct, Inc.	69
InnerDyne, Inc.	13
InSilicon Corp.	82
Mitek Systems, Inc.	85
Monterey Pasta Company	55
North American Scientific, Inc.	1
PFF Bancorp, Inc.	78
Rubio's Restaurants, Inc.	65
Sage, Inc.	93
Somera Communications	47
Southwest Water Company	57
Standard Pacific Corp.	44
Summa Industries	26
Xicor, Inc.	98

State	Ranking
COLORADO	
Mail-Well, Inc.	75
SpectraLink Corp.	22
CONNECTICUT	
International Home Foods, Inc.	76
DELAWARE	
AstroPower, Inc.	6
FLORIDA	
All American Semiconductor, Inc.	91
AmeriPath, Inc.	43
Concord Camera Corp.	5
Exactech, Inc.	8
Extended Stay America	50
Global Imaging Systems, Inc.	38
Sound Advice, Inc.	74
GEORGIA	
EarthLink, Inc.	64
InterCept Group, Inc., The	33
HAWAII	
Cheap Tickets, Inc.	63
ILLINOIS	
Akorn, Inc.	7
INDIANA	
Wabash National Corp.	99
KENTUCKY	
Citizens Financial Corp.	41
MARYLAND	
Ace*Comm Corp.	96
CompuDyne Corp.	15
Integral Systems, Inc.	11

State	Ranking
MASSACHUSETTS	
BTU International Inc.	89
Candela Corp.	14
ePresence, Inc.	17
Moldflow Corp.	59
NetScout Systems, Inc.	48
NETsilicon, Inc.	45
MICHIGAN	
Manatron, Inc.	49
MINNESOTA	
Computer Network Technology	83
PW Eagle, Inc.	21
MISSOURI	
LaserVision Centers, Inc.	39
MONTANA	
Semitool, Inc.	94
NEBRASKA	
Ameritrade Holding Corp.	36
NEW JERSEY	
Dataram Corp.	52
Novidigm, Inc.	25
Opinion Research Corp.	27
NEW YORK	
Actrade International, Ltd.	9
Comtech Telecommunications Corp.	19
Del Global Technologies Corp.	66
Hauppauge Digital, Inc.	28
Interliant, Inc.	81
Richton International Corp.	4
Sevenson Environmental Services, Inc.	100
Take-Two Interactive Software, Inc.	37
Taro Pharmaceuticals Industries Ltd.	53

State	Ranking
NEW YORK, continued	
TD Waterhouse Group, Inc.	34
NORTH CAROLINA	
Embrex, Inc.	12
Kewanee Scientific Corp.	84
Sonic Automotive, Inc.	40
OHIO	
Abercrombie & Fitch Co.	24
PENNSYLVANIA	
ANSYS Inc.	72
CollaGenex Pharmaceuticals, Inc.	97
Kensey Nash Corp.	29
Spectrum Control, Inc.	60
STV Group, Inc.	56
SOUTH DAKOTA	
Daktronics, Inc.	16
TEXAS	
AmeriCredit Corp.	42
Atrion Corp.	62
Tidel Technologies, Inc.	10
TENNESSEE	
AmSurg Corp.	51
UTAH	
Gentner Communications	20
VIRGINIA	
Network Access Solutions	92
WISCONSIN	
Gehl Company	86
WASHINGTON	
Advanced Digital Information Corp.	2

Country	Ranking
CANADA	
Genesis Microchip, Inc.	58
V3 Semiconductor, Inc.	18
HONG KONG	
Chinadotcom Corp.	77
ISRAEL	
BackWeb Technologies Ltd.	54
Camtek, Ltd.	71
Optibase, Ltd.	3
JAPAN	
Trend Micro, Inc.	32

The 100 Best Stocks Under $25 by Industry Group

Industry	Ranking

AUTOMOTIVE

Sonic Automotive, Inc.	40
Wabash National Corp.	99

BUSINESS SERVICES

Actrade International, Ltd.	9
Opinion Research Corp.	27
STV Group, Inc.	56

COMMUNICATIONS

Ace*Comm Corp.	96
AltiGen Communications	90
Channell Commercial Corp.	88
Comtech Telecommunications Corp.	19
Gentner Communications	20
Hello Direct, Inc.	69
International FiberCom	35
Radyne ComStream, Inc.	30
Somera Communications	47
SpectraLink Corp.	22
Spectrum Control, Inc.	60

COMPUTER

Internet

Cheap Tickets, Inc.	63
Chinadotcom Corp.	77
EarthLink, Inc.	64
ePresence, Inc.	17
Interliant, Inc.	81
Network Access Solutions	92
Optibase, Ltd.	3

Networking

Computer Network Technology	83
Global Imaging Systems, Inc.	38

Industry	Ranking

COMPUTER, *Networking, continued*

NetScout Systems, Inc.	48
InterCept Group, Inc., The	33
Trend Micro, Inc.	32

Products

Advanced Digital Information Corp.	2
Dataram Corp.	52
Drexler Technology Corp.	61
Hauppauge Digital, Inc.	28
Sage, Inc.	93

Semiconductors

Amtech Systems, Inc.	87
California Micro Devices Corp.	70
Camtek, Ltd.	71
ESS Technology, Inc.	95
Galileo Technology Ltd.	31
Genesis Microchip, Inc.	58
NETsilicon, Inc.	45
Semitool, Inc.	94
V3 Semiconductor, Inc.	18
White Electronic Designs Corp.	79
Xicor, Inc.	98

Software

ANSYS, Inc.	72
Avant! Corp.	46
BackWeb Technologies Ltd.	54
InSilicon Corp.	82
Integral Systems, Inc.	11
Manatron, Inc.	49
Mitek Systems, Inc.	85
Moldflow Corp.	59
Novadigm, Inc.	25
Take-Two Interactive Software, Inc.	37

DISTRIBUTORS

All American Semiconductor, Inc.	91
Bell Microproducts, Inc.	68
Richton International Corp.	4

Industry	Ranking
ELECTRONICS	
Alpha Technologies Group, Inc.	80
Digital Video Systems, Inc.	73
ENVIRONMENTAL	
Sevenson Environmental Services, Inc.	100
ENERGY	
AstroPower, Inc.	6
FINANCIAL	
AmeriCredit Corp.	42
Ameritrade Holding Corp.	36
PFF Bancorp, Inc.	78
TD Waterhouse Group, Inc.	34
FOOD AND BEVERAGE PRODUCTION	
International Home Foods, Inc.	76
Monterey Pasta Company	55
INSURANCE	
Citizens Financial Corp.	41
LODGING	
Extended Stay America	50
MANUFACTURING	
BTU International Inc.	89
CompuDyne Corp.	15
Concord Camera Corp.	5
Daktronics, Inc.	16
Gehl Company	86
Kewaunee Scientific Corp.	84
Mail-Well, Inc.	75
PW Eagle, Inc.	21
Summa Industries	26
Tidel Technologies, Inc.	10

Industry	Ranking

MEDICAL PRODUCTS

Abaxis, Inc.	23
Atrion Corp.	62
Candela Corp.	14
Del Global Technologies Corp.	66
Embrex, Inc.	12
Exactech, Inc.	8
InnerDyne, Inc.	13
Kensey Nash Corp.	29
North American Scientific, Inc.	1

MEDICAL SERVICES

AmeriPath, Inc.	43
AmSurg Corp.	51
LaserVision Centers, Inc.	39

PHARMACEUTICALS

Akorn, Inc.	7
CollaGenex Pharmaceuticals, Inc.	97
Taro Pharmaceutical Industries Ltd.	53

REAL ESTATE DEVELOPMENT

Catellus Development Corp.	67
Standard Pacific Corp.	44

RESTAURANTS

Rubio's Restaurants, Inc.	65

RETAIL

Abercrombie & Fitch Co.	24
Sound Advice, Inc.	74

UTILITIES

Southwest Water Company	57

Index

A

Abaxis, Inc., 67–69
Abercrombie & Fitch Co., 70–72
Access equipment, 140
Accessory products (thermal
  management), 239
Accutrade, 106, 107
Ace*Comm Corp., 286–88
Active cooling components, 239
Actrade International, Ltd., 25–27
Adelphia, 103
Advanced Clearing, 107
Advanced Digital Information Corp., 4–6
Advertising panels, 47
Age-Related Macular Degeneration
  (ARMD), 19
Agricultural implements, 256, 257
Aharoni, Amir, 7
Aharoni, Amos, 25
AIDS treatment, 290
Airteq, 44
AirTouch, 139
Akorn, Inc., 19–21
Alba, Manuel, 91
Albertson's, 163
All American Semiconductor, Inc., 271–73
Allied Signal, 235
Alltel Communications, 139
Alpha Technologies Group, Inc., 238–40
Alternative energy, 16–17
Alternative Reality Technologies, 110
AltiGen Communications, 268–70
AMAT Network Management System, 287
Amazon.com, 64, 119
Ambulatory surgery industry, 151–52. *See
  also* Surgical procedures
AMD, 244
America's Travel Store, 187
AmeriCredit Corp., 124–26
AmeriPath, Inc., 127–29
Ameritrade Holding Corp., 106–8
AmeriVest, 107
Ames Department Stores, 109
Amit, Rafi, 211
AMP's Signal Conditioning Products, 178
AmSurg Corp., 151–53

Amtech Systems, Inc., 259–61
Analog semiconductors, 208
Analytical modeling, 80
Angio-Seal, 85–86
Animal health products, 67
ANSYS Inc., 214–16
AOL, 191
Apex, 14
Apparel, 70–71
Apple, 11, 172
Application Flow Management, 143
Application hosting, 242
Application Service Provider, 241
Architectural engineering, 167
Arthur Andersen, 64
Asset recovery services, 140
AstroPower, Inc., 16–18
Atmoscan, 259
ATMs, 28, 97
Atrion Corp., 184–86
AT&T, 64, 139
AT&T Broadband, 103
Audio Perfect, 58
Audio/video-conferencing equipment,
  58–59, 206
Aupperle, Kenneth R., 82
AuRA hip, 23
Aust, Jonathan P., 274
Austin, Charles E., 34
Austin Powers video game, 109, 110
Auto dealerships, 118–19
AutoFile Update Manager, 161
Automated Document Recognition, 253
Automated Optical Inspection, 211
Automated tape library, 5
Automatic teller machines, 28, 97
Automation systems, 260
Automobile financing, 118, 124
AutoNation, 148
Avant! Corp., 136–38
Aved Memory Products, 272

B

BackWeb Technologies Ltd., 160–62
Baillie, A. C., 100
Bang & Olufsen, 220

Bank of America, 94
Banking, 97, 101, 232–33
Banyan Worldwide, 49
Barkat, Eli, 160
Barnes & Noble, 64
Barnett, Allen M., 16
Barrington, Michael R., 124
Bass Hunter 64, 110
Batch processing tools, 281
Battat, Emile A., 184
Battle of Britain, 110
Bay Networks/NETGEAR, 91
Bell, W. Donald, 202
Bell companies, 139
Bell Microproducts, Inc., 202–4
Benjamin, Floyd, 19
Bertan High Voltage, 197
Beshouri, Peter, 220
Best Buy, 109
Betty, C. Garry, 190
Beyond.com, 73
Bio-absorbable polymers, 86
Biomet, 23
Biotechnology company, 1
Black Bass Lure Fishing, 110
Blair, Robert L., 283
Blockbuster Entertainment, 148
Blood analysis systems, 67
Bloomberg financial news service, 8
BMC, 242
Bowmar Instrument Corp., 235
BP Amoco, 56
Brachytherapy, 1–2
Branding, 80
Brannon, Robert A., 148
Brant, Ryan, 109
Brewer, Charles, 190
British Telecom, 73, 95
Broadband communications network, 103–4
Broadband equipment, 56, 89, 263, 275, 283
Broadband Studios, 110
Broadview Injection Molding, 76
Brokerages, online, 100–101, 106–7
Broker life insurance, 122
BTU International Inc., 265–67
Builders, 130–31
Bumblebee tuna, 226
Bursaplex, 35
Butler, Lawrence, 238

C

California Micro Devices Corp., 208–10
Calnetics, 76

Cameras, 13–14
Camtek, Ltd., 211–13
Cancer treatments, 1–2, 290
Candela Corp., 40–42
Cantwell, Wayne C., 244
Canyon Mold, 76
Carabetta, Michael R., 73
Car dealerships, 118–19
Cardiac procedures, 85–86, 184
Cashman, James E. III, 214
Cataract surgery, 116
Catellus Development Corp., 199–201
CBE Technologies, 11
CBS, 50
CD-ROMs, creation of, 8
Cellular phones, 17
Century Supply, 10–11
CFK/Skintonic, 41
Chamberlain, Steven R., 31
Chan, Fred S. L., 283
Chang, Steve, 94
Channell, William Jr., 262
Channell, William Sr., 262
Channell Commercial Corp., 262–64
Character recognition products, 253–54
Cheap Tickets, Inc., 187–89
Chef Boyardee, 226
Chemical waste disposal, 298
Ch'ien, Raymond K. F., 229
China, Internet and, 284
Chinadotcom Corp., 229–31
Cigarran, Thomas G., 151
Circuit boards, 265, 269
Cisco Systems, 52, 64, 91, 94, 142–43,
    209, 235, 244
CiscoWorks 2000 network management
    console, 143
Citizens Financial Corp., 121–23
Citizens Security Life Insurance, 121
Civil engineering, 167
Client/server enterprise software, 97, 98
Clothing store chains, 70–72
Coaxial cable, 103
Coca-Cola, 94
CollaGenex Pharmaceuticals, Inc., 289–91
Collins, John W., 97
Co-located hosting, 242
Communications equipment, 139
Communications products, 271
    broadband, 56, 89, 103–4, 263, 275,
        283
    filtering equipment, 178
    solar energy and, 17

systems, satellite-based, 55–56, 88–89
Compaq, 11, 52, 94
Compaq/Digital, 154
CompuDyne Corp., 43–45
Computer(s), 271
    computer-aided design (CAD), 215
    computer-aided engineering (CAE), 214
    data storage, 4–5
    memory circuit boards, 154–55
    peripherals, 202
    platforms, 202
    television and, 82–83
Computer Network Technology, 247–49
Comtech Telecommunications Corp., 55–57
Concord Camera Corp., 13–15
Conferencing systems, 58–59
Connectivity products, 5
Construction equipment, 256–57
Construction projects, 130–31, 166–67
Consumer electronics, 292
Contamination cleanup, 298–99
Converging, 268
Conveyor components, 77
Copiers, 112, 113
Copper connectivity products, 263
CopperNet, 274
Cordless XLT, 206
Corechange, 50
Corporate image, 80
Corrections industry, 43–44
CorrLogic, 44
Cosmetic procedures, 40–41
Counterfeiting, 181
Court administration software, 145
Cox Communications, 103
Crayola, 14
Crossland Economy Studios, 149
Customer information, research/analysis, 79–80
Cutrer, L. Michael, 1

D

DaimlerChrysler, 49, 175
Daktronics, Inc., 46–48
Data communications, 91, 98
Data modeling, 80
Dataram Corp., 154–56
Data storage area network, 247
Data transmission, 88
Dedicated hosting, 242

Del Global Technologies Corp., 196–98
Dell Computer, 5, 154, 172, 242
Denavir, 289
Dental products, 289
Detention hardware/security systems, 43–44
Diffusion furnaces, 254
Digital audio/video chips, 283
Digital cameras, 13–14
Digital devices, 244
Digital subscriber line (DSL), 274, 284
Digital transmission, 88
Digital TV, 278
Digital Video Systems, Inc., 217–19
Digital video technologies, 7–8, 172, 217–18
DirecTV, 56
Disk storage, 4–5
Disposable cameras, 13–14
Distributed Call Measurement System, 286
D-Link, 91
DOCTUS, 254
Document imaging software, 113
Drexler Technology Corp., 181–83
Drexler, Jerome, 181
Drugs, 157–58, 289
DSL, 284
Duggan, Brian, 88
Duke Nukem video games, 110
Dulude, Marc J. L., 175
DuPont, 175
Dura-Plate trailer, 295
DVDs, 8, 172, 217
Dynamic Cooling Device, 41
DynaRad, 196

E

EarthLink, Inc., 190–92
e-commerce, 28
ECO Resources, 169, 170
eDoctor Global Network, 95
Ehrlich, Jerry, 295
Eibeler, Paul, 109
Eisenberg, Ran, 7
Electro-mechanical devices, 239
Electronic Buyers News, 203
Electronic commerce, 73–74
Electronic design automation (EDA), 136
Electronic Designs, 235
Electronic equipment, filtering and, 178
Electronic funds transfer, 97–98

Electronic information display systems, 46–47
Electronic presentation systems, 113
Electronics designers, 136
Electronics Environment, 221
Elia, Michael A., 298
e-mail, 224
Embedded systems, 133–34
Embrex, Inc., 34–36
Energy, solar, 16–17
Enhanced Security Module, 161
Entertainment software, 110
Envelopes, 223–24
Environmental Protection Agency, 298
Epoch 2000, 32
ePresence, Inc., 49–51
Ericcson, 49
ESS Technology, Inc., 283–85
E-TAD, 26
Ethernet switches, 91
e-wrap technology, 74
Exactech, Inc., 22–24
Excimer lasers, 115–16
Executive headsets, 206
Exports, 26
Extended Stay America, 148–50
Extruded heat sinks, 239
Eye care, 19–20
Eye laser surgery, 115–16

F

Falcon Belting, 76
Faroudja Inc., 278
Fassler, Leonard, 241
Fax machines, 112, 113
Federal Communications Commission, 59
FedEx, 295
Feld, Bradley, 241
Ferry, William P., 49
Fiber optics, 17, 262, 263, 293
Filtering equipment, 178–79, 209
Financial services, 100–101
Financing
    auto, 118, 124
    mortgage, 125, 232
Firestone, Dan, 139
FirstAmerica Automotive, 119
First Omaha Securities, 106
Fisher, A., 172
Fitting, Robert C., 88
Fitzgerald, Albion, 73
Flat panel monitors, 173, 236, 272, 277

Flood, Frances M., 58
Food companies, 163–64, 193–95, 226–27
Fountains, decorative, 11
Frontier Software, 143
Fruehauf Trailer Services, 296
Fuji, 175
Fujitsu, 5, 172, 277
Furnaces, 265
Furniture, wood and metal, 250–51

G

Galeotos, Sam, 187
Galileo Technology Ltd., 91–93
Gallagher, Brian M., 289
Garnier, Anton C., 169
Gartner Group, 94, 241
GearHead Entertainment, 110
Gehl, William D., 256
Gehl Company, 256–58
Gendex-Del, 196
General Dynamics, 287
General Motors, 64
Generic drugs, 157–58
Genesis Microchip, Inc., 172–74
GentleLASE system, 41
GentlePeel, 41
Gentner box, 59
Gentner Communications, 58–60
Georgia-Pacific, 224
Global Imaging Systems, Inc., 112–14
Glover, E. Alexander, 205
Goldberg, Bruce M., 271
Goldberg, Paul, 271
Gorfung, Mordechai, 7
Gough, Thomas L., 31
Grand Theft Auto, 110
Graphics, 172
Gray, Bruce, 292
Green card, 181
Greenlight.com, 119
Groupware hosting, 242
Gruverman, Irwin J., 1
GST Industries, 76
GTE, 64, 94, 139
Guidant, 209
Gulden's mustard, 226

H

Haddock, Richard M., 181
Hair removal products/services, 40
Halkey-Roberts, 184
Haratunian, Michael, 166

Hard disk drives, 202–3
Hardware, 4–5, 202–3, 247
   digital video, 7–8
   document imaging, 113
   for embedded systems, 134
   Internet server, 236
   maintenance, 11
   telecommunications billing, 286
Hardware platforms, 236
Hartley, Michael J., 187
Hathaway, Lawrence K., 226
Hauppauge Digital, Inc., 82–84
Health insurance, 122
Heartland Express, 295
Heart procedures, 85–86
Hello Direct, Inc., 205–7
Hewitt, R. Lance, 163
Hewlett-Packard, 11, 42, 91, 94, 154, 175,
   244
High speed access, to Internet, 274–75
Hip replacements, 22
Hitachi, 172
Holland, Bruce, 64
Hollywood Pinball, 110
Homebuilders, 130–31
Home entertainment, 220–21
Honda, 182
Hongkong.com, 229
Horner's Syndrome, 20
Hospital products, 20
Hosting, 242
Hotel industry, 148–49
Hribar, Herb, 241
Hsu, Gerald C., 136
Hu, Gilbert, 268
Hudson, Thomas, 247
Hughes Network Systems, 56
Huizenga, H. Wayne, 148
Hunter, 10
Hyundai, 53, 260
Hyundai Electronics, 218

I

IBM, 5, 11, 52, 154, 172, 203, 242
Image processing, 172–73
Imaging systems, medical, 196–97
Impact VCB boards, 83
Import/export, 26
Industrial process engineering services,
   167
Information panels, 46–47
InformationWeek, 74

InnerDyne, Inc., 37–39
Inovoject system, 34–35
inSilicon Corp., 244–46
Insular Inc., 59
Insurance
   dental, 121–22
   fire and casualty, 121
   health, 122
   life, 121–22
   vehicle, 118
Integral Systems, Inc., 31–33
Integrated circuits, 136, 292
Intel, 209, 260, 244
Intelligent Character Recognition, 253
InterCept Group, Inc., The, 97–99
Interliant, Inc., 241–43
International Data Corp., 4
International FiberCom, 103–5
International Home Foods, Inc., 226–28
International Soccer, 110
Internet
   banking, 97, 98
   digital video, 7–8
   high speed access, 274–75
   hookups, 262
   infrastructure, 271
   -related initiatives, 283
   security, 94–95
   server hardware, 236
   service providers, 103, 190–91
   services, 48–49
   spam problem, 160
   transactions, 26
   transmissions, 88
   Web-hosting data centers, 241
InterScan VirusWall, 95
ipTrend, 95
Irrigation components, 77
Irrigation systems, 10–11
Irritrol, 10
ISPs, 103, 190–91

J

Jack of All Games, 110
Jackson, Donny R., 97
Jeffries, Michael S., 70
Jewel, 163
Jimenez, George T., 286
Johns Hopkins University's Applied
   Physics Laboratory, 20
Johnson, George D. Jr., 148
Johnson, Thomas S., 112

Johnson & Johnson, 23
Joint replacements, 22–23
JVX accelerator, 245

K

K. Aufhauser & Company, 107
Kahane, William M., 199
Kalb, Jeffrey C., 208
Kaufmann, Joseph W., 85
Kealy, Joseph P., 103
Kensey Nash Corp., 85–87
Kentucky Insurance Company, 121
Kewaunee Scientific Corp., 250–52
Keystone, 14
Klein, Raphael, 292
Klobnak, John J., 115
KLSI, 53
Knee replacements, 22–23
Kodak, 14
Kooper, John N., 19
Korea Telecom, 287
Kornberg, Fred, 55
Kroger, 163
Kuo, Mali, 217
Kurtenbach, Aelred J., 46

L

Label printing, 223
Laboratory facilities, 127–28
Laboratory products, 250
Lampert, Ira B., 13
Laparoscopic surgery, 37
Las Vegas Cool Hand, 110
LaserCard, 181
Laser drilling inspections, 211
Laser-etched information, 181
Laser systems
    cosmetic/medical procedures, 40–41
    laser vision surgery, 115–16
LaserVision Centers, Inc., 115–17
LearnIt, 205
LeClic, 14
Legacy, 10
Lego, 175
Levenick, Mark K., 28
Levitt, Aaron, 157
Levitt, Barrie, 157
Libby's, 226
Liberty Life Insurance Company, 121
Lighting, outdoor, 11
Lim, Ming Seong, 88
Limited, The, 70

Liquid crystal flat panel, 173
Loans
    auto, 124–25
    mortgage, 125, 233
Lockheed, 235
Locks/locking devices, 44
Lodging industry, 148–49
Logistics Command, 55
Lotus Notes/Domino, 242
Love Canal, 298
Lucent Technologies, 52, 56, 94, 175, 235, 244, 260

M

McDonald, Ken P., 151
McDonald, Stephen D., 100
McQuary, Michael S., 190
Magnum, 281
Mahoney, Gerald F., 223
Mail-Well, Inc., 223–25
Managed care organizations, 128
Manatron, Inc., 145–47
Manchester, Eli Jr., 250
Marcuson, Randall L., 34
Marek's disease, inoculation, 34
Marketing research/analysis, 79–80
Master Tek International, 170
Materials management services, 140
Matra MHS, 92
Mavity, William G., 37
MCI WorldCom, 64, 94
Medical devices, 184
Medical imaging systems, 196–97
Medical procedures, 40–41, 85–86,
    115–16, 151, 184
Medical products, 19–20, 67–68, 271
Medical services, 127–28
Memory circuit boards, 154–55
Memory modules, 272
Memory products, 236
Merck & Company, 289
Metastat, 290
Metropoulos, C. Dean, 226
Meyercord, Wade F., 208
Microchips, 136, 235–36, 292
Microcomponents, 271
Microprocessors, 52
Microsoft, 64, 242
Microsoft Network, 191
Microwave equipment, 140
Midnight Club, 110
Midwest Surgical Services, 116

Military systems, filtering equipment and, 178
Miller, Edward M., 217
Miniaturization, 136, 239
Minolta, 134
Mission Studios, 110
Mitek Systems, Inc., 253–55
Mitsubishi, 172
Mitsubishi Chemical America, 62
Mobile data communications, 55–56
Modems, 283
Moldflow Corp., 175–77
Monitors, liquid crystal panel, 173
Monkey Hero, 110
Monster Truck Madness, 110
Monterey Pasta Company, 163–65
Morris, Clifton H., 124
Motorola, 56, 73, 175, 244, 260
MPEG, 8
Multimedia presentation, 58
Mumford, John B., 205
Mutual Building and Loan, 232
Myocardial Protection System, 184

N
N*Usage, 287
N*Vision, 287
NASA, 31
National Cancer Institute, 290
National Oceanic and Atmospheric Administration, 31
NEC, 8, 134, 172, 277
NET+Embedded, 134
NET+Imaging, 134
NetPlus Voice and Data Network Management System, 287
NetScout Systems, Inc., 142–44
NETsilicon, Inc., 133–35
Network Access Solutions, 274–76
Network consulting/design/ management/support, 11
Networked systems, 112
Networking systems, for electronic devices, 133–34
Network Solutions, 242
New, James C., 127
New Mexico Utilities, 169, 170
Nintendo 64/Nintendo Game Boy, 109
Non-Spil drug delivery system, 158
Norment Security Group, 43
Norshield, 44
Norstan, 64

Nortel Networks, 52, 209
North American Scientific, Inc., 1–3
Novadigm, Inc., 73–75

O
Office Rover, 206
OfficeScan, 95
Office services, medical practices, 128
OneMain.com, 191
Online brokers, 100–101, 106–7
OnMoney, 107
Operational Art of War, The, 110
Opinion Research Corp., 79–81
Oppen, Peter van, 4
Opteform, 22
Optetrak knee system, 22–23
Optibase, Ltd., 7–9
Optical components, 77
Optical fiber cable, 103
Optical inspection systems, 211
Optical memory cards, 181–82
Optical technology, 5
Orion AOI systems, 211
Orthopedic implants, 22–23
Outpatient laboratories, 127
Outpatient surgery centers, 151

P
Pacific Commons, 200
Pacific Western Extruded Plastics Company, 62
P/Active, 208
PAM cooking spray, 226
Panasonic, 64
Paredine, 20
Passive components, 272
Pasta Store, 163
Pathology services, 127–28
Pavey Envelope & Tag Corp., 224
Payment system, 25
Payroll services, 128
PC-cillin, 95
PC-to-TV convergence technologies, 83
PE pipes/tubing, 61
Peat, Randall L., 145
Penguin coolers, 239
Periostat, 289
Permanent Resident Card, 181
Personal care products, 70–71
Peterson, Cornelius, 133
Petrilli, F. J., 100
Petty, William, 22

PFF Bancorp, Inc., 232–34
Pharmaceuticals, 19–20, 157–58, 289–90
    poultry innoculation, 35
Philips, 172, 260
Picasso, Gino O., 286
Piccolo, 67
Plastics products, 61–62, 76–77
Plastics simulation, 175–76
Plastron Industries, 76
Plotkin, Kenneth, 82
Polaroid, 14
Polymers, bio-absorbable, 86
Pomona First Federal Savings and Loan, 232
Popat, Narendra, 142
Poultry, inoculation of, 34–35
Power bays, 140
Power conversion, 197
Preneed life insurance, 122
Printing facilities, 223
Processing equipment, 254
Prodigy, 191
Product analysis/forecasting, 80
Property evaluations, 146
PT Telkom, 88
Puorro, Gerard E., 40
PVC pipes, 61–62
PW Eagle, Inc., 61–63

Q

Qualcomm, 235
Quanta Systems, 44
Quest Medical, 184
QuickStrokes, 254

R

Radio frequency electronics, 263
Radioisotope technology, 2
Radio repeaters, 17
Radyne ComStream, Inc., 88–90
Rain Bird, 10
Rash, James T., 28
Rash, James, 61
Raytheon, 56, 244
Real estate development, 199–200
Reddy, Chandrashekar M., 277
Reilly, Paul V., 223
Remediation work, 298–99
Remote control systems, 59
Research/analysis, marketing, 79–80
Resistor networks, 209

Restaurants, 193–94, 227
RFI, 197
Richton International Corp., 10–12
Ricketts, J. Joe, 106–7
Ricoh, 134
Rinehart, Larry M., 232
Rising, Nelson C., 199
RMS Electronics, 263
RoadRailer, 295
Roberts, Kenneth D., 40
Robotic equipment, 254, 271
Rockstar Games, 110
Rockwell, 235
Roenigk, Martin A., 43
Rolls Royce, 215
Rubio, Rafael, 193
Rubio, Ralph, 193
Rubio's Restaurants, Inc., 193–95
Russo, Paul, 172
Rutcofsky, Barry, 109

S

Sabre Appraisal, 146
Safeway, 163, 295
Sage, Inc., 277–79
Sam's Club, 163
Samsung, 53, 92, 209, 235, 260, 287
Santa Fe Pacific Corp., 199
Sanyo, 277
Satellite command and control software, 31–33
Satellite-based communication system, 55–56, 88–89
SBC, 103
ScanMail, 95
Scarborough, Stephen J., 130
Schneider, 295
ScleroPLUS, 41
Scoreboards, 46–47
Security, Internet, 94–95
Security system products/maintenance, 43–44
Seese, Timothy J., 22
Sega Dreamcast, 109
Semiconductor-based networking devices, 133
Semiconductors, 52, 91–92, 202, 208, 235, 244, 259, 265, 272, 280–81
Semitool, Inc., 280–82
Servedio, Dominick M., 166
ServerProtect, 95
Set-top box technology, 284

Sevenson Environmental Services, Inc.,
298–300
Severson, Clinton H., 67
Sharp, 134, 172
Shokrgozar, Hamid, 235, 236
Short, John F., 79
Shumaker, William A., 250
Siemens, 64
Signs, programmable, 47
Silicon chips, 52
Singhal, Anil K., 142
Single substrate processing tools, 281
Sisto, Albert E., 244
Skin treatments, 41, 157
Smith, Bryan Scott, 118
Smith, O. Bruton, 118
Smith, Peter J., 214
SmithKline Beecham, 289
Smugglers Run, 110
Software management, 73
Software
    CAD, 215
    CAE, 214
    client/server enterprise, 97, 98
    communications, 268–69
    digital video, 7–8
    disk storage, 4–5
    document imaging, 113
    EDA, 136
    e-mail, 160
    for embedded systems, 134
    entertainment, 110
    legal and public records retrieval,
        145–46
    network system, 142–43
    plastics simulation, 175–76
    SAN, 83
    satellite command & control, 31–32
    security systems, 43–44
    telecommunications billing, 286–87
Software.com, 50
Solar electric power products, 16–17
Solo, 205
Somera Communications, 139–41
Sonic Automotive, Inc., 118–20
Sony, 49, 172, 277
Sony PlayStation, 109
Sound Advice, Inc., 220–22
Southwest Water Company, 169–71
SpectraLink Corp., 64–66
Spectrum, 281
Spectrum Control, Inc., 178–60
Spell, Harry W., 61

Spell, William H., 61
Sprinkler irrigation systems, 10–11
Sprint, 95
Standard Pacific Corp., 130–32
Standby Electronics, 263
Step (surgical device), 37–38
Stonecipher, Charles, 4
Stonkus, Alexander C., 25
Storage area network (SAN), 247
Storage devices, 202–3
Streiter, Robert C., 238
StudioPLUS Deluxe Suites, 149
STV Group, Inc., 166–68
Suburban Water Systems, 169–70
Sullivan, Fred R., 10
Summa Industries, 76–78
Sun, Dr. Edmund Y., 217, 218
Sun Microsystems, 154
SuperLink broadband, 283
Surgical devices, 20, 37–38
Surgical procedures, 85–86, 115–16, 151,
    184
Surgical services, 127–28
Svendsen, Arthur E., 130
Swanson Analysis Systems, 215
Swartwout, James R., 76
Switchboard.com, 50
Switching equipment, 139
Sylvester, Paul R., 145
Synercom Technology, 239
Systems Integration Group, 104

T

Taiwan.com, 229
Take-Two Interactive Software, Inc.,
    109–11
TalonSoft, 110
Tarantino, R. V., 154
Tarantula Studios, 110
Taro Pharmaceutical Industries Ltd., 157–59
Tatoo removal, 41
TD Waterhouse Group, Inc., 100–102
Technical analyses, 167
Technical services, 11, 140
Telecommunications, 55–56, 139, 205–6,
    208–9, 235–36, 262–63, 275, 293
    billing, 286
    filtering equipment, 178
    solar energy and, 16–17
Telephone headsets, 205–6
Telephone systems, wireless, 64–65
Tempress Systems, 259

Texas Instruments, 172, 260
TheDataPort.com, 58
Thermal management products, 238
Thermal processing systems, 265–66
"Thin film" technology, 206
Thoma, Carl D., 112
Thompson, Raymon F., 280
Thornton, John M., 253
Thrasher, 110
3Com, 209, 235
Tidel Technologies, Inc., 28–30
Timed Access Cash Controller (TACC), 29
Time Warner, 8
Time Warner Telecom, 103
Toxic waste cleanup, 298–99
Toys R Us, 109
Trade Acceptance Draft (TAD), 25
Traffic information, 17
Transmission equipment, 140
Transportation
    engineering management, 166–67
    terminal signs, 47
    solar energy and, 16–17
Travel, 187–88
Trend Micro, Inc., 94–96
TrenTech, 44
Triton IP/Triton T1, 269
Truck trailers, 295–96
Trugman, Leonard, 196
TSMC, 92

U

U.S. Air Force, 31
U.S. Army, 55
U.S. Department of Defense, 167
U.S. Department of State, 44
U.S. Government, 56
U.S. Immigration and Naturalization, 181
Ultralight, 205
UltraNet, 247

V

V3 Semiconductor, Inc., 52–54
Vaccines, poultry, 34–35
van der Wansem, Paul J., 265
Varicose veins cosmetic procedures, 40–41
VetScan, 67
Viacom, 73
ViAlta.com, 283
Video card, for computers, 82–83
Video conferencing equipment, 206
Video games, 109–10

Video processing products, 278
VideoTalk, 83
Video technologies, 7–8, 217–18
VideoWizard, 83
Vioxx, 289
Virtual hosting, 242
Virtual Integration Associates, 53
Virus protection system (computer), 94
Vision care/surgery, 19–20, 115–16
Voice-processing equipment, 206

W

Wabash National Corp., 295–97
Wachman, James C., 115
Wafer carrier cleaning systems, 281
Wal-Mart, 109
WAN management system, 142
Warfarin tablets, 157
Warning displays, 17
Waste Management, 148
Wastewater treatment, 169
Water supply systems, 169–70
Waterhouse Securities. *See* TD
    Waterhouse Group, Inc.
WealthWeb service, 107
Web-hosting data centers, 241
WEBrowz, 254
Web site design, 49
Webvan, 163
Wells, Darrell R., 121
Wells Fargo, 73
Whang, Jong S., 259
White Electronic Designs Corp., 235–37
Wide area networks (WANs), 91
Willenz, Avigdor, 91
Williams, Anthony, 109
Williams, Nicholas, 274
Winding cores, 77
WinTV, 83
Wireless equipment, 140, 235
Wireless image-capture devices, 14
Wireless telephone systems, 64–65
Wood furniture products, 250
Work surfaces, 250
World Wrestling Federation, 227

X–Z

Xerox, 52, 134, 175
Xicor, Inc., 292–94
Yie, Charles D., 175
Yip, Peter, 229
Zambakkides, John, 52